Germany and the Transnational Building Blocks for Post-National Community

Donald G. Phillips

PRAEGER

Westport, Connecticut
London

Library of Congress-Cataloging-in-Publication Data

Phillips, Donald G., 1965–
    Germany and the transnational building blocks for post-national community / Donald
G. Phillips.
        p. cm.
    Includes bibliographical references and index.
    ISBN 0–275–96490–6 (alk. paper)
    1. Germany—Economic policy—1990– 2. Germany—Economic conditions—1990– 3.
Europe—Economic integration. I. Title.
    HC286.8.P48   2000
    338.943—dc21   00–025467

British Library Cataloguing in Publication Data is available.

Library of Congress Catalog Card Number: 00–025467
ISBN: 0–275–96490–6

First published in 2000

Praeger Publishers, 88 Post Road West, Westport, CT 06881
An imprint of Greenwood Publishing Group, Inc.
www.praeger.com

Printed in the United States of America

The paper used in this book complies with the
Permanent Paper Standard issued by the National
Information Standards Organization (Z39.48–1984).

10 9 8 7 6 5 4 3 2 1

thanks to:

Ew. Hochwürden Claudia Mumdadmoraydaad

Contents

Contents

Abbreviations and German Terms Used in this Book

AG	*Aktiengesellschaft* – PLC
BdA	Confederation of German Employers' Associations
BDI	Federal Association of German Industry
Bundesrat	Upper chamber of Federal German parliament, membership consisting of *Länder* governments
Bundestag	Lower chamber of Federal German parliament
CAP	Common Agricultural Policy (EC)
CDU	Christian Democratic Union
CEEP	European Centre of Enterprises with Public Participation and of Enterprises of General Economic Interest
CFSP	Common Foreign and Security Policy (EU)
CSCE	Conference on Security and Cooperation in Europe
CSU	Bavarian Christian Social Union
DASA	DaimlerChrysler Aerospace, formerly German Aerospace
DGB	German Trades Union Federation
DIHT	German Association of Chambers of Industry and Commerce
EC	European Community
ECB	European Central Bank
ECI	European Currency Institute
ECOFIN	Council of Economics and Finance Ministers (EC)
ECSC	European Coal and Steel Community
EDC	European Defence Community
EEA	European Economic Area (formed by EC, EFTA members)
EEC	European Economic Community
EFTA	European Free Trade Area
EMS	European Monetary System
EMU	European Monetary Union
EP	European Parliament
ERM	Exchange rate mechanism (EMS)
ERT	European roundtable of industrialists – TNE lobbying association
ESC	Economic and Social Committee of the European Community

ESCB	European System of Central Banks
ETUC	European Trade Union Confederation
EU	European Union
FAZ	*Frankfurter Allgemeine Zeitung*
FDP	Free Democratic Party
FRG	Federal Republic of Germany (pre-1990, also known commonly as West Germany)
GATT	General Agreement on Tariffs and Trade
GDR	German Democratic Republic (also known as East Germany)
GEC	General Electric Company
Grundgesetz	The Basic Law, the FRG constitution
ILO	International Labour Organization
ISO	International Organization for Standardization
JCMS	Journal of Common Market Studies
Land	State in FRG
Länder	Plural of *Land*
Landtag	*Land* parliament
MP	Member of Parliament
MEP	Member of the European Parliament
NATO	North Atlantic Treaty Organisation
OECD	Organisation for Economic Co-operation and Development
QMV	Qualified majority voting – EC Council voting procedure
PLC	Public limited company
SAMAK	Forum of Nordic Social Democrats and trade unions
SEA	Single European Act
SED	Socialist Unity Party of Germany, ruling Communist party in GDR
SPD	Social Democratic Party of Germany
TNE	Transnational Enterprise
TUC	(British) Trades Union Congress
UAW	United Automobile Aerospace and Agricultural Implement Workers of America
UNICE	Union of Industrial and Employers' Confederations of Europe
WTO	World Trade Organization

Introduction: The Extraordinary End of the Cold War

This book assesses prospects for social coherence in a world state system where non-state forces are becoming increasingly significant. In attempting to answer the basic question – what can the building blocks of social coherence in Europe be – my focus is post-Cold War Germany. A study focussing on Germany is appropriate for one outstanding reason: following the collapse of the Soviet Union, the Federal Republic has become central to Europe's future.

The 40-year division of Germany into two states had been accompanied by as-pirations towards European unification as an antidote to extreme nationalism. Both this division and these aspirations were consequences of the catastrophe of the Second World War. But the realization of a European intercommunity perspective was, by force of Cold War circumstance, essentially a Western perspective, both for West Germany itself and its new partners in states to the west. This had to change on 3 October 1990, as at a stroke, the Federal Republic of Germany (FRG) included 17 million East Germans with a different perspective. How much would this change bring new Eastern perspectives? How much would it buttress already existing West-ern perspectives? On unification, for the first time in their history, Germans have gained "State unity with freedom and sovereignty."[1] Nevertheless, this step was not attained in isolation. Unification was made possible only within an overall framework of steps towards a greater European unity: in response to fears from Germany's neighbors that unification would result in different German government policy, the Federal Republic played, and perhaps equally important, was seen to have played, a key role in the negotiation and agreement of the Maastricht Treaty on European Un-ion (EU) on 9-10 December 1991. At Maastricht, agreement was reached on a com-mon currency, the Social Chapter and a political union.

The decisions made or avoided at Maastricht continue to set the agenda in Europe, as the Continent or at least the Western richer part of it, as represented by its political and economic leaderships, determines the merits and means of striving to-wards closer European union. These leadership groups were able to reach a consensus such that all other issues were and are subordinated to debate on European currency union and its subsequent implementation. However, as I will show in this book, commensurate consensus on issues of social coherence between as well as within increasingly interdependent societies of national states has not been achieved: for example European Council, Commission and Parliament have issued statements on the social blights of racism and unemployment.[2] However, many would claim that such statements do not address the actual needs of the more vulnerable in the European Union.

As an example, it could be argued that the German government failed in its duty to non-Germans following unification: in both Western and Eastern Germany, the foreign community was subjected to racist violence. Nonetheless, I would contend that that no European institution is in a position to achieve significant change, however much its members individually or collectively may feel they wish to do so, without acting in concert with other bodies inside and outside Europe: private as well as public, local and regional as well as states.

Unless such steps are taken, the EU will face increasing criticism. I (and I hope many others) would argue that the EU risks being subsumed by the means not the ends of its original goals of achieving the integration of Europe's peoples. If the EU does not prove itself capable of answering such criticism, then opponents of the Community, who already see its structures as incapable of fulfilling the wishes and the needs of the peoples of Europe, will grow in number. Thus, unless these criticisms are met, strains on the existing consensus on European Monetary Union (EMU) will also increase, perhaps to breaking point. As is indicated by the example of German currency union since 1990, the introduction of a common currency alone offers no panacea towards improving the quality of Europeans' lives. Many are excluded or feel themselves excluded from the benefits of moves towards European integration thus far. Accordingly, it is the aim of this book to show that the institutions of European integration are only one way of fashioning a greater social coherence in Europe in an interdependent world, with the emphasis that the term "Europe" does not entail the EU alone, and that the EU is only part of Europe. Moreover, Europe's population is only a small fraction of the world's population. In line with these aims, I would argue for a greater consciousness of "community." A pertinent definition which highlights the current state of contemporary European integration can be found in the *Routledge Encyclopaedia of Philosophy*. In it, Allen Buchanan writes on community: "Each member thinks of furthering the community's ends primarily as gains for us, not as a gain for themselves that happens to be accompanied by similar gains for other individuals in the group."[3]

I would argue that Buchanan's definition of community is in many respects the antithesis of the state of Europe inside and outside the EU. Moreover, it could be implied that the gains for the *us* in this definition could only be made at the expense of excluding a *them*.

I would argue that only by a consideration of detail on policy options from various perspectives can possible criteria be found for an emergence of a consensus on community from an association of individuals: not only for the retention of already existing frameworks, but also for the establishment of new structures. I argue that institutional models for democracy are not ends in themselves, but only one means of fashioning more inclusive societies.

CONSENSUS IN GERMANY AND EUROPE

In the light of the above, at this point some explanatory remarks about the use of the term *consensus* are appropriate also. I would see the definition of the concept of consensus as that Edward Shils gives us in the *International Encyclopaedia of the Social Sciences*, namely that three elements are necessary for the functioning of consensus:

(1) a common acceptance of laws, rules and norms, (2) attachment to the institutions which promulgate and apply the laws and rules ... (3) a widespread sense of identity or unity which discloses to individuals who experience it, those features in respect to which they are identical and therefore equal. The sense of identity diminishes the significance of the differences on which dissensus and hostile sentiments would otherwise focus.[4]

With the aid of Shils' definition, it can be seen that in the case of Germany, it was the appeal of a common identity or unity, which predated and survived the Cold War, which diminished the differences between two 40-year-old states and was a persuasive factor in East Germans launching themselves into the unification process in 1990. In voting for unification, the population of East Germany not only confirmed the vitality of this shared, national, identity. By accepting the West German consensus on laws and institutions without significant articulated reservation, they also implicitly trusted that the system which they accepted "overnight" on accession to the Federal Republic would overcome the societal differences stemming from 40 years of existence of two German states on German soil.[5]

We must draw into consideration a further aspect in relation to German unification. Prior to 1989, common acceptance of laws, norms, along with institutions in the FRG was not based on a specifically German context, or even a West German context, rather a Western/Western European context. In the forty years preceding 1989, the Western European context became the West German context. The government and people of the Federal Republic had entered into this compact at the price of a practical disavowal of identification of common interest with the East German government and population.[6]

At the same time, in Western Europe as a whole, the post-Second World War search for common ground had led to collective acceptance of rules and norms in reaching agreement on common institutions as a means of creating a Europe-wide consensus. These were not seen as ends in themselves, but functionalized as a means of surmounting divisive national identities which had led to areas of conflict culminating in two world wars. These institutions would serve as the basis for the creation of a common European sense of identity, as an alternative to divisive national identity. The creation of a new greater sense of unity would in turn gradually strengthen the regulation of a stable consensus on laws and the institutional fabric of European society.

However, this ideal had not been reached by the time that forces favoring German unification became so overwhelming that it did indeed come to pass. (I use a passive sentence construction here because it helps to underline my point that the diversity of forces acting upon the course of events make it difficult for us to determine one individual force, interest or actor. With this caveat in mind, I would state that the aim of this work is, by a consideration of detail from various perspectives, to identify forces that may have acted upon the course of events.[7]) Indeed German unification came to pass very quickly.

Once the realization dawned that the attainment of one German state was unavoidable, to compensate, (Western) European leaders, fearing that a return to alternative focuses of identity – national identity – would damage the consensus that had been achieved in Western Europe, hermetically reared under Cold War protection prior to 1989, hurriedly sought to reach agreement on more encompassing norms and institutions at the European level. It seemed that fears on the part of Western European leaders (although perhaps not their electorates), not Eastern hopes for the future were the primary motivation.

THE REACTION TO THE END OF THE COLD WAR

These fears of an uncertain future quickly obscured optimistic hopes of a "peace dividend." Perhaps fears stemmed in part from Western political leaders' surprise that the Cold War had ended so quickly. Surprise at the turn in events, along with fear, were prevalent in social science circles too. Indeed, eighties arguments about a crisis of the enlightenment continued, although the principal specific reason for them having started in the first place – the possible end of humanity itself in the event of the failure of Cold War nuclear deterrence – had disappeared with the implosion of the Soviet Bloc.

Ideas discussed in Hans Jonas' work *The Imperative of Responsibility*, for example, published in 1984 and calling into question the ethic of trying to save mankind, continued to exert influence.[8] Lothar Schäfer attempted an interpretation of Jonas' work, conforming to prevalent liberal capitalist practices with his critique of *The Bacon-project*, published in 1993.[9] Immanuel Wallerstein specifically linked his 1991 analysis with the erosion of "the premises of Baconian-Newtonian science."[10] For many, the conclusion was, if not the end of the belief in Enlightenment *per se*, nevertheless that "the connections between the development of human knowledge and human self-understanding have proved more complex" than the pilots of the Enlightenment had originally supposed.[11] Another commentator influenced by Jonas surmised that "it becomes more and more difficult to hold on to a linear conception of history as progress."[12]

On the other hand, an optimistic prognosis regarding the future was regarded by many as inapplicable, as being particularism in a universalist guise. Francis Fukuyama's essay *The End of History* following unification and his proponence of the existing precepts of liberal capitalist democracy became the object of international controversial debate after 1989. Fukuyama claimed, for example, that technology, in that it is developed according to the laws of nature, and not of human beings, made the "limitless accumulation of wealth" possible.[13] In opposition to this optimism, Immanuel Wallerstein for one argued that 1989 represented the "demise not of Leninism alone but of both ends of the great ideological antimony of the twentieth century, the Wilsonian versus the Leninist eschatologies."[14]

However, it is my view that such preoccupations with ends, be they the end of the Cold War or the end of history itself, are too particularist in the search for a wider sense of social coherence. Fukuyama's belief that the problems confronting Western democracy could be solved on the basis of (Western) liberal principles[15] does not take account of the energies unreined with the release of people, their ideas, their experiences, their resources previously confined and subordinated to a different agenda in the East under the Cold War. We in the West may be uncertain what these ideas and experiences may be exactly, but we should nevertheless consider them.

In this sense, in the search for ways towards a greater social coherence, merely a brief look at the philosophy of history can show us that uncertainty is a constant companion in our search for understanding of the historical process. As I wished to indicate by showing the post-Cold War complexities of reaching consensus in Europe at the beginning of the Introduction, efforts in extending consensus to obtain a greater social coherence across contemporary European society must take account of the linkage between a recognition, on one hand, of fundamental uncertainty concerning dilemmas posed by the nature of our existence, and on the other, the corresponding partiality and the possible contradictory nature of solutions that we attempt in response. As a response to uncertainty, we may be tempted, with the perspective of the seemingly overwhelming weight of human experience behind us, to follow Karl Jaspers and perhaps imagine "seeing history thus far taking shape."[16] But, this is not Fukuyama at the *end* but Jaspers at the *beginning* of the Cold War, in 1949. Moreover, Jaspers was not seduced by the idea. Instead he argued against partiality, a view which I would share:

History is factually open. I hold myself open for the future. This is a posture of waiting and searching for the truth, even of not yet knowing about that which is already here, but which can only be understood by the future. With this basic posture, even the past is open, it lives on – its decisions are not the last, but only the latest, they can be over-turned.[17]

Therefore, although we can view 1989 as a caesura of colossal importance, it should nevertheless be borne in mind that there are innumerable parallel endings and beginnings, societal as well as individual. The Cold War was only one of these processes. It may certainly help us in our analysis to think, to write, to read, in terms of "the end of the Cold War" (as is often the case in this work), but to choose to focus on an end of a process may not be helpful nor necessarily correct, certainly if seen from the perspective of future generations, who might curse the lost opportunities of our present if we allow this partiality to limit our ambitions. By analyzing only a part of history, our understanding is partial too. If, however, we attempt to understand more of the whole, an attempt also which will inevitably be incomplete, we can see that the end of the Cold War could give us the chance to start something new.[18] Our understanding will also be modest. But if we recall the views of Karl Popper on the pursuit of knowledge, we can realize that the academic recognition of the universal nature of uncertainty is a prerequisite towards overcoming differences, towards extending a consensus that is socially coherent.[19]

To underline the argument for the need to act despite uncertainty: it is conceivable that the past, in Jaspers' sense, is "incomplete" and the Cold War may return. We might actually find ourselves currently in an interregnum of comparative opportunity. Accordingly, we can and should use our knowledge that the greatest uncertainty of all, the threat of the end of mankind itself, has moved into abeyance, to stimulate our imaginations to be open to positive impulses to prevent the return of the ultimate danger. Perhaps then we would be able to surmise that it is not an inherent, inevitable reaction of mankind to wander off after the necessary end of every Iliad into an unnecessary Odyssey. Accordingly we should meet tendencies to play down the extent of outstanding problems of limited resources and ever greater global consumption (also present before the end of the Cold War) with skepticism.[20]

How then to find pragmatist approaches which reflect societal needs, which have a chance of reflecting the contradictory factors listed in the analyses above? As the best response to inherent uncertainty, we should be open to a pluralistic approach, based upon dialogue between as many individuals and interest and expertise groups as possible.

In recognition that new impulses are required, many Western politicians favor a search for what they themselves call a "third way," and have staged seminars to back up their declared attempts to find it.[21] Romano Prodi, now president of the European Commission, has criticized the initiative, if we can label it as such, as having little in the way of content.[22] However, in fairness, they are only at the beginning. British Prime Minister Tony Blair has himself acknowledged the sketchiness of the third way by describing it as an "attempt" to reformulate values of social justice, democracy and freedom for the modern world.[23] It remains to be seen whether the German Social Democrat-led government will develop any interest in the attempt rather than the slogan.[24] So, unless/until the initiative moves considerably beyond its Anglo-Saxon origins (to open up to Eastern Europe for example) and its participants bear in mind narrowness implicit in the term "third way," we should view it too with skepticism.

ORIENTATION OF DISCUSSION ON EUROPEAN AFFAIRS

In this book, two broad areas of study will be explored to try to take account of contradictions exposed by the uncertainties caused by the end of the Cold War. I will argue that where we attempt to define community solely by criteria of geographical demarcation and exclusion of others, we will encounter problems. We should look for means to extend parameters for inclusion wherever possible. The two main sections following this introduction focus on these two broad areas:

- Part I. Problems of Community: The European Intercommunity Perspective on Building Blocks for Social Coherence
- Part II. Chances of Community: Transnational and Transinstitutional Parameters for Greater Social Coherence

Material on the subject matter covered by these two sections is already vast. However, I would identify three deficiencies to approaches in existing studies. First, many are unidisciplinary, and thus while (hopefully) benefiting from a wealth of in-depth detail, the narrowness of scope may tend to heighten the seeming importance of the area under consideration, thereby giving no balanced picture in a wider context, which is what I would seek to do.

Second, specifically as a reflection of the formulation of actual policy on the broad issues of European integration, studies are made from a perspective of the Continent taken from the West and from the top downwards: occicentric and peremptory. In respect to policy formulation, I would agree with Anthony Smith, who has seen the "over-reliance on elites and leaderships," and also observed that "the European project has been constructed functionally through the actions and programs of business, administrative and intellectual elites of that national state and who have sought to build the economic infrastructure and political framework of a wider European union."[25] This imbalance has been reflected in most academic and media debate, which is conducted by a community of scholars, political figures and journalists whose considerable expertise and insight stem from a primary focus on European institutional integration.

Moreover many of these scholars – in Britain, for example, Helen and William Wallace, in Germany, Werner Weidenfeld – have been coopted themselves into the same European elite described by William Wallace himself as consisting of "national ministers, senior officials, the informal policy community, business and bankers" that are the locus of their expertise.[26] For example, William Wallace, now a member of the British House of Lords, was one of the speakers at *Fazit: Nation* conference in Berlin in May 1998. Along with Wallace, the list of speakers was a typical cross-section of the elite Wallace himself has described, including then Christian Democratic Union/Christian Social Union (CDU/CSU) parliamentary leader Wolfgang Schäuble and French Interior Minister Jean-Pierre Chevènement.[27]

In this field of study, it is difficult to distinguish between media commentary and scholarship. Scholars contribute articles to the news media. Published studies contain papers provided by such figures as former British Cabinet Minister Shirley Williams [see Robert Keohane and Stanley Hoffmann (eds.), *The New European Community* (Boulder: Westview Press, 1991]. Another, *Towards Greater Europe? A Continent without an Iron Curtain* (Oxford: Blackwell, 1992) is coedited by David Marquand, former advisor of Tony Crosland in the British Foreign and Commonwealth Office, and, together with the coeditor of this volume, Colin Crouch, also editor of the *Political Quarterly*.

Furthermore, Williams and her former Labour cabinet colleague Merlyn Rees serve on the journal's editorial board. While this study also shares Wallace's view that trust between national elites and national electorates has been weakened by the practices and ambiguities of European Community government,[28] it may be that such a restricted circle of debate and a level of understanding of integration processes is not itself enough.[29]

Third, I would contend that a further imbalance to many such studies of European integration is additionally the focus of "international relations." For historical reasons, Anglo-Saxon scholars have also dominated research on international relations in a disproportionate manner.[30] In this book however, I will focus on the effects of European and transnational integration processes upon communities, which are not only increasingly shaped by them, but also – as we shall see – increasingly capable of doing some shaping of these processes themselves.

GERMANY AS THE KEY TO POST-NATIONAL SOCIAL COHERENCE

I would point out that the use of the prefix supra- in the term "supranational approach to integration" between European states implies an improvement on the perceived value of national identity. If the supranational approach had contained either real or perceived benefits over the status quo, then we would no longer have an international order based upon the nation-state system. Therefore, in my discussion, unless concerned with supranational characteristics of European institutional integration, I prefer the term "transnational integration," implying the strengthening of bonds between national group identities and nation-states, which nevertheless leaves these groups intact, and is perceived as no hierarchical threat to existing identities by the groups concerned.

In this book, I desire to explore means of understanding and then identify levels of integration in relation to the culture of the FRG, the state central to the European integration process right from its inauguration. The question arises: does the post-Second World War establishment of internationalist impulses stemming from Germany serve a hegemonic German interest, or do they serve greater mutual goals? In post-Cold War Europe, the resolution of this issue is a crucial point in the analysis of prospects of overcoming still existing divisions in the creation of European-wide consensus. As Manfred Henningsen has pointed out, the subject of the infamous March 1990 Chequers seminar of then British Prime Minister Margaret Thatcher, perhaps because she herself attached so much importance to the realization of the British national interest – whatever this might be – was the German national character:

not however the ability of German business to get its way transnationally. It is exactly this successful border crossing that characterizes the dynamic of European agreement from the Coal and Steel Community of the six original member states in 1952 until the admittance of Sweden, Finland and Austria to the European Union in 1995 and the long waiting list of EU hopefuls.[31]

Henningsen does not define what he understands by the term "German business," and his formulation is also unfortunate because it seems to imply that German business operations alone are characterized by transnational activity to survive in the international marketplace. However, the fact that Henningsen links the issues of international activity of German business with Thatcher's seminar shows clearly that a consideration of the role of German business forms a crucial part in the analysis of whether transnational interests are mutual or hegemonic.[32]

A study of post-Second World War European developments centered on Germany would seem to be a powerful argument also against the view of Wallerstein, who has claimed that globalization will see increasing involvement by states in enterprises.[33] It would seem to me that the opposite contention holds true. As I will discuss more fully in Chapter 8, not just nation-states but supranational forms of institutional organization are also becoming obsolescent in some senses.[34] Nonetheless, we should remember that the growing transnational tendencies of business are only one aspect of globalization.[35]

FOCUS AND SOURCES OF THIS BOOK

As we will see, the meaning and significance of national and European political institutions is subject to increasing skepticism. Accordingly they should not be the sole focus of discussion. So, to explore these themes, I truly have attempted to spread my sources as widely as possible. This study does not claim to be definitive. As the work of one author, the viewpoint is inevitably particularist: but the aim is a synthesis of as much clarity and as much wholeness as possible.

I include literary as well as economic and political sources. In addition to a wide-ranging academic input, I have also used sources in journalistic and other comparable media.[36] I am well aware of the flaws and dangers of an overreliance on such sources, but think their use essential for two reasons. First, many of the events covered are recent, and have not yet received extensive or, in some cases, any academic study. Thus a circumspect use of sources from the quality media is while unavoidable, very helpful.[37]

Second, much of this book is about the popular reception of events. In this respect, I bear in mind that the nature of media reporting and popular debate can be instrumental in the further course of events as much as the events themselves. Thus on one hand, the influence of aspects of popular debate on further events may only be short term and tangential, but on the other hand, it is important to assess the nature of this influence and not discard it without evaluation. In this respect, the pattern of historical processes can be compared to a French-plaited ponytail. We can see new strands being woven in and replacing the old strands which had previously formed the body, but becoming too short and thin, are later to twist out to become extraneous wisps.

I would not argue for a radical change in the conclusions of narrower studies. I would however lay emphasis on a different prioritization and/or relativization. The presentation of these issues together in this study is an attempt to reflect the practical reality faced by the communities which are faced collectively with these issues, and in so doing is an attempt to argue that our understanding of one area, and consequently our inclination to act to offer a solution in that area, should not be carried out at the cost of neglecting others. Let me clarify further what I mean by this by citing the analysis of former Federal (West) German Chancellor Helmut Schmidt in 1993. Schmidt's locus of interest was what he saw as four main crises facing Germany: "Unification crisis, economic crisis, asylum crisis and crisis of trust all at the same time ... we must return to the standard of living of the end of the eighties and bivouac there for a considerable time."[38]

Schmidt's partial solution, outlined in his article, was to concentrate on solving the economic crisis first. Given better economic conditions, Schmidt argued the remaining three crises could be solved also. However, Schmidt's analysis was essentially based on Western European and not German premises: the living standards of the end of the eighties that he refers to are implicitly Western and not Eastern. Hence the applicability of his solution was primarily in the West, not the East. Indeed, although we cannot do so here, we could make a case for the applicability of his solution to all of Western Europe. This then is the basic problem: the well-being of society is dependent on frequently contradictory forces. Forces and agents of forces in German society have their counterparts and parallels world-wide. As Schmidt, the realistic pragmatist par excellence of the Cold War era, might care to admit, he may be overly optimistic concerning contemporary global society's capacity to solve economic problems. The tendency is that any sector of society is unwilling to accept a cut in its standard of living unilaterally. Furthermore, in a world of limited resources, economic problems never disappear, but are transported to other locations on the globe, or are delayed to a later point in time.[39] Afflictions in the German economy spread to other parts of Europe, which in turn affect other parts of the globe. In turn other problems, whether new, or virulent strains of the old, come ranging their way in; in the ever more interdependent global society, the manifold variety of predicaments demands a manifold variety of partial solutions. These are inevitably contradictory at times. The wave effects of these solutions recall the defraction process as demonstrated during a ripple tank experiment in a school physics lesson: partial solutions either doubling the trough of despond, or at times canceling each other out to leave a flat calm surface. Unlike a school experiment, however, despite the end of the Cold War's threat of nuclear oblivion, it seems more difficult to cater for practical human needs.

STRUCTURE OF THIS BOOK

As described previously, this work is henceforth divided into two main parts.
- Part I. Problems of Community: The European Intercommunity Perspective on Building Blocks for Social Coherence

This part gives a brief account of the history of (Western) European integration, seen from the German perspective. Explanations lying behind the limitation of European institutional regulation and legislation to narrow economic aspects are offered. Two questions arise from this limitation, namely: what are the chances and pitfalls for community –from EU level to local level – arising out of the concentration of business encouraged by the development of European integration? What are the chances of a substantial measure of social consensus – as currently exists for example in the social market economy of the Federal Republic of Germany – being extended to a heterogeneous Europe?
- Part II. Chances of Community: Transnational and Transinstitutional Parameters for Greater Social Coherence.

This part deals with further possible answers to the issues considered in Part I. Multipolar characteristics of the decision-making process in Europe are shown, reflected in the nature and scope of lobbying work of interests which transcend the EU and indeed Europe as a whole. Aided by an analysis of major companies formerly perceived as being German, but which are increasingly transnational in character, like companies of comparable scope world-wide, I argue that approaches to integration couched in institutional terms alone are insufficient and must be balanced with extra-institutional approaches.

Based on these themes, the hypothesis is that any conclusions regarding the future building blocks for post-national social coherence can only be valid if a wide number of frequently contradictory forces pertaining to the developments discussed in this chapter are taken into account. What exactly is the role of a national government in post-Cold War Europe? What is under way in German society has parallels with events elsewhere in Europe. Equally, these developments on the larger scale, not only in Europe but also in the world beyond, have ramifications for developments in Germany too. No action is complete without reaction. Therefore, where forces are diffuse, can we speak of a German influence on these processes? I would argue that we can, but only inasmuch as we may speak of German influences in the plural, which by all means may act to contradict or cancel the other out.

NOTES

1. Fritz Ullrich Fack, 'Die Deutschen gewinnen die Einheit in Freiheit', *Frankfurter Allgemeine Zeitung (FAZ)*, 2/3.10.1990, p. 1. [Note: dates are presented in European style – day, month, year.]

2. For example, at Maastricht, the Council issued a *Declaration on Racism and Xenophobia*. The declaration, while recalling previous European Community (EC) declarations on racism, noted that racism was still growing inside and outside the EU, an implicit acknowledgement that previous statements on the topic had had no effect. [Source: Annex IV, Commission of the European Communities, *Legal instruments to Combat Racism & Xenophobia. Comparative assessment of the legal instruments implemented in the various member states to combat all forms of discrimination, racism and xenophobia and incitement to hatred and racial violence* (Directorate General Employment, Industrial Relations and Social Affairs. 200, rue de la Loi, B-1049 Brussels, Dec. 1992).] In 1993 the Commission published a white paper on Growth, Competition and Employment. In it, the Commission set the goal of halving the Community's unemployment levels by the year 2000. However, the feasibility of the aspiration was undermined by a seemingly infinite number of factors, not least of which is the accession to the Community since then of three new member states bringing additional competition to the labor market. It is now a different Community. [Kommission der Europäischen Gemeinschaften, *Wachstum, Wettbewerbsfähigkeit, Beschäftigung. Herausforderungen der Gegenwart und Wege ins 21. Jahrhundert.* Weißbuch (Bulletin der Europäischen Gemeinschaften, Beilage 6/93).]

3. Allen Buchanan, 'Community', in Edward Craig (ed.), *Routledge Encyclopaedia of Philosophy*, Volume 2 (London, 1998), pp. 464-465 (p. 464).

4. Edward Shils, *The Concept of Consensus*, in David L Sills (ed.), *International Encyclopaedia of the Social Sciences Volume 3* (London: Macmillan Company and The Free Press, 1968), pp. 260-266 (pp. 260-261).

5. The precept that soil could have a national identity is spurious, but it seems to be a generally accepted convention, and therefore I use it here for purposes of discussion.

6. This is not to say that symbolic affirmations of unity with the East were discontinued, quite the contrary, especially on the anniversaries of the 1953 uprising and the 1961 erection of the Berlin Wall.

7. For example, in his study *Deutschlandpolitik in Helmut Kohls Kanzlerschaft*, published in 1998, Karl-Rudolf Korte concludes that the collapse of the SED regime in autumn 1989 occurred neither because nor in spite of Kohl's *Deutschlandpolitik*. See Karl-Rudolf Korte, *Deutschlandpolitik in Helmut Kohls Kanzlerschaft. Regierungsstil und Entscheidungen 1982-1989* (Stuttgart: Deutsche Verlags-Anstalt, 1998).

8. Hans Jonas, *Das Prinzip Verantwortung* (Frankfurt/Main: Suhrkamp, 1984). Here we can read such thoughts as "The choice of humanity's destruction touches on the question of existence of mankind and this necessarily leads to the question ... whether anything rather than nothing should be" (p. 97).

9. Lothar Schäfer, *Das Bacon-Projekt* (Frankfurt/Main: Suhrkamp 1993), p. 147.

10. Immanuel Wallerstein, 'Introduction: The lessons of the 1980s', in his *Geopolitics and Geoculture* (Cambridge University Press, 1991), pp. 1-15 (p. 13).

11. Anthony Giddens, 'Risk, trust, reflexivity,' in Ulrich Beck, Anthony Giddens

and Scott Lash, *Reflexive Modernization* (Cambridge: Polity Press, 1994), pp. 184-197 (p. 184).

12. John B. Thompson, *The Media and Modernity* (Cambridge: Polity Press, 1995), p. 37.

13. Francis Fukuyama, *The End of History and the Last Man* (London: Penguin Books, 1992), p. xiv. The flaw in Fukuyama's argument is exposed succinctly by Karl Popper's discussion of Kant's *Kritik der reinen Vernunft* where the former sums up the latter: "Human understanding invents the laws of nature." [Karl R. Popper, 'Über Wissen und Nichtwissen' in his *Auf der Suche nach einer besseren Welt* (Munich: Serie Piper, 1987), pp. 41-54 (p. 48).]

14. Wallerstein, *Geopolitics and Geoculture*, p. 2.

15. Fukuyama, p. xxi, p. 288. Fukuyama listed the problems of democracy as being drug abuse, homelessness, crime, the destruction of the environment, consumption excess.

16. Karl Jaspers, *Vom Ursprung und Ziel der Geschichte* (Munich: R. Piper, 1949), p. 329.

17. Jaspers, pp. 320-321.

18. On analyzing history as a whole, see Jaspers, p. 332.

19. See Popper, pp. 41-54, especially: "Scientific research is indeed the best method for us to discover more about ourselves and about what we do not know. It leads us to the most important insight that we humans are very diverse in respect to the minor details about which we perhaps know something. However, in our infinite lack of knowledge we are all the same." (pp. 52-3). Giddens states in his essay 'Living in a Post-Traditional Society', with only a passing acknowledgement to Popper's views on knowledge, that the latter applied these only specifically to science. [in Giddens, *Reflexive Modernization*, pp. 56-109 (pp. 86-87).] However, we can see that Popper clearly meant that his views be applied to everyday life in general because he prefaced the passage quoted above by recalling Isaac Newton's experience: "Newton speaks for all of us when he says 'I do not know how I appear to the world. To myself I appear like a boy playing on the seashore. I enjoyed myself inspecting a pebble here and there that was smoother than the others, or a more attractive mussel – and all the while the great ocean of truth lay before me undiscovered.'"[Popper, p. 52.]

20. See Ernst Tugendhat, 'Die Hilflosigkeit der Philosophen angesichts der moralischen Schwierigkeiten von heute', in his *Philosophische Aufsätze* (Frankfurt/Main: Suhrkamp, 1992), pp. 371-382.

21. Lorenz Jäger, 'Neue Arbeit,' *FAZ*, 19.6.1998, p. 41; Jacob Heilbrunn, 'Europa wird Amerika nicht folgen', *Die Zeit*, Nr. 46, 5.11.1998, p. 15.

22. 'The third way revealed', *The Economist*, 19-25.9.1998, p. 54.

23. Ralf Dahrendorf, 'Politik: Eine Kolumne' in Karl Heinz Bohrer and Kurt Schell (eds.), *Merkur* 593 Heft 8 August 1998 (Stuttgart: Klett-Cotta, 1998), pp. 710-714 (p. 713).

24. Schröder's preferred slogan is "The new centre." Both slogans were claimed in a joint SPD and British Labour party declaration presented by Blair and Schröder in June 1999 to be "policy," the document concluding that this "Policy of the third way and the new centre" might become "Europe's new hope." Joint declaration cited in Werner A. Perger, 'Kampfansage an die alte Garde', *Die Zeit*, Nr. 24, 10.6.1999, p. 10.

25. Anthony Smith, *Nations and Nationalism in a Global Era* (Cambridge: Polity

Press, 1995), p. 127.

26. William Wallace, *Regional Integration: The West European Experience* (Washington D.C.: The Brookings Institution, 1994), p. 21.

27. 'Schäuble: Ost-Erweiterung der EU nicht verschieben', p. 2; Jean Pierre Chevènement, 'In den Nationen liegt die Zukunft Europas', p. 14; Wolfgang Schäuble, 'Für sich allein ist jedes Land den Abhängigkeiten stärker ausgeliefert', p. 15. All articles published in *FAZ*, 15.5.1998. See also the contribution of William Wallace, 'Was an ihre Stelle treten könnte', *FAZ*, 4.6.1998, p. 11.

28. Wallace *Regional Integration*, pp. 60–1.

29. Anglo-Saxon influences are also clearly discernible in the sources cited in studies by German scholars of European integration, e.g. in Bertold Dietz et al. (eds.), *Die soziale Zukunft Europas* (Gießen: Focus, 1994); Michael Kreile (ed.) *PVS Sonderheft 23 1992* (Opladen: Westdeutscher Verlag, 1992); in this Anglo-Saxon environment, German scholar Peter Lange, based in the United States, with his 'The Politics of the Social Dimension', has contributed to Albert M. Sbragia (ed.), *Europolitics* (Washington D.C.: Brookings Institution, 1992).

30. This domination can be traced to the foundation after the First World War of the Royal Institute of International Affairs; it can also be linked to the fact that following both world wars continental Europeans had no influence on the shaping of the global state system. As Anthony Giddens has pointed out, "Both the League of Nations and the United Nations were mainly the result of American thought and planning. The British Government was the only one among the European nations to play an active role in the drafting of the charters of both organizations." [Anthony Giddens, *The Nation-State and Violence* (Cambridge: Polity Press, 1992), p. 258.] There is indeed a vast amount of German-language literature on Europe, European integration, and the like, but the balance of overall discussion is dominated by an international community of scholarship, removed from national and regional debate, and influenced by the origins of the study of the subject "international relations" in the USA and the UK.

31. Manfred Henningsen, 'Die politische Verfassung Europas', in Bohrer and Scheel (eds.), *Merkur*, Mai Heft 5 (Stuttgart: Klett-Cotta, 1998), pp. 454-461 (p. 454).

32. David Marsh alluded to the same question in 1990 by quoting Ernst von Weizsäcker's 7 January 1937 *Auswärtiges Amt* memorandum about Germany's need for the presentation of a peaceful image to the world abroad if its foreign policy aims were to be realized. See Marsh, *The New Germany: At the Crossroads* (London: Century, 1990), p. 342.

33. Wallerstein, *Geopolitics and Geoculture*, p. 10; also the same view in his earlier essay 'The withering away of the states', in *The Politics of the World Economy* (Cambridge University Press, 1984), pp. 47-57 (p. 55).

34. See, for example, Jean-Marie Guéhenno, *Das Ende der Demokratie* [*Le Fin de la Démocratie*] (Munich: Artemis & Winkler Verlag, 1994), pp. 165-166.

35. See Anthony Giddens, *Beyond Left and Right: the Future of Radical Politics* (Cambridge: Polity Press, 1994), p. 4; also in his contribution to *Reflexive Modernization*, p. 96.

36. The demarcation between stratified academic and general popular debate is not so strong in Germany compared with English-speaking countries. The *Bundeszentrale für politische Bildung*, for example, publishes and delivers the weekly newspaper *Das Parlament* jointly with the journal *Aus Politik und Zeitgeschichte*. Friedrich Karl Fromme,

Fritz Scharpf and Christian Graf von Krockow, prominent media figures, serve alongside the likes of Charles Taylor on the editorial advisory committee of *Zeitschrift für Politik*. Not only do my footnoted sources thus cite references to newspaper articles by academics, they and the bibliography reflect the authorship of articles by political and business figures published in academic journals.

37. I would very much lay emphasis on treating these sources with circumspection. Thus I would set more store on the media's reporting of data, less so on the opinions contained in the articles. Pressing newspaper deadlines necessitate judgements made in haste to conform to the needs of the story. For example, in an *FAZ* supplement on Germany's 100 largest companies, one could find the opinion that "Siemens ... is developing constantly, and is making itself indispensable in the production of computer chips." The question, is however, for whom is Siemens indispensable? As we shall see in Chapter 11, although Siemens is indispensable as an employer for many of its employees, clients and the market found Siemens' very dispensable as a producer of computer chips, and this caused problems for firm and workforce. See Christian Geinitz, 'Im Club der Großen hat sich die Sitzordnung verändert', 'Die 100 größten Unternehmen', 40. Folge (*FAZ* supplement), 7.7.1998, p. B 12.

38. Helmut Schmidt, 'Hände weg von der Steuerschraube', *Die Zeit*, Nr. 10, 5.3.1993, p. 1.

39. That solutions relying upon parameters of economic growth alone will not succeed is shown by a report prepared by the Swiss Federal Council for Foreigner and Refugee policy: "Switzerland, Western Europe, North America, Japan, Australia and some South East Asian states, along with some Central and Eastern European states in the near future, are gradually developing into islands of material affluence in a world of deprivations. It is becoming ever clearer that an imitation by third world states of this form of life could only lead to an ecological collapse ... The recognition is growing that the characteristics of our western civilisation form cannot serve as a model for a globally sustainable world societal order." See *Swiss Federal Council on Foreign and Refugee Policy Report 15 May 1991*, cited in Bernd Hof, *Europa im Zeichen der Migration: Szenarien zur Bevölkerungs- und Arbeitsmarktentwicklung in der Europäischen Gemeinschaft bis 2020* (Cologne: Deutscher Instituts-Verlag, 1993), p. 21. A UN Development Program 1998 report comes to similar conclusions. The authors plea for goals that make possible a minimum level of consumption for all. See Ulrike Meyer-Timpe and Fritz Vorholz, 'Die letzte Lüge', *Die Zeit*, Nr. 38, 10.9.1998, pp. 23-24.

Part I

Problems of Community: The European Intercommunity Perspective on Building Blocks for Social Coherence

The focus of Part I will be concentrated on the effects and pressures of interstate integration on communities' social coherence in Europe. This part of the book will give a synopsis of the evolution of (Western) European institutional integration from the German perspective. It serves as a necessary initial framework for a discussion of further aspects of integration affecting post-war Europe in dramatic measure upon the end of the Cold War: extrainstitutional integration at the transnational level. These aspects will be discussed in Part II.

Although the focus here in Part I is on the effects and pressures of interstate integration, I will at times use the term "intercommunity" to express this idea also, reflecting my aim to discuss the effects of these developments upon societies as a whole. We should also recall the desires of proponents of the original drive towards integration in Europe to focus upon the concept of "community" as a means of eliminating state conceptions, hence the naming of the European Coal and Steel Community (ECSC). This emphasis continued in the titles European Economic Community (EEC) and European Community (EC) (until they were replaced or overshadowed by the term EU under the Maastricht Treaty). Where I discuss these Communities, I will use upper case. Nevertheless, Europe's political elite's agreement at Maastricht to accentuate the bond between states, in the name European *Union* is perhaps an indication that the institutional means to integration risks losing focus on the community aspect of integration.

Accordingly, in Part I, I aim to show why institutional mechanisms are not enough alone to achieve greater European unity. I will focus on the effects of institutional approaches upon social coherence in Europe in the chapters: "The Single European Act," "Reactions to the Single European Act: The Western Path to Maastricht," and "EMU and the Establishment of Greater Interdependence." On this basis, I will show the insufficiencies of these approaches in the penultimate chapter, "The Limits of EU Integration and the Possibilities of Functionalism." Nonetheless, before moving on to a discussion of transinstitutional approaches to extending transnational social coherence in Part II, in the final chapter "Parameters and Limits of Democracy in Europe," I will discuss how institutional mechanisms already in existence can be better attuned to citizens' needs.

Leading up to these objectives, however, as an initial stage towards finding possible building blocks for social coherence, let us now trace briefly the history of (Western) European integration from the immediate post-Second World War period to current post-Cold War times. We will see initially how transnational market forces, not the inaugural drive towards supranational institutional regulation, have come to play the dominant role in steps to integration.

2

The Movement from Supranational Regulation to the Transnational Market

In this chapter we will examine reasons for a switch in emphasis from the idealistic steps towards European integration in the immediate post-Second World War period to the pragmatic economic preoccupations in the Community of the mid-eighties.

The popular aspiration to build a unified Europe following 1945 was a reaction to the conflict of interests between sovereign states, which had resulted in two world wars with catastrophic effects, not just in Europe, but world-wide. Furthermore, the additional factor of the widening ideological divide between East and West directed the supranational focus more strongly in Western European states, yet limited it also solely within Western Europe until 1989. Nonetheless, as I discuss in more detail elsewhere, the fact of the division meant that Western European conceptions concerning identity and goals of post-1945 integration were not subjected to the rigorous questioning that might otherwise have occurred had there not been the external threat from the Soviet Bloc.[1]

Initially, despite ideological division, steps in Western Europe towards integration took place with astounding imagination and willingness to make things work. Widespread enthusiasm stemmed from hopes among many that things in the second half of the twentieth century could only be better than in the first half. Idealistic calls for a United States of Europe (most famously made in a speech by Winston Churchill) notwithstanding however, the first major step towards integration also incorporated immensely pragmatic considerations. This step was the creation of the ECSC under the Treaty of Paris in April 1951. Although the relinquishment by its six member states (Belgium, France, Germany, Italy, Luxembourg and The Netherlands) of their sovereignty over coal and steel production to a supranational High Authority was a revolutionary step, the inauguration of the ECSC had two practical aspects. First, the creation of the ECSC could help rebuild Europe, and second, within this greater need, it made the rebuilding of the German coal and steel industry politically acceptable to other European states, particularly France. The ECSC additionally linked homogeneous aspects of need to heterogeneous need. It fulfilled French needs for security: German coal and steel production, subjected to the control of the Community's High Authority, would no longer be able to fuel the cravings of militarism in Germany. Under the aegis of the ECSC's High Authority, the coal and steel production of the Ruhr could be freed from stringent Allied controls in place since 1945, and deployed to the urgent needs of rebuilding Europe following the destruction of war. This was the common need.[2] The new Federal Republic of Germany meanwhile also gained immeasurably in symbolic acceptance from its fellow states: in that its fellow signatories gave up a measure of their own sovereignty in equal measure to it, the Federal Republic actually gained in sovereignty in relative terms.[3]

The social, consensual approach of the ECSC was a reflection of the terms of the power equation within Germany itself. Capitalism, and the capitalists of German heavy industry in particular, were severely discredited because of their association with and advocacy of the Nazis' armament policies. So discredited was capitalism that it was even scorned in the Ahlen political manifesto of the CDU in the British Zone of occupation in 1947. The manifesto famously contained the following passage:

The capitalist economic system has become inappropriate for the state and social interests of the German people. Following the terrible political economic and social collapse resulting from criminal political policies, a new order from the bottom up can be the only possible consequence. The content and goal of this social and economic new order can no longer be the capitalist striving for profit and power but the well-being of our whole people.[4]

Much of post-war public opinion in Germany viewed the market economy as an antisocial form of organizing society. Although the market economy was to prevail ultimately under the aegis of Ludwig Erhard (who attacked the planned economy at the CDU party congress in February 1949 as "the most unsocial possible, and only the market economy is social"[5]), the prevailing mood contributed to workers' representatives being accorded a say in the decisions of the ECSC High Authority. Within the Federal Republic, the position of those inside the CDU who favored a new order of industrial organization was reinforced as both steel workers and miners voted overwhelmingly (95.87% and 92.8%, respectively) to strike if necessary in support of company workforce codetermination. The first FRG Chancellor Konrad Adenauer voiced his support for the Ahlen manifesto too.[6] Thus, following negotiations between unions, employers' organizations and the government, the *Bundestag* passed the Parity Codetermination (*Paritätsmitbestimmung*) statute in April 1951, which gave employees equal representation on the supervisory boards of coal and steel companies.[7]

In the ECSC, the union representatives saw an international ally in their aspirations towards greater determination in the running of the industry, and even wider long-term goals of more general social regulation. Meanwhile, the employers saw the freedom of the markets impinged.[8] To date the ECSC remains the high-water mark of the institutional and social consensus approach to European unification.

However, during the course of the fifties the aspirations of many on the union side were disappointed. A number of factors on the international stage contributed to the balance of power shifting back to the free-market forces of capital once more. We can see that these international developments ensured the switch in emphasis from idealistic, revolutionary steps in pursuit of European integration to pragmatic economic preoccupations. The most important factor was the North Korean forces' invasion of South Korea in June 1950. The Korean War was a turning point in West German history, in domestic social policy as well as in foreign policy terms. The heightening of Cold War tensions brought about by the conflict – the battlefield in Korea could have lain in Germany instead – played the major role in the formulation of domestic and foreign policy in Western Europe as a whole.

The effect of hardening Cold War stances was reinforced by reverses to UK and French colonial policies in Suez and Indochina, which all but ended their imperialist ambitions. The political process in the fourth republic in France was debilitated further by the need to restore international prestige and domestic cohesion following the Nazi occupation. These factors had repercussions on these states' foreign policy. Successive UK governments gave expression to their insecurities by pursuing a special relationship with the United States. Meanwhile in France, the result was chronic instability in the process of maintaining coalition government, which played a critical role in the National Assembly's rejection of the statute for the planned European Defence Community (EDC). The plan for the EDC foresaw a supranational authority on parallel lines to its counterpart in the ECSC as a means of simultaneous control and deployment of a rearmed Germany in the defense of the West against the Soviet Union.

FROM THE EUROPEAN MOVEMENT TO THE MARKET

The Treaty of Rome in 1957, which set up the European Economic Community (EEC) and the European Atomic Energy Community (Euratom), was borne of a desire to reprime the political integration process after the failure of the EDC. However there was little in the Treaty to foster solidarity in the more important of the new communities, the EEC. The document was a compromise. While the French government was in favor of a substantial measure of social statute harmonization, others, especially the increasingly economically confident Federal Republic, laid more emphasis on liberal free-market elements. The Treaty of Rome only contained agreement on social issues as secondary elements servicing the primacy of the market, and ensuring freedom of competition.[9] This assignation of priorities has continued up to the present. Consequently, as Mathias Hinterschied, then general secretary of the European Trade Union Confederation (ETUC), pointed out, social policy remains the stepchild of the Rome Treaties.[10]

In West Germany, the freezing of the divide across the Continent between East and West had set the external parameters for the rehabilitation of business. In 1952, Germany's most influential post-war banker, Joseph Abs, had been able to negotiate a settlement of Germany's debts to international creditors. Furthermore, apart from the two notable exceptions of IG Farben and the coal and steel mammoth Vereinigte Stahlwerke, large German firms were able to avoid the fate of being split as the Western allies had originally foreseen. Although the companies law (*Betriebsverfassungsgesetz*) of July 1952 established the principle of collaborative consultation processes between employers and employees in works councils, trades union representatives were unable to extend their achievement of codetermination in the coal and steel industry to other sectors. The unions' goal of parity between capital and labor remained unachieved.[11]

This was an era when Western European economies were booming in the post-war reconstruction process. We can see two symptoms of the boom in the FRG. First, it was a period that saw the first of the Federal Republic's *Gastarbeiter* agreements. Second, business also lobbied successfully to dilute Erhard's Cartels legislation, passed in 1957. The latter left not only "Dr. Ludwig Erhard ... putting a brave face on the emasculation of his plans, which has occurred largely under pressure of the powerful Federation of German Industry," but as the same contemporary column in *The Economist* observed, was to have knock-on effects for the rest of Europe also: "A less mild and flexible law would have been more propitious for the fruitful working of the coming European common market and the proposed free trade area."[12]

In the narrower sense during the Cold War, the term "European integration" came to encompass solely Western European unification. Along with higher profile political rapprochement between French and German governments, business and finance in Germany were also firm supporters of European integration. For example Fritz Berg, the first Federal Association of German Industry (BDI) president, consistently strove to form close relationships with French counterparts.[13]

However the iron curtain was no barrier to business, which continued to build up trade with Eastern bloc states, not least in Germany, despite acute ideological sensitivities resulting from Cold War division. For example, despite massive tensions over the successive crises in Berlin, German firms were delivering pipes in massive numbers to the Soviet Union: on average, 170,000 a year in the period 1959-62. In 1963, with a further 163,000 outstanding orders, firms involved – Mannesmann, Hoesch, Phoenix Rheinrohr – supported by the opposition Social Democratic Party of Germany (SPD), unions and Adenauer's junior coalition partner Free Democratic Party (FDP) lobbied hard against an export ban. They failed, but the controversy resulted in contemporary discussion whether an export-oriented state such as the Federal Republic would not be better off separating politics from business.[14]

In political/institutional terms, the Economic Community was to be hampered in progress towards the founding fathers' goals of European integration by the Luxembourg compromise of 1966. It seemed that the assertion of traditional conceptions of state interest meant that any member inclined to halt further steps to integration could do so. Nation-state interests continued to assert themselves above supranational community interest. Thus although the period up until the 1973 oil crisis saw higher economic growth rates in the EEC than in the USA or UK,[15] the period was marked by little progress towards further political integration. From 1966 to 1985, with the exception of its increase in membership, and the beginning of direct elections to the largely powerless Parliament in 1979, the Community found itself locked in a political and, following the oil crisis, an economic stasis. Until the mid-eighties, the Community's capacity to achieve the intended common market remained limited save the exceptions of the agricultural, coal and steel sectors, along with the achievement of a customs union. Economic performance was not improved to any great extent in the short term by the inauguration of the European Monetary System (EMS) and its exchange-rate mechanism (ERM) in 1979. EMS, not based on any Community treaty articles, was in the judgement of Nicol and Salmon, "a hybrid – not entirely inside, not entirely outside it."[16] In 1982, 66% of the EC budget remained in the agricultural sector, an indication of the Community's inability to address more pressing urban economic problems in the world's oldest industrial region.[17]

The mood concerning the Community's future was so pessimistic that a term coined in an *Economist* leader "Eurosclerosis" became a general catchword. In terms of its original medical meaning, sclerosis demands practical medical steps to help individuals affected by it. Ruminations concerning the person's ideal physical appearance, or plastic surgery, will not improve his or her health. If we bear this in mind, we should not be surprised that in the next chapter, in our examination of the Single European Act, we will continue to observe the continuing domination of pragmatic economic considerations in the evolution of the European integration process.

NOTES

1. See companion volume to this work: Donald Phillips, *Post-National Patriotism and the Feasibility of Post-National community in United Germany* (Westport, CT: Praeger, 2000).

2. Although these aims also coincided with UK policy, the UK government rejected membership on nationalist grounds. Prime Minister Clement Attlee stated that a major area of British industry could not be "controlled by a foreign committee." See David Mitrany, 'The Making of the Functional Theory: A Memoir,' in his *The Functional Theory of Politics* (London: LSE Martin Robertson & Co Ltd, 1975), pp. 3-46 (p. 36).

3. The FRG was not, for example, to become a full member of the Council of Europe, set up like the FRG itself in May 1949, until May 1951, the month following the Treaty of Paris. Although the FRG was invited to join the Council of Europe in spring 1950, other non-founder members – Greece, Turkey and Iceland – acceded before it. See Martin Westlake, *A Modern Guide to the European Parliament* (London: Pinter, 1994), p. 6.

4. Cited in Volker Berghahn, *Unternehmer und Politik in der Bundesrepublik* (Frankfurt/Main: Suhrkamp, 1985), p. 202.

5. Cited in Christoph Buchheim, 'Was ist sozial an der Marktwirtschaft?', in Wolfgang Benz (ed.), *Sieben Fragen an die Bundesrepublik* (Munich: Deutscher Taschenbuch Verlag, 1989), pp. 53-68 (p. 58).

6. Needless to say, some on the political left doubted Adenauer's sincerity. The author has heard, for example, a Communist Party of Germany (KPD) member (released in 1945 from concentration camp imprisonment to become a political office holder in the US-occupied zone in the immediate post-war period) dismissing Adenauer's support for the Ahlen declaration as merely "a formulaic declaration." Nonetheless, Adenauer's support was a reflection of the historical constellation of the time.

7. See Wolfgang Däubler, *Das Arbeitsrecht 1* (Reinbek: Rororo, 1993), pp. 629-631.

8. See Beate Kohler-Koch, 'Interessen und Integration. Die Rolle organisierter Interessen im westeuropäischen Integrationsprozeß,' in Michael Kreile (ed.), *PVS Sonderheft 23 1992* (Opladen: Westdeutscher Verlag, 1992), pp. 81-19 (pp. 84-85).

9. Hans-Wolfgang Platzer, 'Sozialpolitik und soziale Integration in der Europäischen Union: Bedingungen, Perspektiven und Grenzen im Spannungsfeld von Markt und Politikintegration', in Bertold Dietz et al. (eds.), *Die soziale Zukunft Europas* (Giessen: Focus, 1994), pp. 42-62 (pp. 50-51).

10. Mathias Hinterschied, 'Binnenmarkt und Sozialraum im Binnenmarkt '92 Perspektiven aus deutscher Sicht', in Werner Weidenfeld (ed.), *Strategien und Optionen für die Zukunft Europas Arbeitspapiere 1* (Gütersloh: Bertelsmann Stiftung, 1988), pp. 45-50 (p. 45).

11. See Däubler, *Das Arbeitsrecht 1*, pp. 383-385.

12. 'Bonn's Elastic Cartel law', *The Economist*, 20.7.1957, p. 227.

13. Arnulf Baring, *Im Anfang war Adenauer* (Munich: Deutscher Taschenbuch Verlag, 1971), pp. 321-323.

14. Hans-Peter Schwarz, *Geschichte der Bundesrepublik Deutschland: Die Ära Adenauer 1957-1963* (Stuttgart: Deutsche Verlags Anstalt, 1983), pp. 300-301.

15. See Loukas Tsoukalis, *The New European Economy: The Politics and Economics of Integration* (Oxford University Press, 1993), pp. 22-24.

16. William Nicol and Trevor Salmon, *Understanding the New European Community* (Hemel Hempstead: Harvester Wheatsheaf, 1994), pp. 152-154 (p. 153). EMS was legitimized as part of the Community under the Single European Act.

17. Figure cited by Claus Eiselstein, 'Die Rolle des internationalen Wirtschaftsrechts in der Krise', in Joseph Mako and Armin Stolz (eds.), *Demokratie und Wirtschaft* (Vienna: Böhlau Verlag, 1987), pp. 266-299 (p. 290). Limited Commission reform under the aegis of Agricultural Commissioner Ray MacSharry, principally in lowering beef and cereal prices, saw the Common Agricultural Policy (CAP) portion of budget being reduced to under 50% of EU spending by the end of the nineties, nonetheless a very high figure. See 'Goodbye to Berlin', *The Economist*, 20.3.1999, p. 20; 'EU-Ausgaben sollen um 3,4 Prozent wachsen', *FAZ*, 30.4.1998, p. 19; Stephen George, *Politics and Policy in the European Union* (Oxford University Press, 1996), pp. 189-191.

3

The Single European Act

Only from the mid-eighties onwards did a dynamic arise for changes in the Community which resulted in agreement on the Single European Act (SEA). In this chapter, we will examine how the pragmatic parameters of the SEA nonetheless have played a substantial role in the development of revolutionary societal processes. I will argue that these changes will presage wider changes to existing sociopolitical norms of liberal representative democracy.

Initially, the combination of the dynamic Commission presidency of Jacques Delors, large businesses' concerns over global competitiveness and UK government advocacy of free-market economics gave the internal parameters for change. The extra-Community factors of German unification and the disappearance of the Soviet Union supplemented these at the start of the next decade.

When Delors became president of the Commission in 1985 "[his] major contribution was to focus states' attention on the one issue – the single market – that was acceptable to the three major actors, Britain, West Germany and France."[1] Delors' task was facilitated by the move away from socialist interventionism by the François Mitterrand government, together with Margaret Thatcher's proponence of the primacy of the market and deregulation. Impetus came also with the Community's expansion to twelve members. These political trends were harnessed to business' concerns that production throughout the EEC was becoming progressively less competitive in comparison to Japan or the USA. Indeed, the actual formulation of the plan for the single market was the remit of leading European businesses, not the Commission.

The origins of the Commission's White Paper on the SEA can be traced to the work of a European roundtable of industrialists (ERT) chaired by the then head of Volvo, Pehr Gyllenhammar in 1983.[2] Although Volvo's Swedish base was then outside the EEC, Gyllenhammar attracted most of the Community's leading transnational businesses to his deliberations. These included representatives of Philips, AEG, Olivetti, Shell, Siemens, Fiat, Daimler-Benz, MAN, Thyssen and Robert Bosch. The tangible resulting focus of the consultations was a thesis paper written by the head of

Philips, Wisse Dekker, entitled "Europa 1990."[3] The contents reflected business concerns about the necessity of European merger or cooperation to win enough economies of scale to compete economically and technologically with Japanese or American competitors.[4] Western Europe's political leadership agreed to many of these proposals when they were taken over by the Commission in the shape of the SEA at the Luxembourg summit in December 1985. Their agreement resulted in the introduction of the single market on 1 January 1993, which officially freed the movement of goods, services and labor within the Community.

WIDER IMPLICATIONS OF THE SINGLE EUROPEAN ACT

In general, as we have seen already in regard to the continuance of interbloc trade when the Cold War was at its coldest, business is a continuous and all-pervasive process. In this section, let us link this property with the effects of the SEA on the Community.

The then head of the Deutsche Bank, Alfred Herrhausen, in a speech entitled "The changing world economy," delivered frequently during the mid-eighties, gives an illuminating view of business fears and hopes contemporary to the establishment of the European single market:

We often cannot tell what might be good or bad or what consequences might follow ... as the developments brought by modern communication, information and transportation technologies have now resulted in people being joined with each other in a system of global participation. What happens, or indeed does not happen, politically or economically in one part of the globe is not without consequences for the rest of the world.[5]

Here, we should note that the SEA has played a part in the development of even higher levels of business and financial activity, one of several societal processes that are progressively outflanking political positions contoured solely by geographical positions. Traditional forums for political and social activity, hitherto much more limited in geographical scale, are increasingly losing relevance in communities' everyday activities. On the wider scale, although the SEA provided for the free movement of labor, capital is inherently more fluid than people, or even manufactured goods. In 1986, foreign exchange turnover was only 25 times that of world trade. By the beginning of the nineties, annual turnover on the foreign exchange markets was 70 times that of world trade. During this time, daily turnover on the foreign exchange markets increased from $200 billion to $1,000 billion.[6]

Thus, we should investigate how communities' actions and social policies can better take account of revolutionary changes in political and social processes, where the importance of geographical factors is diminishing. I would argue that our societies would be better served first by incorporating business more in democratic decision making. Second, we could envisage extending democratic decision making into business, to overcome periods of political deadlock within and between communities. I will expand these thoughts later in Part II of this book.

But before we do so, it is necessary to retain the institutional focus of this part of the book. Many commentators see the EU as a suitable replacement for nation-states. But as we shall see in the remainder of Part I, the alternative institutional focus of the

EU is itself as much an insufficient parameter bounding conceptions of community as the same nation-states that agreed to the establishment of the single market.

It seems that many of Europe's political leaders were taken by surprise at the revolutionary implications of the creation of the European single market. But in view of the above remarks by Herrhausen, is it any wonder that the single market has had revolutionary implications? The nature of the European integration process, since its beginnings under Jean Monnet and Robert Schuman, has been one of utilizing the pragmatism of functionalism to secure the fundamental ideal of avoiding war between heterogeneous interests and perceived identities. Integrationist steps have been carried out by a process of stealth, a habit well practiced by businessmen in boardroom coups and takeover and merger bids, but foreign to politicians who revel in the grand public gesture and the telegenic moment. At the close of the Luxembourg summit that approved the SEA, François Mitterrand remarked that "[the Single Act] goes in the right direction, [but that]... France has a more ambitious view of what Europe could do." Meanwhile, Margaret Thatcher referred to the act as "a modest decision."[7]

But out of small acorns, oaks can grow. Moreover, plants invariably grow in directions that are most clement for them, not where we would necessarily like them to grow. This is the case with the single market, which has grown in directions most clement for the market. Nonetheless, the SEA also included a majority voting provision in the Council on certain policy areas related to setting up the Internal Market, and as a counterweight to this, also for the first time, the provision of the right for the European Parliament (EP) to amend Community legislation. Prior to the SEA, the Parliament had only the power to delay.[8] Thus, in two respects we can see that the signing of the SEA, although the product of a coalescence of nation-states' economic interests, proved to be an acknowledgment of the necessity of multipolar decision making and discussion in response to an increasingly interdependent world.

First, the SEA acknowledged the necessity of multipolar decision making in respect to freeing the operations of business from the constraints of national parameters. The existence of the SEA was in turn to foster this dynamic further. Second, in doing so, the SEA fostered the prerequisite for multipolarity in that it curtailed democratic accountability of state governments to their own parliaments. As we shall see, subsequent European treaties have encouraged this trend further, and have led to resentments expressed in national legislatures and other representative segments of public opinion throughout Europe. Previous shortcomings of nation-state-based liberal representative democracy tend to have been forgotten. Instead, the loss of influence and curtailment of scope to carry out changes within traditional parameters of parliamentary democratic legislature have prompted many to concentrate on "democratic deficit." New shortcomings brought by the move to supranational organization are seen in terms of divisive hegemonic concepts of power. These should be becoming increasingly outdated, but for many, as we shall see, they are not.

Discussing potential for democracy in Europe, Juliet Lodge has discerned that after the SEA, many Members of Parliament (MPs) at state level have seen Members of the European Parliament (MEPs) as a group as actual or potential rivals rather than as allies. I would agree with her assessment that "the democratic legitimacy problem has to be addressed from a variety of perspectives ... the issues of defining and rectifying the EU's democratic deficit by reference to the sociopolitical norms of a bygone age may no longer be entirely appropriate."[9]

Accordingly, in subsequent chapters to this, I will argue that it is inappropriate to see potential solutions in terms of the hegemony of a supranational parliamentary authority or even a return to national parliamentary democracy. I will argue in Part II for an extension of democracy to embrace non-parliamentary arenas instead.

So far we have seen how idealistic steps taken towards the ideal of European integration had become progressively usurped as a motive in Western Europe by pragmatic economic considerations, largely at the behest of elite business interests. As a last Western European coda to this, in the next chapter we will examine the limited capacity of employee representatives to respond to the Single (Western) European Act, before we move on to a consideration of what happened when these pragmatic steps encountered the challenge of the end of the Cold War, marked most dramatically of all with the end of divided Germany.

NOTES

1. Robert J. Keohane and Stanley Hoffmann, 'Institutional Change in Europe in the 1980s', in Keohane and Hoffmann (eds.), *The New European Community* (Boulder: Westview Press, 1991), pp. 1-39 (p. 24).

2. Andrew Moravcsik: 'Negotiating the Single European Act,' in Keohane and Hoffmann, pp. 40-84 (p. 44).

3. Harald Fiedler, 'Der EG-Binnenmarkt aus Sicht des DGB', in Friedrich-Karl Feyerabend (ed.), *Europa 1992, Binnenmarkt, Europäische Union* (Giessen: Verlag der Feber'sche Universitätsbuchhandlung, 1993), pp. 57-76 (pp. 64-65).

4. Keohane and Hoffmann (eds.), p. 22. Ironically, echoing Herrhausen's remarks on this page regarding the global unpredictability of the consequences of actions, Volvo sold its car division to Ford in 1999.

5. Alfred Herrhausen, *Denken – Ordnen – Gestalten* (Berlin: Wolf Jobst Siedler, 1990), p. 193.

6. Norbert Walter, 'World Financial Markets: Trends and Options for Globalization', in Werner Weidenfeld and Josef Janning (eds.), *Europe in Global Change: Strategies and Options for Europe* (Gütersloh: Bertelsmann Foundation Publishers, 1993), pp. 45-64 (p. 45).

7. Albert Bressand (quoting *Le Monde*, 4.12.1985), 'EC Policy and Diplomacy', in Jonathan Story (ed.), *The New Europe* (Oxford: Blackwell, 1993), pp. 314-327 (p. 319).

8. See Westlake, pp. 26-27.

9. See Juliet Lodge, 'The European Parliament' in Svein Andersen and Kjell Eliassen (eds.), *The European Union: How Democratic Is It?* (London: Sage, 1996), pp. 187-214 (p. 214).

4

Reactions to the Single European Act: The Western Path to Maastricht

As we have seen, business played an essential role in the formulation of the SEA. As an understandable reaction therefore, the SEA and the 1992 project, according to one commentator, "raised fears among European unions and the European left that integration will promote an erosion of workers' existing social benefits (or at least prevent any extension of such benefits) and that it will weaken labor's position in industrial relations institutions."[1] Fears common throughout Europe that the SEA would accelerate the regional division of labor were especially marked in Germany, where organized labor has achieved more than most in terms of social stability.[2] Although German employees were among those with perhaps the most to lose, these fears were common throughout Europe. Stephen George, who subscribes in great part to the neofunctionalist approach to European integration, has pondered nonetheless that neofunctionalism could not explain why pressure to form the SEA "was able to overcome the resistance to freeing the market that came from other groups."[3]

In attempting to identify fundamental deficits of current approaches to European integration, I will discuss the deficits of neofunctionalist analysis and approaches and compare these with original functionalist precepts in Chapter 6. Here, however, we can clarify George's puzzlement as to why neofunctionalism could not explain the lack of resistance at the European level to freeing markets with the following simple answer. Before the signing of the SEA, there were no such groups capable of resisting. Before the SEA, national union leaderships had lacked the necessary motivation for action at the European level. As opposed to capital, which is deployed wherever the investor believes he can obtain the best return for his money, union activity is dependent on human relationships established at a local level to motivate collective campaigns. This handicaps the appeal of action undertaken on a wider scale.[4] Indeed, both the acronym and organization of the ETUC stand for a confederation, *not* a federation of interests. Moreover, unions did not have the resources to represent the interests of their members at the European level commensurate with changing times and the more fluid affiliations of potential or actual employers. In Germany for example, German Trades Union Federation (DGB) or individual union representatives saw themselves increasingly pressured by lack of resources and time.[5]

Furthermore, attempts to coordinate particular labor interests at the European level were caught up in ideological conflicts, bringing a further handicap to unions' activities expanding beyond a national focus. The work of the ETUC had been limited since its inaugural year in 1973, by the contrasting, contrary political and economic traditions of its constituent members. Any international activity was viewed as optional and supplementary.[6]

Thus, European trade unions were not consulted in the drafting process of the SEA. Unlike employers, who were primarily responsible for the realization of the SEA, the ETUC only reacted following the publication of the Commission white paper. Its input on its formulation was nil. The opportunity for organized labor articulating its views in a coordinated manner was further debilitated in that ETUC congresses were held only once every three years. It took over two years for the ETUC executive committee to publish a draft program calling for extended social and regional policies as a reaction to the single market. The program was to be discussed at the organization's 1988 congress in Stockholm. The 1985 Milan congress had taken place before agreement on the SEA was reached.[7] Since the end of the Cold War, ideological strains in the ETUC have disappeared, but as Wolfgang Merkel has pointed out, the organization remains a substantially ineffectual and largely reactive lobbying mechanism.[8]

As a result, as the former British cabinet minister and noted prointegrationist Shirley Williams argued, the SEA had little to commend it to the people of Europe, its completion being the "main objective of the business lobby and of those European governments responsive to business interests."[9]

Social issues have always been neglected at European levels, whether through lack of agreement, as at the time of the EEC's inauguration, or simply lack of focus of potential conduits for their articulation. At the 1969 Hague Summit, Willy Brandt argued that social justice should not be considered by the Community as an appendage of economic growth, and that an effective social policy would enable people to identify with Europe more.[10] It may be that Brandt was influenced through his close personal links to the region by the social provisions agreed upon in the Nordic Council integration process among the much more culturally homogenous Scandinavian countries. However, nothing came of Brandt's arguments. Prospects for a more equitable approach to social justice have been made all the more problematic since then, as the Community has become all the more socially and culturally diversified, with the accession of Spain and Portugal concurrent with the signing of the SEA, along with that of Greece some four years before.[11]

Nevertheless, concerns within the ranks of organized labor about prospects of future social imbalances in the Community were quelled somewhat by the extension of German industrial consensus pertaining to social aspects of the European single market. In July 1989 a joint declaration between DGB and the Confederation of German Employers' Associations (BdA) agreed "that in making the European internal market reality, the social dimension is essential."[12] This declaration was undoubtedly more significant in facilitating agreement later that year on the Social Charter than the ETUC's own conference and lobbying documentation in October.[13] German employers' keenness on social aspects of the social market was not out of altruism, but borne out of fear that their home market was more regulated and had more social provisions than any other. Nevertheless, subsequent political and economic developments, as we shall see, raise "the big question for the future of trade unions in Europe ... whether the German model will survive."[14] I would argue that it can only survive if it is conceived of by non-Germans as well as Germans as a post-national rather than specifically German model, and it can only survive by means of grassroots approaches to post-national organization.[15]

In response to union lobbying efforts, in December 1989, 11 of then 12 members of the EC signed the Social Charter. Although most European unions saw the charter for what it actually was, a declaration of intent rather than a covenant of rights, the British Trades Union Congress (TUC) saw it as positive because it went further than was possible in British domestic politics. Nonetheless, most recognized that binding social demands had no realistic chance of being implemented before the advent of the single market. Therefore, unions focussed their activity on advocating an extension of parliamentary democracy at the European level, hoping that more extensive social provisions could be accomplished within the EC institutional and democratic reform process.[16]

However, in the same month as the Social Charter was signed, Western European discussions in the social field, not to mention parallel negotiations towards prospective monetary union, were being considerably distracted by the end of the Cold War in general and the German unification process in particular. This was the catalyst that forced the hurried negotiation process that culminated in the Maastricht Treaty. It is this process which now becomes the focus of our study.

THE ANTECEDENTS OF EMU: THE PATH TO MAASTRICHT THROUGH THE BERLIN WALL

I will now discuss how Western European uncertainty over the prospect of German unification was instrumental in achieving agreement, rather than mere discussion, about EMU.

During the eighties under EMS, member states' monetary policies were subordinated increasingly to the interest rates set by the Bundesbank, and the increasing strength of the D-mark. In January 1988 French Finance Minister Edouard Balladur, frustrated at German dominance of European monetary policy, had proposed a European central bank charged with overseeing a common currency.[17] In their frustrations at D-mark dominance, the French government overcame inclinations against the supranational nature of a common currency, which had led President Georges Pompidou to oppose the EEC's first proposal on monetary union, the Werner Report in 1970.[18] However, the Germans were divided in their responses to Balladur's proposal. Foreign Minister Hans-Dietrich Genscher, with his long-standing commitment to European integration, was in favor.[19] The head of the Bundesbank, Karl Otto Pöhl, and Finance Minister Gerhard Stoltenberg were reserved. As a result, the Federal cabinet endorsed monetary union, but only as a long-term goal. Nevertheless, despite German misgivings, not to mention outright British opposition, the European Council meeting in Hanover in 1988 agreed that a Council Committee chaired by Jacques Delors, and consisting largely of central bank governors, should prepare a report on

EMU.[20]

The following year, however, everything changed utterly: one by one the Communist regimes in Eastern Europe crumbled. The pragmatic functionalist approach of the Western European business and administrative elite to integration was suddenly faced with extraordinary radical changes in the East. These changes were symbolized by the miraculous vision of floods of individuals streaming from totalitarian uniformity through the Berlin wall. The fall of the wall on 9 November 1989 heralded the swift move towards German unification and a seemingly less certain future for all of Europe. The telegenic images of renascent German joy apparently underlined the appeal of the national model of state organization once more, a seismic shift which threatened to overturn all integrationary steps to stability in Western Europe undertaken in the four decades before. In October Jacques Delors had warned: "Where there is no big vision the people perish."[21] But both the "vision" and the "people" that he had in mind were not the same as those resurrected in the imaginations of those demonstrating in East German cities following 9 November. As I discuss in more detail in the companion volume to this book, after the wall came down, the pre-9 November demonstration chants of "We are *the* people" [Wir sind *das* Volk] changed to "We are *one* people" [Wir sind *ein* Volk].[22] It seemed that the Western technocratic proponents of the European vision were, like W.B. Yeats' Caesar, alone with his maps in his tent, naught but long-legged flies on the stream.

Faced with Eastern European instability and anxious about the prospect of German unity, the French president had called upon the EC to speed up its own integration in October 1989. In November, with France occupying the presidency of the Council, he visited all of the other community leaders seeking support for EMU, and called an extraordinary Council meeting without prior consultation of other governments on 18 November. Mitterrand was also notoriously the last Western leader to visit Communist-governed East Berlin, on 20-21 December.[23] Before the true costs or nature of German unification became apparent, general perceptions were that as a result Germany could only grow stronger. In this, Mitterrand's fears bore similarity with those French leaders of a generation before that had prompted the establishment of the ECSC to preempt any resurgence of German military hegemony over Europe. The argument advanced then, in an editorial in *Le Monde* in 1945 was: "If the Ruhr should come out from under the control of Berlin, the question of a central administration for the rest of Germany would lose much of its importance."[24] Half a century later, by interchanging the then Ruhr and Berlin power symbols with their successors, the D-mark and Frankfurt, historical parallels between the ECSC plan and the French impetus to the work of the Delors' committee are strikingly discernible. Delors himself, speaking in October 1989, quoted Genscher's moral exhortation, urging that "the German people should behave in such a way that its (*sic*) existence is seen as a piece of good fortune, or, indeed a necessity for the whole (of Europe)."[25]

Delors' Committee's study, *Report on Economic and Monetary Union in the European Community*, had been published in April 1989. Initially, the German government was largely unenthusiastic in its responses, knowing that a scheme to replace the D-mark would be electorally unpopular. Perhaps but for the fall of the wall, consensus might have been forthcoming on the plan put forward by the Euroskeptic British government in September on development of the ecu as a parallel trading currency to national currencies.[26] But after the wall fell, everything changed.

Federal German government activity began to be characterized by multilateral communication and negotiation with all partners in locations from Moscow to Washington. On the day before he announced his ten-point plan on German and European unity to the *Bundestag* on 28 November for instance, Chancellor Kohl suggested to French President Mitterrand that an intergovernmental conference on institutional reform, including a strengthening of the EP, should be an accompanying counterweight to negotiations on EMU. Many in France, however, saw this step as a delaying tactic in the process towards EMU.[27] French disquiet at the rapid pace towards German unification, for example, led to support at the highest level for Poland. A joint Franco-Polish government press conference, attended by both presidents and prime ministers on the subject of the Oder/Neisse line, had led itself to tensions in telephone conversations between Kohl and first Delors and then Mitterrand on 13 and 14 March. However, in the light of the now increasingly runaway movement towards German unification, the French government gradually cast aside previous inhibitions on supranational political organization during the first three months of 1990. Thus, French and German governments began working on a joint initiative to present to other EC governments on 15 March.[28] Added impetus to the initiative was given as the pace of German unification was quickened further by the East German election results on 18 March.

At an extraordinary European Council meeting in Dublin on 28 April 1990, the Delors report, German unification with its consequences for the Community and the EC's relations to Eastern Europe were all on the agenda. The agenda was primed by Mitterrand and Kohl's joint proposal to the other ten leaders to open negotiations on European political union, as well as discussing a currency union, as a means of stressing Germany's commitment to Europe:

In face of the revolutionary changes in Europe and in view of the creation of the internal market and the realization of an economic and currency union we believe it necessary to speed the process of the political construction of Europe's twelve [EC member states].[29]

The Council agreed to move towards political union as well as EMU. The fact that the proposal was made, and that the Council was held only weeks after the East German election results had set course firmly towards swift unification in Germany, can probably be seen as crucial in encouraging perceptions favoring commensurate urgency on both political reform and EMU. At a further Council meeting in Dublin on 25-26 June, attended also by the newly elected non-Communist East German Premier Lothar de Maizière and Foreign Minister Markus Meckel, the 12 Community leaders agreed to set up an intergovernmental conference on political reform under the banner of political union in parallel to that on EMU.[30]

The first phase towards EMU began on 1 July 1990, the same date as the actual currency union in Germany. The first phase emphasized the goals of states' currency stability and budgetary discipline, and a liberalization of capital markets to make possible the integration of European capital markets.[31] The first phase had been agreed at the Madrid Council meeting in June 1989 against strong UK government opposition. But it was only following the Dublin Council meeting agreement in 1990, that in Tsoukalis' judgement, "economic and political integration appeared to be almost unstoppable."[32]

THE ECONOMIC AND POLITICAL INTEGRATION OF PEOPLES AS WELL AS STATES?

In this chapter we have reviewed how Western European leaders, confronted with the turbulence of Eastern Europe in general, and specifically with the uncertain prospect of German unification, agreed to assess further steps towards dismantling barriers of diverse state interests, cultures and issues of national prestige. On the basis of evidence considered in this chapter, we would seem to have strong reason to suspect that they otherwise might have continued to deem these barriers as being insurmountable. We have seen how plans towards monetary union and a measure of social union had come to naught when the Community had numbered only six. Moreover at this time, the Community was indubitably far less heterogeneous as a unit in terms of economic performance, social structure and cultural tradition than in 1989.

Nonetheless, the end of the Cold War in Europe spelled simultaneously the need to acknowledge a greater interdependence and diversity within and across former bipolar bloc structures. Both these aspects were reflected, emphasized in varying magnitude according to point of view, in debate within the Community at the time over whether widening or deepening the terms of membership should be of primary importance. The need to take account of interdependence transcending former bloc structures was acted upon by the Community itself with its incorporation of former East Germany upon German unification. However, national homogeneity between the two German states obscured diversity. This was more apparent in more objective comparisons between Eastern and Western European political and economic systems. Thus, in the absence of national bonds between other parts of Europe on either side of the former ideological divide, there has been less solidarity between the richer West and the poorer East. However, across a continent no longer dominated by bloc politics as the primary foreign policy consideration, there were substantial reasons for the growth of layers of inner-bloc and interbloc interdependence. First, there was a need to coordinate Community policies regarding Eastern Europe. Second, Eastern European states were dependent upon Western European states as role models and a source of investment. Third, Western European states were dependent on the stable development of their Eastern neighbors precluding any significant new security threat. Finally, Western European states that had remained neutral were now free to move closer towards Community membership, motivated on one hand by political and economic policy coordination needs within other former non-Soviet bloc states, and on the other, mutual concerns about Eastern Europe.

Moreover, as the Continent as a whole retreated from state regulation of society, we should probe further whether we could seek to widen the applications of Tsoukalis' judgement cited above, concerning the inexorable nature of economic and political integration following the Dublin Council meeting. His remarks were actually concerned with states' economic and political integration, not necessarily concerned with citizens of those states, and exclusively pertaining to members of the (Western European) Community. In this respect, we should recall that in Eastern Europe, with the collapse in upon itself of the Comecon system, the contrasting danger in this period was rather more one of economic and political disintegration (although it was certainly a period of opportunity for differential individual self-expression and ability to take decisions, which had been longed for by many). Did the move towards economic and political integration at a horizontal state level in the Community therefore imply an accompanying universal trend to vertical disintegration within states across Europe? Although fears continue that a single market and EMU will see the erosion of nation-states' social provisions, I will argue that there are considerable factors that could provide a commensurate counterbalance to this trend, which may also correct problems of Eastern/Western European integration that the supposed solution of the national bond between Western and Eastern Germany has not been able to solve.

Therefore, over the course of this work, I would hope to show that Tsoukalis' judgement may be applied more widely than to EMU participating states in the EU, namely to Eastern Europe, and to the world beyond. Additionally, they may be applied in vertical terms within states, former national demarcations punched through or made meaningless by transnational forces. But we would be ahead of ourselves to consider these issues in this part of the book. Transnational and transinstitutional developments towards interdependence, between sectors and private companies transcending states, will form the basis of discussion in Part II.

Nonetheless, in the next chapter, although an examination of the EMU implementation process comes to the fore, we should bear in mind that these many factors discussed above remain significant longer-term policy issues all the while that Western Europeans were preoccupied with only one facet of movement towards a greater degree of interdependence. EMU issues form only one element of an overlapping number of interdependent frameworks.

NOTES

1. Peter Lange, 'The Politics of the Social Dimension', in Sbragia (ed.), pp. 225-256 (p. 226).

2. Peter Glotz, 'Ausbruch aus der Wagenburg. Über die Zukunft der Gewerkschaften', *Neue Gesellschaft/Frankfurter Hefte* (*NG/FH*) (Bonn: Friedrich-Ebert-Stiftung), 11/88, pp. 1034-1046.

3. George, p. 200.

4. See Hans-Wolfgang Platzer, *Gewerkschaftspolitik ohne Grenzen: Die transnationale Zusammenarbeit der Gewerkschaften der neunziger Jahre* (Bonn: Dietz Verlag, 1991), p. 165.

5. See, for example, the view that union personnel see themselves increasingly as "servant girls for everything" in Ralf Sitte and Astrid Zegler, 'Partnerschaft in Europa. Warum werden Gewerkschaften nicht an der EU-Strukturpolitik beteiligt?' *WSI Mitteilungen* 12/1994 (Cologne: Bund Verlag), pp. 735-744 (pp. 743-744).

6. Platzer, Gewerkschaftspolitik ohne Grenzen, p. 148.

7. Platzer, *Gewerkschaftspolitik ohne Grenzen*, p. 168. The program (published as Formation of the European Social Space in the Internal Market, Brussels February 1988) called for (1) European social laws, (2) European social dialogue with employers, (3) European social policy which could be implemented at national and regional level, albeit

with the proviso that these European laws should not preclude the retention/ provision of higher social standards at national level, (4) demand for active expanded regional policy to combat inequality.

8. Wolfgang Merkel, 'Das Demokratie-Effizienz-Dilemma', *FAZ*, 24.4.1996, p. 12.

9. Shirley Williams, 'Sovereignty and Accountability', in Keohane and Hoffman (eds.), pp. 155-176 (p. 164).

10. Mark Hall, 'Industrial Relations and the Social Dimension of European Integration: Before and after Maastricht', in Richard Hyman and Anthony Ferner (eds.), *New Frontiers in European Industrial Relations* (London: Blackwell, 1994), pp. 281-311 (p. 286).

11. See Michael Kreile on the obstacles to integration of political systems and cultures, as opposed to business operations in Kreile, 'Einleitung', *PVS Sonderheft 23 1992*, pp. vii-xix (p. xiv).

12. Platzer, *Gewerkschaftspolitik ohne Grenzen*, p. 169.

13. For details of ETUC measures, Platzer, *Gewerkschaftspolitik ohne Grenzen*, p. 146.

14. Jelle Visser, 'European Trade Unions: the Transition Years', in Hyman and Ferner (eds.), pp. 80-107 (p. 101).

15. In Chapter 3 of Phillips, *Post-National Patriotism*, I discuss this idea in more detail.

16. Platzer, *Gewerkschaftspolitik ohne Grenzen*, p. 172.

17. Wayne Sandholtz, 'Choosing Union Monetary politics and Maastricht', in B.F. Nelsen and A.C.-G. Stubb (eds.), *The European Union*, (Boulder: Lynne Rienner, 1994) pp. 257-290 (p. 281); Konrad Handschuch, *D-Mark ade! Das Maastrichter Experiment* (Frankfurt/Main: Fischer, 1994), pp. 66-71.

18. See Tsoukalis, pp. 176-182, on economic reasons leading to the Community abandoning implementation of the Werner proposals; for political divisions leading to abandonment see Peter Hort, ' Allen Rückschlägen zum Trotz ging es immer wieder voran: Pierre Werner war von der Logik der Währungsunion immer überzeugt', *FAZ*, 2.5.1998, p. 3.

19. Arguing against any possibility of Bonn pressure to postpone monetary union in 1997, Helmut Schmidt quoted Genscher's warnings about the likely reaction of the FRG's European partners should EMU fail: "then it would be ice-cold for Germany." Schmidt, 'Aufgeschoben ist aufgehoben', *Die Zeit*, 13.6.1997, p. 1.

20. Sandholtz, p. 281; Jacques Delors, 'A necessary Union', pp. 51-64; Emil Noël, 'Reflections on the Maastricht Treaty', in Ghito Ionescu, Isabel da Madareiaga and Ernest Gellner (eds.), *Government & Opposition*, Vol. 27 no. 2. (London: L.S.E., spring 1992), pp. 148-157 (p. 148).

21. Jacques Delors in his Bruges speech citing Monnet, who had quoted F.D. Roosevelt, whose speech writers in turn had taken the line from *The Bible*, Proverbs 29:18. [Jacques Delors, 'A necessary union' (Text of Delors October 1989 Bruges speech), in Nelsen and Stubb (eds.), pp. 51-64 (p. 56).]

22. See Part II, Chapter 5 of Phillips, *Post-National Patriotism*.

23. Horst Teltschik, *329 Tage: Innenansichten der Einigung* (Berlin: Siedler Verlag, 1991), pp. 37, 94-96.

24. *Le Monde*, October 1945 cited in Alan Bullock, *Ernest Bevin, Foreign Secretary, 1945-51* (London: Heinemann, 1983), p. 149.

25. Delors, p. 62.

26. George, p. 221.

27. Joachim Bitterlich, 'Anfangs frostig, später europäisch', *Die Zeit*, Nr. 20, 7.5.1998, p. 2.

28. Teltschik, pp.173-176. According to Bitterlich, the basic draft on political union was ready by the end of February (the same month that Kohl offered *German* currency union to the GDR). See Bitterlich.

29. 'Gemeinsame Initiative des französischen Präsidenten, François Mitterrand, und des deutschen Bundeskanzlers, Helmut Kohl vom 18. April 1990 zur Vorbereitung der Europäischen Union', in Werner Weidenfeld (ed.), *Maastricht in der Analyse* (Gütersloh: Verlag Bertelsmann Stiftung, 1994), pp. 103-104; also Noël, p.148; Dieter Wild, 'Land der Lügen', *Spiegel*, 20/91, 13.5.1991, pp. 186, 188; Jacques Attali, ' "Hinter all dem steckt Kohl" ', *Spiegel*, 42/95, 16.19.1995, p. 166.

30. Teltschik, p. 287.

31. See Deutsche Bundesbank, *Die Geldpolitik der Bundesbank* (Frankfurt/Main: Deutsche Bundesbank, 1995), p. 16; Handschuch, p. 72.

32. Tsoukalis, p. 70.

5

EMU and the Establishment of Greater Interdependence

In this chapter examining the path towards EMU, I will argue that as no part of an increasingly interdependent state system is wholly independent or dependent, we can talk perhaps more appropriately of influence over the status of one's own community and of others.[1]

Here, I mean community to apply in terms of sectoral interest as well as in the geographical sense. Thus, we must also consider interdependence between sectors and companies transcending states. In the course of this chapter, I will consider interdependence between sectors as well as states. I will, however, only consider interdependence specifically between companies in Chapter 11, by a study of "Siemens, BMW and the Transnational Challenge to Social Coherence."

Helen Wallace has outlined the importance of identifying who participates in, and not who governs Europe.[2] Accordingly, despite the growing consensus for a stronger president of the Commission in 1999, which had superseded states' inclination to demand a weaker Commission in 1992-98,[3] we should bear in mind that there is no suggestion that remaining sovereigns of states will be replaced in time by a single sovereign of Europe. Thus we should eliminate traditional perceptions of sovereignty from our thinking, just as sovereigns have been supplanted by the primacy of constitutional democracy.[4] In the contemporary state system, sovereignty is defined still as deriving from the people, but where increasingly there are *peoples* and not *a people* living in states, it is a principle to be rejected, or very substantially modified.[5]

In this chapter, we will see that the independence and supranational nature of the central bank, perhaps what can be dubbed the "post-nationalization" of money, brought about by the introduction of the euro, served to camouflage EMU's fundamentally political nature.[6] But, as has been pointed out by de Grauwe, although EMU's elimination of transaction costs and price uncertainty among participating states will bring economic benefits, theoretical and empirical evidence is weak that monetary union will stimulate growth.[7] Thus, although arguments that the introduction of the single currency will be good for the European economy may well be true, we would do well to remember that monetary union is not undertaken purely in pursuance of an agenda dominated by economic factors.

We have already examined political fears arising from post-Cold War uncertainties as instrumental in casting aside previous inhibitions on supranational political organization. For Germany, France and Italy, furthermore, it was an extension of political objectives of the ERM of the EMS, which they had seen as strengthening European coherence vis-à-vis the United States,[8] that is an aspiration that Europe will be able to compete with the USA in a rivalry for hegemony. As I noted in remarks concerning Germany in the Introduction to this book, one of the crucial questions in regard to contemporary international society is whether transnational interests are mutual or hegemonic in intent. I noted also, in the paragraph preceding this one, that growing interdependence should provide compelling reasons for the concept of hegemony, both within Europe and globally, to become increasingly irrelevant.[9] However, EU aspirations to hegemony, in reaction to current US economic hegemony, mean that thus far it has not. Furthermore, as noted by Adam Watson, the hegemony of the great powers (and we may include the parts and sum of the EU in this appellation) in terms of political ideas as well as economic wealth in relation to the rest of the world is increasing and "the risk is not that they will do too much, but rather that they will do too little."[10]

Indeed, three factors would rather lead us to share Watson's conclusion: first, preoccupations within EU member states about overcoming remaining prejudices among themselves; second, linked partly with the first factor, increasingly irrelevant questions of inner-European hegemony; third, the focus on competition with North American and Asian rivals. Member states' preoccupations with their own affairs obscure the effects of Community integration on those parts of Europe, which lie outside its borders and on the world beyond. But it would be a pity if this continued, for the EU has a potentially valuable global contribution to make, which extends beyond its undoubted economic advantages. I would argue that the evolution of the Community has another significant advantage. Its members' progress in overcoming centuries of internal European strife has given them the extraordinary chance to set aside hegemonic sovereign perceptions of power in favor of adopting the hegemony of doubt as a means of understanding and settling disputes instead. The inherent value of the reflexive sharing of doubt concerning self and others is, for example, reflected in the French verb *douter*. Alone, as in English, this verb means "to doubt." However, in its reflexive form, *se douter* has the connotation of "to suppose, to realize." Sharing doubt and the exploitation of difference, to promote understanding and cooperation rather than conflict, could be of obvious benefit to global development.[11]

In this chapter, therefore, I will argue first that an analysis of the EMU process provides compelling impetus for a consideration of European integration that accentuates interdependence. Second, an understanding of EMU as a multipolar process will help us discard traditional structures of hierarchically based representative territorial democracy.[12] I will thus argue that an examination of aspects of EMU implementation and the debate about the manner of its implementation may lead us to be increasingly skeptical about traditional conceptions concerning hegemony. Prospects of the euro becoming more important than the dollar would not in any case seem to be high.[13] We may see thus that the successful implementation of EMU could provide a solid basis for the advancement of conceptions of power based on sharing influence, and the rejection of formulations of power derived from methods of coercive domination.

NEGOTIATION AND HETEROGENEOUS PREFERENCE INTENSITIES

The purpose of this section is to focus on how multipolar perspectives facilitate agreement in processes of negotiation. Nonetheless, in the remainder of this chapter, we will see that an agreed solution based upon multipolar perspectives, these in turn subjected to a manifold variety of pressures, is bound to be partial only. With further pressures building at a later juncture, amendment to the original agreement is not only likely: it is desirable.

The process of negotiation in the immediate aftermath of German unification culminated in the summit meeting that agreed the Treaty on European Union in Maastricht on 9-10 December 1991. The member states reached agreement on three elements: on EMU; on a package of political reforms bracketed under the term political union; on a Social Chapter, an extension of the earlier Social Charter.[14] I will discuss the latter two parts, in Chapter 7. But in this chapter, as a first step towards our objective of discarding traditional structures of hierarchically based representative democracy, I would like to concentrate on a discussion of the Treaty provisions on EMU.

As I noted in discussing the establishment of the ECSC, the exploitation of heterogeneity of need played a fundamental part in the success of the Schuman plan. Heterogeneous requirements also played a role in the negotiation of Maastricht, the French proposing the establishment of a European Central Bank to overcome the hegemonic power of the Bundesbank, and the Germans preferring stronger supranational political bonds. These differences in political requirements, which Lisa Martin has identified as "Heterogeneous Preference Intensities," were instrumental in bringing about agreement at Maastricht, perceived as a means of embedding united Germany even more firmly in a European framework.[15]

However, as we shall see, the equivocal nature of agreement achieved at Maastricht on political union and the close time proximity of the negotiation process to German unification have combined to diminish the preference intensity subsequently for political union. In respect to the march of time onwards from German unification, continuing internal problems of unified Germany and the focus of Germans inwards upon themselves have perhaps facilitated a partial subsidence of neighbors' fears of the dangers of German hegemony. This factor, combined with attendant differences among commentators and government as to how to overcome obstacles to political union, has contributed further to it becoming less favored. On the other hand the equivocation over political union has resulted in the growing view that EMU is *the* core element of political union, although it was originally seen as complimentary to it.[16] Thus, differences about political union have spilled over into tensions over practicalities of EMU implementation, culminating in controversy over the national identity of the president of the new European Central Bank in 1998. (The French government wanted a Frenchman, although a Friesian from The Netherlands subsequently got the job.)

Furthermore, in the run-up to EMU, both commentators and policy makers asked, "can there be a central bank without a corresponding political authority?" As both Loukas Tsoukalis and Karl Otto Pöhl have surmised, there is no real precedent for such a development.[17] (We can rule out any parallel with monetary union between the German states in 1990, because the period of time was too short, and it was also accompanied by a social union.) Now, we need not fear the unprecedented for its own sake. This is shown by the unprecedented events of German unification and the collapse of totalitarianism in 1989. Nonetheless, as a result both of uncertainty and the lack of consensus in perceptions, let alone arrangements for political union in Europe, this has caused difficulties for EMU. Indeed, the difficulties of EMU reflected behavioral patterns and perceptions stemming from the very sociopolitical parameters whose increasing obsolescence and political undesirability was actually reflected in the very agreement on monetary union, which strictly speaking was intended to make them further obsolete.

Nevertheless, the seeming inevitability of closer economic interdependence between EMU participating states will heighten the preference intensity for political regulation once more. I will argue in Chapter 7, however, and in Part II also, that the preference intensity may be better amplified within additional, non-hierarchical and transinstitutional parameters. I will argue that these are necessary supplements to the pale duplicates of representative state parliamentary models agreed upon at Maastricht and subsequently at Amsterdam in 1997.

EMU: "THE CLARITY OF UNDERTAKING" TOWARDS GREATER INTERDEPENDENCE

Let us now turn to the technical details of EMU to understand the precise nature and scope of the contractual interdependence that the signatories to Maastricht agreed upon. The Delors Committee report was the basis for the monetary union provisions agreed at Maastricht. These were to be the outstanding point of agreement at Maastricht. As Emile Noël has pointed out, the parts of the Treaty relating to economic and monetary union share the same strengths as the original ECSC and EEC Treaties of the fifties. These are a

clarity of ... undertaking, [a] provision of timetable, [a] solidity of its institutions and the irreversible character of the process which has been engaged upon, which could not be blocked by a state or by a minority of states. This resulted in a dynamism of progress, ... and in a confidence on the part of economic actors, thus making a major contribution to the success of the undertaking.[18]

The Treaty set out that the second phase towards EMU would begin on 1 January 1994, with the foundation of the European Currency Institute (ECI) to oversee the technical preparations for the introduction of the new currency. The third phase was to begin at the earliest on 1 January 1997, at the latest on 1 January 1999. On this date, those states judged by the ECI and Commission to have fulfilled economic criteria set out in the Treaty would join EMU following approval by the Council of Economics and Finance Ministers (ECOFIN). Exchange rates of state currencies were to be fixed permanently at a set rate, and the European Central Bank (ECB) would come into being, superseding the ECI and controlling monetary policy and overseeing a European System of Central Banks (ESCB).[19] The irrevocably welded currencies would be replaced subsequently by a common currency, at a juncture and with a name not decided at Maastricht. Under Treaty Article 105, echoing the practices of the Bundesbank, the primary goal of the ESCB was price stability. Subordinated to this goal was the support of the ESCB for the general economic policy of the Community.[20]

The French government thought itself satisfied, having achieved a clearly time-tabled escape plan from D-mark hegemony over EC monetary policy. Meanwhile, the German negotiators were satisfied too, the new bank's statutes being modeled on the independent status of the Bundesbank. Karl Otto Pöhl claims to have viewed the setting up of the Delors Committee as "one of the darkest moments" of his term in office as Bundesbank president, but on his insistence, the resulting report laid out that the ECB was not to be subordinated to political control.[21] Thus, the Bundesbank itself reacted more than favorably to the agreed constitution of the new institution.[22] The Bundesbank subsequently published the view that the Treaty ban on the ESCB financing state deficit was stricter than the Bundesbank law before its amendment in 1994.[23]

In keeping with the clarity of the Treaty, the timetable was fulfilled. The name of the new currency, euro, and the date of 1 January 1999 for the beginning of EMU were decided upon at the European Council meeting in December 1995.[24] In March 1998, the ECI and Commission presented their reports on the convergence criteria, and after this, in May, the European Council meeting in Brussels gave the go-ahead for 11 states to participate in the third stage from 1 January 1999. Euro currency is set to be introduced to circulation from 1 January 2002.[25]

Despite the clarity of the ECB's independence, the bank's status as only one part of a greater political and economic framework would seem to give indications of an emerging multipolarity and interdependence of power in Europe rather than a hegemony of power. I understand this interdependence both in the relationships between sectors and those between states.

INTERDEPENDENCE BETWEEN FINANCIAL AND POLITICAL SECTORS

Before I discuss interdependence between states, let me first turn to a consideration of interdependence between financial and political sectors. On taking office, the first ECB President Wim Duisenberg, the former Dutch finance minister and head of The Netherlands' central bank, emphasized that the bank's ruling council (consisting of the six members of the bank directorate and presidents of member national banks) had the duty to explain and present its decisions to the public. This required as much openness and transparency as possible, including regular discussions with the EP, he said.[26]

The Treaty gives all internal monetary policy powers to the ECB, but nonetheless article 111, paragraph two directed that the EU Council was to lay down a general orientation on external exchange rate policy with EMU trading partners, on the basis of recommendations made from the Commission or submissions from the ECB. This interaction rather than concentration of power has been seen by some negatively as a blurring of responsibility.[27] But a single telescoped view of the world is less comfortable and is much more easily shaken and blurred than that brought by the dual perspective of binoculars. Thus, we should not view such a dual perspective negatively. The Bundesbank president at the time of the Maastricht Treaty, Helmut Schlesinger, has rebutted claims of politicians to a potentially significant role in the formulation of policy. In a letter to *Die Zeit*, he has recalled his insistence during the negotiations, in a telephone call with Finance Minister Theo Waigel, that the *influence* of the Council to provide general orientations should remain merely that, and not a *power* to *give* the more specific "Guidelines" favored by the other eleven. Even so, the wording of Treaty article 109, which Schlesinger quotes in his letter, where the word "formulate" (*aufstellen*) is linked to "general orientations " shows starkly the interdependence between both sides. My understanding of the meaning of "general orientations" is that it is linked with the possibility of movement in many directions subsequently. But the possibility of the Council deciding upon a *given* direction of policy, a guideline, is strongly implied by the Treaty's wording, with the use of the term "formulate." Nonetheless any significant difference between the meaning of guidelines and orientations is further negated, and with it an implied subsequent curtailment to independent ECB policy, if we recall that the original meaning of orientation comes from the prescripted building alignment of church naves on west-east axes.[28]

But this does not rule out the view that the financial sector has powers over the politicians. Indeed, contradicting my view of interdependence, Schlesinger's successor as Bundesbank president, Hans Tietmeyer, seemingly gave voice to a hegemonic perspective, namely that the financial markets hold sway over the politicians. Speaking at the World Economic Forum in Davos in 1996, Tietmeyer stated that in the light of growing political and economic integration, financial markets had the chance to discipline the politicians: "I have ... the impression that most politicians are still not aware just how much they are controlled today by the financial markets, indeed that they are ruled by them."[29]

Little wonder that the question has been posed: "A dictatorship of the Bundesbank?"[30] Indeed, it very well may be that in making these remarks, Tietmeyer believed in the primacy of economics over politics. His decades of experience in European financial politics (Tietmeyer also worked on the 1970 Werner report on EMU) have indeed provided solid grounding for such an instinctive view. However, we should recall also that, as head of the Bundesbank, Tietmeyer's primary responsibility was to ensure currency stability, and at the time he had especially good reason to be hawkish in his insistence that the convergence criteria agreed at Maastricht be adhered to. He may have feared that some members of the Federal government might have been tempted to distance themselves from pledges to abide strictly to the Maastricht criteria on the public deficit: higher than expected unemployment levels were exacerbating existing strains in balancing the Federal budget caused by unification. Moreover, he may have had good reason for these fears. The following year, in an attempt to cover the Federal Exchequer's deficit ballooning way above the Maastricht convergence criteria due to the new spiraling cost factor of unemployment in addition to the burden of unification, Germany's Finance Minister Theo Waigel announced a plan to revalue the Bundesbank gold assets more in line with actual market prices.[31]

His plan, however, outraged the public as well as the Bundesbank, and Waigel had to climb down.

But there can be no question of dictatorship of one sector over another. As Tietmeyer himself acknowledged, writing on the occasion of the fiftieth anniversary of the D-mark, "The success story of the D-mark would be incomplete without mentioning the broad consensus on stability among societal groups in Germany."[32] Even in one sector, currency stability in Germany is also dependent on currency stability elsewhere in the world. It is further dependent on innumerable political, social and environmental factors. As pointed out by Norbert Walter, the world trend towards financial deregulation, liberalization and electronic trading means that there is "greater interdependence of world financial markets and higher volatility of interest rates and asset prices." Even so, despite his admission of the volatility of markets, Walter sees the role of world financial markets as a policeman punishing unsound government policies.[33] We may in response wonder, who controls the policeman? However, we should resist the temptation to find appropriate measures to shackle the police, but ensure that the communities under questioning get a "fair trial," and provide a credible explanation for their actions to other sectoral and geographical communities. The world financial markets are an integral part of these communities. On the other hand, we should look to means of encouraging appropriate social and political forums of discussion which could undertake a counterbalancing scrutiny of the volatile processes of the financial markets. In terms of trade, World Trade Organization (WTO) General Director Renato Ruggerio specifically stated that other organizations than his, such as the International Labour Organization (ILO), should be the responsible forums for discussion of social and environmental standards, and that "the solution cannot come by making the WTO a global policeman."[34]

Furthermore, returning to Tietmeyer's Davos remarks, we should bear in mind that he was addressing an audience comprising members of the world's financial and economic elite, whose primary concern was the financial markets. Like Tietmeyer, they knew that although there may be persuasive economic reasons in its favor, the question of monetary union was itself a fundamentally political decision. To underline why this should be so, we can see that a strategy of using an existing trusted currency rather than the creation of a new currency would have served the needs of transnational business at lesser risk. Indeed, following financial crisis in South America, Argentinian President Carlos Menem floated the idea of the introduction of the US dollar as the official currency of Argentina.[35] The extension of the use of the D-mark to the whole of the EU, for example, would have just as well served business needs of avoidance of extensive cost/risk evaluation and contingency planning to cope with currency exchange fluctuations. But this option would have been politically unpalatable to many, if not all, of Germany's partners.

By way of a further concrete illustration that the agreement on EMU was a political decision, we can see that businesses in Europe took different stances on the prospect of a common currency following Maastricht. Larger businesses tended to be for; smaller businesses against. Martin and Schumann have pointed out that many of those who campaigned against the single currency, or favored a delay in its introduction, were those who had much to lose (or feared they had much to lose) from a departure from the preeuro status quo. In defense of their point, Martin and Schumann cite an *Economist* prognosis, that if enough people with money believe that the euro will fail then it will fail.[36]

The same remains the case today, and we can see Tietmeyer's remarks made to the World Economic Forum in this light. Accordingly, I would argue that there is no question of any actual control of the financial markets over the politicians or vice versa. There is an interdependence, for were the euro to fail, this would have calamitous effects for many of the major investors on the financial markets. Thus, both political and financial sectors have a joint responsibility to ensure the success of the project. We can understand responsibility as not only having to account for the needs, practices and goals of specialists in one's own sector. Responsibility also entails the requisite capacity to respond (and help formulate new responses) to the needs, practices and goals of other sectoral and geographical communities, and thereby contribute to the collective good of society in general.

Perhaps then we can see Tietmeyer's remarks as part of the ongoing negotiation process that has increasingly characterized European integration since the SEA, and which became even more marked following 9 November 1989, between all states and participants across all interest sectors. If it had been up to Tietmeyer alone for example, there seems to be little doubt that Italy would have failed to obtain founder membership of EMU. Right up until the successful candidates for EMU were announced in May 1998, Tietmeyer remained against Italian membership.[37]

In this section, we have assessed only a small part of the intricacies of interdependence which play a part in the economic and political discussions on the introduction of EMU. In Part II, we will examine aspects of wider global transnational and transinstitutional interdependence. For the moment though let us remain within the narrower confines of states.

INTERDEPENDENCE BETWEEN STATES

Let me now turn to a consideration of interdependence between states. This is not as advanced as between functional sectors. We can see this simply if we remember that the SEA established a single market, not a single suprastate structure in general.

As I noted above, tensions in the run-up to the implementation of the third stage of EMU reflected behavioral patterns and perceptions stemming from sociopolitical parameters whose increasing obsolescence and perceived political undesirability were actually the genesis for agreement on monetary union, and also the agreements on European integration before it. However, I would argue that a consideration at this point in our study of tensions over EMU implementation could give important indicators of the chances and dangers of greater interdependence. Perhaps we can compare hardened conceptions of national prestige confronted by the attractions of economic interdependency to lobsters, tempted by the bait into the trap: once in, there is no way back. The lobsters can then be plonked in the boiling pot, the shells cut away leaving the meat for universal consumption. Thus, the elimination of the invertebrate carapace of nation removes an obsolescent obstacle to closer and wider interdependent relationships. Few can afford lobster; similarly, nationalist perceptions are a luxury also, which we could exchange in favor of acquiring a more balanced, interdependent worldview. But before this can be accomplished, pincers pose dangers.

Here we should recall Stanley Hoffmann's sixties critique of European integration. Hoffmann had suggested that nationalism would prove to be a barrier to integration when areas of what he defined as "high politics" as opposed to "low politics" became subjects for debate. "High politics" he saw as key national totems of status and security – foreign policy and defense.[38]

However we can see that in the history of the Federal Republic, these totems have been acquired only in conjunction with becoming embedded within transnational organization. Having started at a base point of no sovereign control over the defense of its territory, political integration has been less a matter of "high politics" for the Federal Republic compared with other states in the European integration process. Germany has had less to lose politically, because with the Nazis, it lost everything. In making these remarks, I leave aside the continuities of economic organization in Germany (I will discuss these in Part II, Chapter 9). Thus, the encouragement of European integration has been very much a matter of "high politics" for the Federal Republic as it was seen that the process brought considerable political and economic advantages.

On the other hand, in the absence of other national totems, the D-mark has become a matter of "high politics" instead, its allure and status arguably reinforced for both West and East Germans by the experience of German monetary union in July 1990. Tellingly, in the light of subsequent hard D-mark versus soft euro arguments, immediately after Maastricht, a *FAZ* business leader column can be seen as evidence of the D-mark as high politics, that faced with British obstinacy during negotiations, Kohl was "the good European, ... who receiving almost no benefit in return, relinquishes the D-mark."[39] Six years later, Arnulf Baring's conclusion on currency union was that "no-one says that we owe this risky project not to aspirations to European unification, but to ill-devised French-US coercion in 1990."[40]

In his deployment of "we," Baring meant Germans, not Europeans. It could be said that German perceptions concerning the prospect of currency union are similar in quality to UK misgivings and sensitivities regarding European integration, based on the traditional English (N.B. *not* Scottish) understanding of Parliament as the expression of sovereignty. Moreover, just as Britain's island status has safeguarded the British State against military conquest from its foundation, so has the D-mark protected Germany against invasions of price instability undermining hard-won postwar Federal German affluence. Accordingly, insular German perceptions that the Maastricht agreement foresaw the prospect of the end of the mark, but not the end of the franc, or the guilder, or any other currency, recalls the apocryphal English newspaper headline "Fog in the Channel – Continent Cut Off." Even the unanimous judgement in October 1993 of the Federal German constitutional court that the Maastricht Treaty was compatible with the *Grundgesetz* included the judges' strong insistence that the economic convergence criteria of EMU be maintained.[41]

We can see the strength of attachment to the D-mark further in *Handelsblatt* commentator Hans Mundorff's attempt ultimately to argue that Germans are the best Europeans because they are prepared to give up the D-mark. Writing following the Mölln racial murders in November 1992, he also stated that the cosmopolitanism of German consumers' activities was proof enough that the behavior of the vast majority of ordinary citizens was far from xenophobic.

Most Germans are profoundly xenophiliac. Millions of tourists spend their holidays abroad, they eat in Greek or Italian or Turkish restaurants, their children learn foreign languages as their main subjects in school. The Germans are the best Europeans, and their passion for Europe is such that the German government is prepared to exchange the Deutsch-Mark (sic) for an artificial currency.[42]

We can see that Mundorff supported his claim that Germans were willing to give up their currency with further components of economic or competitive nature. On the other hand his article did not include evidence of social and cooperative components, approaches which might tend to buttress efforts at mutual understanding in greater measure. Nor did it acknowledge that opinion poll evidence right up the final go-ahead for EMU in May 1998 has shown a consistent majority *opposing* its introduction. According to opinion poll evidence in April 1998, 62% of German voters were opposed to the introduction of the euro.[43]

In response to popular opinion in Germany to the effect that "we are giving up more than you are," the Federal government lobbied hard for the name euro, instead of the technical-sounding ecu, and for the ECB to be located in Frankfurt as an attempt to bolster popular acceptance of EMU.[44]

In his speech marking retirement from active politics at the party conference to elect his successor as CSU leader, Theo Waigel reflected Germans' attitudes to these two linked areas of "high politics," first in respect to their desires for European integration, but second, widespread popular opposition to giving up control over currency. First of all, he described the political union achieved at Maastricht as a "quantum leap in European policy." As we shall see in Chapter 7, "Parameters and Limits of Democracy in Europe," Waigel was rather immodest in his claim on this point, perhaps as a reaction to the more nationalistic tone consistently struck by his party rival and successor as CSU leader, Bavarian Premier Edmund Stoiber. On the other hand, Waigel was keen to play down any significance of loss in terms of "high politics" resulting from acceptance of EMU, by dint of emphasizing that his personal involvement in its nascence guaranteed its future: "The EURO is written in my handwriting and also the name stems from me!"[45] In a booklet issued by the Federal Finance Ministry in 1996 to publicize the euro, Waigel was at pains to point out the significance of Frankfurt as the location of the ECB:

The setting up of the European Central bank in Frankfurt/Main is an important success for Germany, but also an advantage for the whole of the European Union. For with this step, the future common European currency falls in the tradition of stability of the D-mark. Thus, the home of currency stability in Germany and in Europe is and will remain Frankfurt.[46]

However, the Federal government's need to take account of domestic popularity of the D-mark in its negotiations on the move to EMU, and its success in persuading its partners that accordingly giving up its currency was an issue of key national prestige, progressively made the issue "high politics" for its partners also. We have already seen that the French government was the primary instigator of EMU at the end of the eighties as a reaction to Bundesbank hegemony over financial policy. Yet Bundesbank hegemony was all the more confirmed following Maastricht in the dramatic repercussions of its high interest rate policy to reestablish control of the money supply following the inflationary boom of German unification. The July 1992 decision, to raise interest rates to the highest levels in Germany since 1931, set off a wave of currency speculation, that in the short term forced the UK and Italy to leave the ERM of EMS in September, and which culminated ultimately in heavy market speculation on the French franc at the end of July 1993. At a crisis sitting of the EMS committee on 1 August, a Sunday, in a bid to restore prestige, the French even proposed that the D-mark should leave EMS, and the French franc should become the anchor currency for Europe instead. All the others, led by the Dutch, were against, and the currency bands were opened to allow 15% differential, a potential difference of 30% in exchange rate variation.[47] The ERM spring had been sprung.

Nonetheless, the EMS turbulence, combined with the success of German negotiators in gaining agreement of EU partners that EMU was to occur very much on their terms, led some to see EMU not as an expression of European integration but of German hegemony. This was especially the case in France. The French had been against the name euro, for example, preferring to retain the name used during the EMS, the ecu, which as well as standing for European Currency Unit was also a French gold coin during the Middle Ages.[48] Stephen George has pointed out that perceptions that high unemployment was connected with the government tying France's currency to the D-mark, the so-called *franc fort* policy, resulted in growing anti-EU popular attitudes. Despite widespread opposition, notably from former President Giscard, who argued that rates of interest set by the Bundesbank in Frankfurt/Main damaged French exports, French government finance policy did not change.[49]

Against this background, perhaps we can see growing reasons for the French government in particular, but other Europeans also, viewing steps towards further EU economic interdependence not as measures promoting European cooperation, but serving German monetary and economic hegemony instead. Thus, the stability and growth pact in 1997, proposed by the Germans to their EU partners to ensure continued strict control of the Maastricht deficit criteria additionally following the beginning of EMU, was only agreed despite massive French resistance. The word "growth" in the pact's title was the face-saving measure that secured French agreement.[50] Despite German attempts to explain the mechanism as a core political as well as economic need, the French did not accept it as such, and this was ultimately to result in the crisis of the selection of the first president of the ECB. This crisis overshadowed the European Council meeting held in May 1998 to confirm the participants and start date of EMU. In the next section, we will try to understand why the selection process of the first ECB president was so difficult.

EXCHANGE AND EXPLANATION IN THE EMU PROCESS

In this section we will focus in on traditional hegemonic behavioral patterns as an obstacle to greater interdependence. To help understand these, we will look at the concepts of *extortion*, *exchange* and *explanation* as methods of achieving agreement in international political negotiation, as discussed by Lisa Martin. She notes that the first two concepts have problems of credibility in negotiation processes in organizations among interdependent states. First, in processes of *extortion*, states threaten steps that are likely to harm their own interests. Second, in processes of *exchange*, states, by giving up previous advantages, might still be seen by others as not really giving them up. Third, *explanation* involves one side showing its negotiation partners "linkages" between different functional areas. If the explanation is not convincing, then credibility is also a problem. The supposed linkage is seen by others as an unsubstantiated claim and therefore in terms of unconvincing extortion or exchange bids.[51]

With regard to the EMU process, I would like to concentrate on the latter two concepts, *exchange* and *explanation*. As we saw in the previous chapter, in the run-up to Maastricht, at face value at least, the Germans offered to give up control over monetary policy, and the French agreed to a measure of political reform that would cede state legislative power to the Community. However, as I will argue in this section, in terms of exchange, the Treaty of European Union largely failed the credibility test, because different parties placed different emphasis on the weight of the items subject for exchange. Moreover, I would argue that one of the items subject for exchange was not even negotiated at Maastricht. This was German unification.

As we saw in Chapter 4, "Reactions to the Single European Act: The Western Path to Maastricht," the French government hurriedly committed itself to negotiation on political union in addition to EMU, because of its uncertainty over the prospect of German unification. The German government, on the other hand, can be seen to have coupled its commitment to EMU with negotiation over political union. The German government saw political union as a means of stressing its commitment to European integration, and as a strategy of making EMU a more attractive prospect to its electorate.[52] However we can see that it was easier to arrive at agreement on EMU than political union in 1990-91 for three reasons. First, because it represented a plan to replace D-mark hegemony over Community monetary policy, which the French did not want (and it is more often than not easier to describe what one doesn't want as opposed to what one wants). Second, EMU was a logical extension of the single market introduced under the SEA. Third, the French and the German governments were only two of twelve parties negotiating the Maastricht Treaty. In particular the presence of the Euroskeptic British at Maastricht combined with the French preference for political union not being as strong as for EMU ensured that Community political reform was not as far-reaching as the German government would have wished. As we shall in Chapter 7, "Parameters and limits of Democracy in Europe," Maastricht was criticized by a wide spectrum of opinion in Germany on this aspect.

Thus, if we considered the exchange of EMU for political union alone, we could see that such was Kohl's desire to prove himself a good European that in accepting a hollow concept to political union he scorned traditional bartering approaches in European negotiation, where "negotiators ... link accumulated 'credits' and 'debits' across issue areas."[53] But this does not alone explain the imbalance of the Maastricht agreement. We can see that at Maastricht, an imbalance in exchange arose in two respects: first, in that there was a greater preference for economic aspects than political aspects of union in the Community as a whole, and second, in the establishment of the parallel intergovernmental conferences in the run-up to Maastricht, the German government's core aim had not by any means been the establishment of *European* political union but to secure European partners' political support for *German* political union.

In effect, the exchange that the Germans received for their agreement to EMU was that their partners overcame their prejudices and acceded in reasonably good grace to German unification. In this respect, we can see that Helmut Kohl may have been right to state in November 1989 as point six of his ten-point plan that "the future architecture of Germany must fit in with the future architecture of Europe."[54] However, architecture is subject to change as any brief glance in any European city center street will show. Thus Kohl's point in the same speech concerning Germany can also be applied to European integration too: "No-one knows today what a reunited Germany will finally look like."[55] For the time being therefore, the political price for German unity has become largely EMU alone, but in the light of growing interdependence brought by EMU, this will be subject to renegotiation. As we already know from our consideration of the words of Karl Jaspers in the Introduction, history is never final. Moreover, in the light of growing interdependence, more states are likely to see a clarification in terms of political union as mutually advantageous.

Therefore, seen in terms of exchange, the German government had less to negotiate *for* at Maastricht: the core aim of German unification had already been achieved the year before. However, although the hidden exchange of EMU for German unification is indeed very credible when seen in these terms, we can perhaps speculate that neither side in the negotiation process could admit openly, either to themselves or the other, that this was the core exchange at the heart of the agreement. The Germans could not admit to it because of political infirmity in comparison to their neighbors – it remained largely a political taboo to define themselves in national terms. Germany's partners meanwhile were faced with the difficulty that an admission that German sovereignty was contingent on and curtailed by historical legacies also implied that theirs too would have to be limited ultimately, if the imbalance between Germany and the rest of the Community were one day to be corrected.[56]

Finally, in terms of exchange in interstate negotiation, I would point out that although it is probable that EMU will lead to added pressures for greater political union, the principle exchange actually made at Maastricht itself was not EMU for deeper political union, as many in Germany might have expected it to be on the setting up of the joint intergovernmental conferences in 1990. It was actually that the German government accepted the implementation of EMU, in exchange for its partners' agreement that EMU would be implemented largely according to the existing German model of the Bundesbank.

In terms of the second concept in interdependent states' negotiation, *explanation*, Germans' explanation of the linkages between areas of policy moved from initial lack of success at Maastricht, to being too successful afterwards. It was unsuccessful at Maastricht inasmuch as the link between political union and EMU was not made successfully enough. The unspoken link with German unification was more pointedly significant to both Germans and non-Germans alike. In the years following Maastricht, however, as we noted in discussing Theo Waigel's remarks, German policy makers succeeded in showing their partners that in view of the failure to establish a political counterweight to EMU, it was essential to gain its electorate's trust that EMU would bear all the hallmarks that had made the D-mark so popular. Accordingly, we can see that perceptions in French government circles mounted that there was less and less of a shift from German to supranational control of monetary policy than they had originally anticipated.[57] German agreement to EMU and giving up Bundesbank regulation of its currency was no longer seen as such, but a continuation of Bundesbank hegemony through the backdoor. The link between EMU and national interests made the issue of currency a national prestige issue.

In this light, we can understand that there were powerful underlying reasons of national prestige for the French government to demonstrate to its electorate that the EMU, which had seemingly become progressively German in character, would not in actual fact become a mere pseudonym for the Bundesbank. Opinion polls showed that the French electorate was in favor of the introduction of the euro. However, two-thirds of French voters were opposed to Frankfurt as the location of the ECB.[58]

I will discuss the aspect of nationalism among ordinary citizens as an obstacle to European integration between states in the next chapter. Here, however, we can see that French domestic politics and national prestige combined to play a crucial role behind French opposition from 1997 onwards to the candidature of the serving ECI President Wim Duisenberg to serve also as the first ECB president. President Chirac nominated French National Bank President Jean-Claude Trichet instead. The presence of a second candidate overshadowed both the run-up to the Council and the Council itself.

We can learn two lessons from the fraught nature of the EU Council's difficulties in reaching agreement on the ECB appointment. First, the difficulties at the Council meeting showed the consequences of the concept of "explanation" in the negotiation process, which I discussed earlier, being interpreted as unconvincing by the other negotiating party. The French did not manage to show other EU Council members that sacrifices made by French national prestige demanded a French head of the ECB as compensation. Second, the Council provided further evidence of the ongoing process of bargaining in the integration process in Europe. The compromise finally agreed upon was that Duisenberg was appointed as the ECB president for a term of eight years as laid down by the Treaty of European Union, but beforehand the president-elect made a statement to the president of the EU Council that he would only serve out four years before retiring "voluntarily" at the age of 67. On Duisenberg's "retirement," the Council thus agreed that he be replaced by a French candidate, probably Trichet. Some saw this compromise as breaking the Treaty of European Union. Only days before the Council meeting, Duisenberg had said that he would only take on the job if he were permitted to serve the full eight-year term.[59]

THE DIFFICULTIES AND POSSIBILITIES OF INTERDEPENDENCE

Having reviewed in the previous section the difficulties in the negotiation process concerning the communication of linkages between needs, fears and goals, we shall see now how the Brussels compromise gives us an important indication of both the difficulties and possibilities of European development.

The summit illustrated the difficulty of overcoming the forces of national pride and prestige. The issue of national prestige spilled over from France's stance to other parties too. Dutch Prime Minister Wim Kok described the accession of Duisenberg as ECB president as a victory for The Netherlands.[60] Meanwhile many Italian commentators savored Italy's success in accession to EMU at the first stage as avoiding the drop into the "second division" of nations.[61]

However, in terms of future possibility, we can perhaps see that upon the advent of monetary union, the interdependence established between states is likely to develop to such a degree that doubt in one party concerning the veracity of linkages offered as an explanation by the other party for its negotiation stance is less likely: they too are likely to be affected by the same linkages. Problems of credibility would therefore be less in the negotiation process than in times when the negotiating partners were less dependent upon one another. In the future, given favorable economic conditions, we could hope for the evolution of a continuity of stable ESCB practice that could permit greater freedoms of social organization throughout Europe, in place of perceptions of an outright hegemony of the Bundesbank, or indeed the German state behind it. But the problem is that favorable economic conditions are by no means guaranteed.

With this caveat in mind, to conclude this chapter, we may draw the following lessons from our study of the process towards EMU implementation. It was the clarity of EMU undertaking and its clearly laid out timetable that overcame tensions stemming from national prejudices. However, these prejudices show that more is needed than just a common currency to bring Europe together. They also show that more is required if the chances of the euro's success are to be maximized. In giving evidence to the Financial and European Committee of the *Bundestag*, in the run-up to the Council decision on which states would fulfil the criteria for euro participation, both Tietmeyer and European Commissioner for Currency Yves Thibault de Silguy agreed that EMU would inevitably lead to a closer alignment in states' taxation systems.[62] But, if it is to be "inevitable," this development will entail difficult negotiation. Thus, it may be that the ramifications of problems between states with a high level of interdependence are potentially more serious than those occurring between those with less. In negotiations between interdependent states, a process of extortion may not be credible, because it will damage the interest of the state making the threat also. But states' actions are not always rational. Furthermore, although agreement on EMU has been achieved, there are a considerable number of areas of difference between states, which also could conceivably be elevated to the realm of high politics.[63] The D-mark's period of existence as a key perceived area of high politics for example was (is) relatively short, certainly substantially less than the half-century of its overall existence, but as I discuss elsewhere, there will always be another area for chauvinism and prejudice to focus on.[64] Moreover, hegemonic views within Europe remain, in sectoral as well as national approaches. Perhaps the dangers of remaining hegemonic conceptions, which reached their apogee within precepts of the nation-state, can be given by returning to my lobster metaphor: lobsters roaming freely in the ocean are less dangerous to one another than those condemned and caught, crawling over one another in fishermen's crates.

In this chapter, I have shown that in a relationship where levels of mutual interdependence are steadily increasing, the concept of hegemony should become increasingly irrelevant within Europe because none of the parties involved can do without the other. This applies both in the relationship between economic and social sectors of organization and in the relations between states. The go-ahead for the participation of 11 states in EMU from its inauguration was given despite doubts about the levels of debt in Belgium and Italy.[65] Nevertheless, high levels of debt in *all* EMU member countries curtailed the ECB's room for maneuver in financial policy at the beginning of its tenure.[66]

Accordingly in the next chapter, I will attempt to identify methods that may overcome behavior stemming from hegemonial perceptions, by a discussion of possible new patterns of relationships that could serve mutual interests. For a correction away from hegemonic thinking, I propose to go back to the antecedents of contemporary approaches to European integration and to the functionalist approach of David Mitrany.

NOTES

1. Compare with David Held's point on the result of supranational organization: "The idea of a community which rightly governs itself and determines its own future – an idea at the very heart of the democratic polity is ... deeply problematic." See Held, 'Democracy and the International Order', in Daniele Archibugi and David Held (eds.), *Cosmopolitan Democracy: An Agenda for a New World Order* (Cambridge: Polity Press, 1995), pp. 96-120 (p. 100).

2. Helen Wallace, 'Introduction', in Helen Wallace and Alasdair R. Young (eds.), *Participation and Policy-Making in the European Union* (Oxford: Clarendon Press, 1997), pp. 1-16 (p. 1).

3. On the beginnings of desires of national governments for weaker Commission, see Kohl's September 1992 comments in George, p. 17; also Kohl and Chirac letter opposing development of European central state to Council President Blair: 'Die Kommission befürchtet eine Beschränkung ihrer Rolle', *FAZ*; 10.6.1998, pp. 1-2; on the mood to strengthen Commission, see articles in *The Economist*: 'Crisis in Brussels: Europe has to scratch its head', 20.3.1999, pp. 19-20, 29; 'Europe's next Commissioners', 27.3.1999, p. 36; 'The challenge awaiting Romano Prodi', 3.4.1999, pp. 23-24.

4. See Watson's argument against sovereignty, deploying Barry Buzan's term that it is based on an "anarchophiliac" conception of world order [Adam Watson, *The Limits of Independence: Relations between states in the modern world* (London: Routledge, 1997), p. 3]. Also a discussion of Bull's conception of the "nebulous quality of sovereignty," in Andrew Linklater, *The Transformation of Political Community* (Cambridge: Polity Press, 1998), pp. 193-195 (p. 195).

5. See definition of sovereignty in The Report of The Commission on Global Governance, *Our Global Neighbourhood* (Oxford University Press, 1995), pp. 68-72.

6. In a 1998 interview, former Bundesbank President Karl Otto Pöhl uses the term "denationalization." This is not entirely appropriate, as it implies the idea of privatization. See Heribert Klein, 'Warum haben Sie keine Angst vor dem Euro, Herr Pöhl?' *FAZ Magazin*, Heft 954, 12.6.1998, pp. 42-43.

7. See Paul de Grauwe, *The Economics of Monetary Integration* (Oxford University Press, 1992), pp. 61-92. Paul de Grauwe contrasts high growth in gross domestic product of non-EMS states with EMS states, 1981-90 (p. 75).

8. Tsoukalis, p.187.

9. By "hegemony" in one sense I understand the meaning given in *The Compact Edition of the Oxford English Dictionary* (Oxford University Press, 1971): "the leadership or predominant authority of one state of a confederation or union over the others" (p. 1283). However, Adam Watson in his definition of hegemony writes: "the line between influencing external and internal conduct has always been smudged, and today is particularly so." (Watson, p. 147.) Accordingly, I would understand the term hegemony

applied also to non-state identities, whether sectors of expertise or private interests of capital or labor.

10. See Watson, p. 128.

11. For further discussion of the meaning and usage of doubt, see Chapter 13 of this book, also Chapter 1 of my *Post-National Patriotism*.

12. See George, pp. 52-54; Svein Andersen and Tom Burns, 'The European Union and the Erosion of Parliamentary Democracy: A Study of Post-parliamentary Governance, in Svein Andersen and Kjell Eliassen (eds.), pp. 227-251.

13. Paul de Grauwe points out that the dollar only displaced the pound because of higher US growth. Citing prospects that on the world scale, the size of the EU economy will decline in relative terms, he therefore dismisses the likelihood of the euro becoming the world's leading currency. See de Grauwe's discussion of Richard Portes and Hélène Rey, 'Euro vs dollar: will the euro replace the dollar as the world currency?' in David Begg et al. (eds.), *EMU: Prospects and Challenges for the Euro* (Oxford: Blackwell, 1998), pp. 305-344 (pp. 333-335).

14. At the insistence of the UK government, which refused to sign it, the Social Chapter was kept separate from the main Treaty. Following a change of UK government, however, the Chapter was incorporated in the main Treaty at the Amsterdam summit in June 1997.

15. Lisa Martin, 'Heterogeneity, Linkage and Commons Problem', in Robert Keohane and Elinor Ostrom (eds.), *Local Commons and Global Interdependence: Heterogeneity and Cooperation in Two Domains* (London: Sage, 1995), pp. 71-91 (p. 80).

16. For this view, for example, see: Peter Hort, 'Schatten auf der Währungsunion', *FAZ*, 4.5.1998, p. 1.

17. Tsoukalis, p. 224; Klein, *FAZ Magazin*.

18. Noël, p. 150.

19. The economic convergence criteria for union were: first, on debt: (a) planned or actual public budgetary deficit must not exceed 3% of the Gross Domestic Product (GDP); (b) state debts must not exceed 60% of GDP; second, on price stability: in the two years prior to decision on union, the inflation rate should not be more than 1.5% above the average of the three states with the lowest rate; third, currency stability: the national currency must have remained within the narrow (2.25%) band of EMS without any devaluation or tension within the system as a result of this level.

20. Deutsche Bundesbank, p. 16.

21. See Thomas Hanke, Wolfgang Proissl, 'Die Dolchstoßlegende: Warum das neue Geld die deutsch-französischen Verhältnisse schon seit zehn Jahren prägt', *Die Zeit*, Nr. 20, 7.5.1998, p. 5.

22. *Monatsbericht der Deutschen Bundesbank*, February 1992, cited in Hans Tietmeyer, 'Probleme einer europäischen Währungsunion und Notenbank', in Josef Isenee (ed.), *Europa als politische Idee und als rechtliche Form* (Berlin: Duncker & Humblot, 1993), pp. 35-61 (p. 51).

23. Deutsche Bundesbank, p. 17. This view is also postulated by de Grauwe, p. 161.

24. See brochure published in April 1996 by German Federal Finance Ministry, *Europäische Wirtschafts- und Währungsunion: Der Euro stark wie die Mark*, p. 40.

25. 'Meilenstein für Europa: Die Währungsunion startet mit elf Teilnehmern', in Bundesministerium für Finanzen (ed.) *per Saldo*, pp. 2, 4. Denmark and the UK excluded

themselves from participation; Greece and Sweden failed because of high levels of budget deficit.

26. See interview with Wim Duisenberg: 'Der Euro wird erst langfristig zur Reservewährung', *FAZ*, 29.6.1998, pp. 15, 17. The ECB president is required to account to the EP for ECB interest rate and monetary policy at least once a quarter. See Wolfgang Proissl, 'Mit aller Macht', *Die Zeit*, Nr. 24, 10.6.1999, p. 9.

27. See 'Oskar Bravo', *The Economist*, 20.3.1999, p. 97.

28. See Helmut Schlesinger's letter, 'Falsche Interpretation', *Die Zeit*, Nr. 8, 18.2.1999, p. 36. Schlesinger highlights (for him) the stark contrast between (his italics) the eleven's wish, "to issue *general guidelines* for exchange rates" and article 109 of the Treaty: "that the (EU) Council, acting by a qualified majority either on a recommendation from the Commission and after consulting the ECB or on a recommendation from the ECB, may formulate *general orientations* for exchange rate policy in relation to these currencies."

29. 'Tietmeyer: "Finanzmärkte kontrollieren die Politik" ', *FAZ*, 3.2.1996, p. 13.

30. See Jeremy Leaman, 'Diktatur der Bundesbank?', in Günter Gaus et al. (eds.), *Blätter für deutsche und internationale Politik* 7/93, pp. 802-814.

31. See interview with Theo Waigel, '"Eine Erblast tilgen"', *Spiegel*, 22/97, 26.5.1997, pp, 25-26; various articles in *Spiegel*, 23/97, 2.6.1997, pp. 28ff; *Spiegel*, 24/97, 9.6.1997, pp. 22ff.

32. See Hans Tietmeyer, 'Fünfzig Jahre D-Mark – Perspektiven für Europa', in *50 Jahre DM FAZ Beilage*, 2.6.1998, B1, B3.

33. Walter in Weidenfeld and Janning (eds.), p. 59.

34. See Konrad Mrusek, 'Die Advokaten der Globalisierung: Die Welthandelsorganisation und ihre Fachleute', *FAZ*, 9.5.1998, p. 15.

35. See 'Cool Menem', *The Economist*, 30.1.1999, p. 50. Following his accession to office in 1989, Menem's administration pegged the peso to the dollar.

36. See Hans-Peter Martin and Harald Schumann, *Die Globalisierungsfalle: Der Angriff auf Demokratie und Wohlstand* (Reinbek: Rororo, 1996), pp. 112-118.

37. See, for example, 'Tietmeyer bekräftigt die Zweifel an Euro-Start mit Italien', *FAZ*, 4.4.1998, p. 5.

38. See George, pp. 47-48.

39. Peter Hort, 'Die D-Mark über den Tisch gezogen', *FAZ*, 12.12.1991, p. 15.

40. Quoted by Rudolf Augstein, 'Scheitert Deutschland?' *Spiegel*, 40/97, 29.9.1997, p. 34.

41. For summary of the court judgement on Maastricht, see Bundeszentrale für politische Bildung (ed.), 'Europäische Union', *Informationen zur Politischen Bildung 213* (Bonn: March 1995) p. 23.

42. Hans Mundorf, 'Die Lehren von Mölln', *Handelsblatt*, 15.12.1992, p. 2; in spring 1992, the CSU's Peter Gauweiler labelled the then unnamed euro-currency "*Esperanto-money*." See 'Lafontaine empfielt der SPD die Ablehnung der Verträge von Maastricht', *FAZ*, 6.3.1992, p. 2.

43. See 'Die Zustimmung zum Euro wächst', *FAZ*, 23.4.1998, p. 15. The poll was carried out by opinion poll institute Ipos together with the Federal Association of German Banks. In February 1998 the figure had been 70% against. *FAZ's* support for EMU can be discerned from the headline ["Agreement on euro growing"].

44. The Maastricht Treaty left the bank's site undecided. The decision favoring

Frankfurt/Main was not made until the European Council in October 1993. See 'Zweite Stufe der Währungsunion', *FAZ*, 3.1.1994, p. 9.

45. See Günter Pursch, 'Die neuen Unions-Vorsitzenden Edmund Stoiber und Wolfgang Schäuble demonstrieren Einigkeit', *Das Parlament* Nr. 5, 29.1.1999, p. 21.

46. See 'Fragen zur Europäischen Wirtschafts- und Währungsunion an Bundesfinanzminister Dr. Theo Waigel', in *Europäische Wirtschafts- und Währungsunion*, pp. 50-55 (p. 52).

47. See Handschuch, pp. 97-114.

48. See 'Europäische Union', in *Informationen zur Politischen Bildung 213*, pp. 26-27.

49. 'Der Euro erregt die Gemüter in Frankreich', *NZZ*, 29.11.1996, p. 10.

50. See Martin Weale, 'Monetary and Fiscal Policy in Euroland', in Iain Begg and John Peterson (eds.), *Journal of Common Market Studies (JCMS)*, Vol. 37 no. 1 (Oxford: Blackwell, 1999), pp. 59-85 (p. 60); Peter Hort, 'Schatten auf der Währungsunion', *FAZ*, 4.5.1998, p. 1; Hanke and Proissl, *Die Zeit*, Nr. 20, 7.5.1998, p. 5; for an economic analysis see Barry Eichengreen and Charles Wyplosz, 'The Stability Pact: more than minor nuisance?' in David Begg et al., pp. 65-113.

51. Martin, p. 82.

52. Teltschik records that although the German press universally hailed the April 1990 Dublin summit as a success, Kohl and his team were nonetheless worried by opinion polls indicating German public concern that the introduction of EMU could affect D-mark stability (p. 212).

53. For synopsis of European Council bargaining techniques, see Helen Wallace, 'Making multinational negotiation work', in William Wallace (ed.), *The Dynamics of European Integration* (London: RIIA 1990), pp. 213-229 (p. 214).

54. Teltschik, p. 56. Kohl's ten-point plan, for example, also foresaw the keystone of European architecture as a development of the CSCE process. This may yet prove to be so, but thus far European masons have continued working on other stones instead.

55. For speech in full see Hanns Jürgen Küstes (ed.), *Dokumente zur Deutschlandpolitik* (R. Oldenburg Verlag, 1998).

56. See Teltschik's report of Mitterrand's remarks made to Kohl in Paris on 14 February 1990: "Germany was a historical reality, which one had to get used to, whether one liked it or not. He liked it. He welcomed the suggestion of currency union" (p. 150). On 7 February, Kohl had made his offer of currency union to the GDR, and the D-mark, not EMU, was the currency union in question. But EMU was perhaps the unspoken corollary to Mitterrand's remarks. The conclusion is that rationally, the French had no other choice but to like the Germans, and that the Germans would have no other choice but to accept EMU. For closer analysis of FRG government neurosis about German nationality, see Chapter 15 of my *Post-National Patriotism*.

57. We can speculate that tensions would have been even higher between the UK and German governments in the September 1992 pound crisis had the UK not negotiated an opt out from EMU at Maastricht.

58. See Joseph Hanimann, 'Abschied ohne Tränen: Francfort oder Der Franc ist fort: Die Franzosen und der Euro', *FAZ*, 23.5.1998, p. 35.

59. See 'Ein Kompromiß bei der Amtszeit Duisenbergs macht den Weg frei für die Wirtschafts- und Währungsunion', *FAZ*, 4.5.1998, p. 1; Claus Tigges, 'Der Erste', *FAZ*, 4.5.1998, p. 16.

60. 'Kok spricht von einem Sieg für die Niederlande', *FAZ*, 5.5.1998, p. 4.

61. See 'In Italien "Euphorie" ', *FAZ*, 5.5.1998, p. 4.

62. 'Tietmeyer bekräftigt die Zweifel an Euro-Start mit Italien'.

63. For example, Eichengreen and Wyplosz, in David Begg et al. (eds.) (p. 107), have argued that EMU has diverted attention from discussion on pan-European problems of unemployment and financing pensions. They argue furthermore that fiscal stringency under the stability pact will limit the room for maneuver required to solve these problems.

64. See Chapter 3, Phillips, *Post-National Patriotism*.

65. Claus Tigges, *FAZ*, 4.5.1998.

66. 'Europas Währungshüter treffen sich im Eurotower zum ersten Mal', *FAZ*, 9.6.1998, p. 18. Germany, for example, was admitted to EMU despite having a state debt level of 61% for 1997, above the rate set by Maastricht. Commission and ECI judged benignly, however, that German borrowing was likely to fall below the 60% barrier during 1998.

6

The Limits of EU Integration and
the Possibilities of Functionalism

In this chapter, I am going to investigate further ideas of interdependence and methods of mediating between specialist sectors of interest, not only within the EU, but outside it too. Approaches and analyses of European integration broadly rely upon any one, or a combination of, three groups of ideas:

- Realist or intergovernmental
- Federalist
- Functionalist or neofunctionalist

There is undoubtedly a case for the view that elements of all three are present in the European integration process. I would agree indeed with two commentators who analyze EU politics from a perspective of liberal intergovernmentalism that there can be no general theory on European integration "any more than there exists a theory of American politics."[1] However, in view of parameters that I will identify in this section, I tend to favor the current need to accentuate functionalism as an approach and method of analysis best suited to overcoming differences. In doing so, I will argue that the functionalist approach needs to be developed independent of European state institutions if the integration process is to go further in overcoming remaining differences between communities and sectors of interest. As I stated in the Introduction, my aim in this book is not so much to focus ultimately on the relationship between states, but the relationship in and between communities with differing identities which increasingly traverse state boundaries. The focus of federalist and realist approaches is on state structures. However, as states and institutional sectors are engaged in the process of negotiation of increasing levels of interdependence between themselves, there would seem to be little choice but to place greater emphasis on the functionalist approach. This would maximize cooperation and minimize the division generated by resulting exposed differences between individuals and groups coming increasingly into contact independent of state interlocution.

When individuals want to find out more about each other, and the circumstances in which they might have something in common, they do not after all ask each other initially what form of government they have or what sort of government they would like, but questions concerning their function: parenthood, job, hobby and so forth. Therefore, after a critique of realist and federal approaches, in the chapter ahead, I would like to focus on the potential benefits of sharing of functions between people.

The intergovernmental/realist school dominated international relations post-Second World War.[2] The state-centrist perspective can be seen to be the result of depression and two world wars.[3] Indeed, as I have outlined in the previous chapter, much of the negotiation process surrounding the Treaty on European Union was intergovernmental. However, we also saw that individual states are not entirely in control of the process. We must bear in mind that there are a whole range of pressures bearing on member governments. Thus, we can link the changes wrought by the Treaty and the SEA before it as specifically linked to a substrand of the realist approach, namely multilevel governance.[4] But this perspective by itself is not sufficient to lead to an understanding of forces acting for or against further integration. We should bear in mind too that the purpose of the previous chapter was an examination of a key stage establishing a measure of extragovernmental interdependence.

David Held's study of cosmopolitanism has pinpointed the insufficiencies of the realist approach to the study of international relations, its "statist" approach ignoring the manifold variety of non-state internal and external forces affecting interstate relations.[5] A constituent part of Held's study is what he terms disjunctures: in law, internationalization of political decision making, security structures, culture/identity and world economy, between the formal authority of the state and the "actual practices and structures of the state and economic system at the national, regional and global levels."[6] We can link this point with the post-modern view of Jean-Marie Guéhenno, that institutions, not just those of nation-states, but also those of their nascent replacements in such bodies as the EU, are becoming increasingly obsolescent. However, although I agree with Guéhenno that the new flexible global society can bypass all institutions, not merely those of the nation-state, I disagree with his conclusion that we can detect the end of politics itself.[7] The process of organizational influence and power has become more diffuse,[8] but dramatic statements are unhelpful when we wish to understand. As Anthony Giddens points out, authors' preoccupations with "ends" is an indication that we should reform established structures.[9]

In another paper, Held sees the future of democracy as a "framework of democratic states and agencies."[10] Held envisages the UN charter becoming more than just a statement of intent, along with the growth of regional parliaments, and the advent of supranational referenda. But that his ideas are partially captive to increasingly irrelevant sociopolitical conceptions is shown by his unconvincing defense of what he himself terms a "pipe dream." Further desiring to uphold his point, Held asks who would have "imagined the peaceful achievement of German unification a few years ago."[11] However, this process has taken place within very conventional precepts of state organization.[12] The principle shortcoming of the German unification process has been its unintended overreliance on state structures.[13] Accordingly, we can correct Held's study of cosmopolitan governance, which argues in favor of the establishment ultimately of global supranational authority, by linking it with functional ideas which Held overlooks, and specifically with the ideas of the original outstanding theorist of the functionalist principles refashioned in the original drive towards European unification, David Mitrany.[14]

Some see federalism as the solution to the insufficiencies of European integration. In a 1996 paper, which includes a critique of Mitrany's approach, Murray Forsyth concludes that the technical functional approach now shows "serious limitations, and a more explicit and determined recourse to federal-constitutional principles could help rectify the lack of coherence and balance that has arisen."[15] Now, I would certainly agree with him that greater clarity in application of federal-constitutional principles could go some way to redressing existing problems of the EU. I will discuss these in the chapter following this one. However, I would disagree with him on "the need to posit a federal end-point."[16] Aspects of federalism are only a means, not an ends in overcoming the divisiveness of differentiation between people. In his preoccupation with discussion of various forms of international organization, it seems to me that Forsyth loses sight of this.[17] Moreover, I would disagree with him on the limitations of the functional approach. I would argue that it is the limitation of the functional approach *within* EU parameters that is the problem and not the actual approach itself. The drive of Forsyth's argument is to see the EU as "permanent" and, drawing upon Carl Schmitt's conception of *Freund/Feind,* he sees the 1957 Rome Treaty's establishment of an area without internal frontiers as a crucial delineation between those within and without.[18] But in the post-Cold War era, I would argue that this is not very helpful and we should no longer be drawing geopolitical boundaries. In this respect, I would argue, like many before, that Europe's destination is unknown, and that we should be thinking in terms of new post-territorial structures.[19] Given global and European demographic pressures, drawing such boundaries can only sow the seeds of further societal strife across and within EU borders.

THE LIMITATIONS OF THE EU FUNCTIONALIST APPROACH

We have now identified evidence showing limitations to the realist and federal models of integration. In this section, let us now turn to evidence for the functional approach. As we shall see soon, the limitations of the functional approach *within* EU parameters were criticized long ago by the originator of functionalism, David Mitrany. Mitrany's critique of regional integration in Europe was that it would ultimately only duplicate in much greater measure the problems of already existing interstate rivalry and desires for hegemony in the international order.

Indeed at the beginning of the previous chapter to this, we saw recent evidence for Mitrany's critique of Western European integration. Additionally to the aspirations for the euro to replace the dollar as the world's leading reserve currency, we may view US demands on the EU to drop import barriers to Latin American bananas in a long-running trade dispute as falling in centuries-long traditions of interstate strife.[20] It seems that there are many in Europe who are attracted by the view that closer EU cooperation can lead to winning the battle for economic hegemony with the USA. We can see more recent trends in the tradition of de Gaulle's covetous perception of the "exorbitant privilege" of the postwar economic hegemony of the USA, unrivalled in world history, based on "a large internal market, a high degree of self-sufficiency in basic raw materials and a low external dependence on trade."[21]

Even commentators who see global institutions as becoming more important in regulation of the international order see them in hegemonic terms, the implication being that a possibly damaging interest conflict will ensue, not an attempt to arrive at an equitable consensus. Iain Begg and John Peterson ask whether decisions on external trade once reached internally within the Community will "gradually become 'externally' dictated by WTO rules."[22] But rules need not be "dictated" in a state of hegemony, in this instance US hegemony. In 1997, for example, at the WTO, it seemed to Europeans that negotiations on liberalization of the financial services market were dominated by the US. Moreover, US diplomats signed an agreement only following approval from the national financial lobby.[23] However, to react to hegemonial behavior displayed by another party by desiring to dominate the relationship in her or his place, only perpetuates the principles and hence the dangers of hegemonial order *per se*.

Mitrany identified supremacist aims of the contemporary modern European Community dating back to pre-Second World War analysis of pan-European organization, which he had made in a paper originally published in 1930. He pointed out regretfully that "the aim of Pan-Europa, according to [Count Coudenhove-Kalergi, one of the pioneers of European unity, and founder of the Pan-Europe movement] is 'a federation of states and a customs union for the salvation of Europe, of Western culture and of the white race ... the struggle for Pan-Europa is a struggle against barbarism.'" Mitrany traced the links between this view and continuing exclusivist tendencies in Western Europe, citing a July 1969 BBC radio interview with Jean Monnet in which the latter claimed "European union is a matter of civilization." In doing so, as Mitrany points out, Monnet implicitly ignored the rest of non-EEC Europe, and indeed the rest of the world.[24]

Therefore, we should remember that "Europe" is not an idea encapsulating all that is good, or for that matter evil. Moreover, the term Europe is also contestable as a geographical expression, and the preservation of effective lines of demarcation in geographical terms is increasingly difficult.[25] In view of increasing global interdependence, it is difficult to see where barriers can be drawn, despite some commentators being seemingly captivated by the illusion of the possibility of a geopolitical demarcation and finality of the European integration process.[26]

As an answer to interstate rivalry, Mitrany saw functionalism as a method of separating considerations of power from welfare, in so doing, fostering the common good of mankind. Paul Taylor in his overview of Mitrany's work encapsulated his approach as "the major principles of functionalism are that man can be weaned away from his loyalty to the nation state by the experience of fruitful international cooperation." Indeed, Mitrany himself expressly states that he originally developed functionalism to combat the "political directive," as he terms it, of the "principle of nationality."[27] He believed "(the functional approach) ... should help shift the emphasis from political issues which divide to those social issues in which the interests of the peoples is plainly akin and collective."[28] We can see that for Mitrany, "collective" by his use of it in connection with "akin" is interchangeable with common. Indeed, Stephen George has neatly encapsulated how the original Treaty of Rome, which set up the *Common* Market, is a practical manifestation of this principle of common good, being an "interstate version of the social contract between individuals."[29]

FUNCTIONALISM AND CONTEMPORARY PRACTICES

We have now noted the persuasiveness of Mitrany's critique of European integration. However, this leads us on to the need to correct three insufficiencies in Mitrany's original approach before the relevance of his functionalist ideas can be exploited to the full. That is the task of this section. First, much of Mitrany's theory was developed before the worst evils of racial and nationalist conceptions were perpetrated. So some of his thoughts today seem to be as out of tune as if heard on crackling 78 rpm shellac. For example, although he developed functionalism as a response to correct the negative precepts of nationalism, Mitrany could still write pre-Second World War: "Twentieth century nationalism in allying itself with the new current of social revolution has changed both in character and in purpose. It is positive as nineteenth century nationalism never was, aiming at satisfying positive social needs, at meeting legitimate social discontents."[30]

The datedness of Mitrany's ideas leads us on also to a second weakness, which I have already hinted at. Mitrany's functionalism does not account for the diversity of need and perspective. We have already seen in the previous section that he uses the terms "collective" and "common" interchangeably. Underlying Mitrany's idea of a common good was his assumption of a single homogeneous "international society," which excludes the commonly held contemporary perspective of diversity existing in a framework of global interdependence.[31] Tracing back the evolution of his ideas, Mitrany still believed firmly in Rousseau's common good. He supported his belief by citing from one of Horace's satires, "We are all lost in the woods, the only difference is that we are lost in different directions." The implication of Mitrany's use of the quotation was that there was only one direction out of the woods for all of us to escape, as he termed it, from the "individualist-nationalist period" and its "all-providing collective deity."[32]

However, in view of the manifold evidence of the enrichment to individuals' lives brought within diverse social groupings and traditions throughout Europe and the world beyond, there can surely be no single conception regarding future steps to what is good. We should emphasize the difference in meaning between "common" and "collective." Hence we should emphasize that the aim of integration should be to promote cultural diversity, recalling Bhikhu Parekh's argument, that "cultural diversity ... is a collective good."[33] We may see that each group can know where he or she is in the woods only by ascertaining his or her position in relation to others, and in this process of collaborative dialogue, each group can find the path out of the woods that best suits them.[34]

In his neofunctionalist critique of Mitrany, Ernst Haas argued persuasively in his study of Western European integration, *Beyond the Nation State* (1964), that the considerations of power and welfare cannot be separated, and "the crucial question is: whose welfare is being realized by what means."[35] If a community of interest can be found, then steps towards integration occur. Therefore, as a contemporary critic has pointed out: "It is not the preparedness to contribute to a "common good" which fosters the community process, but the particular advantages, which each group in competition with the other sees in the supranational solution to problems."[36]

Thus, the concept of competition would seem to point us in the direction of an examination of the role of business and a correction of the third insufficiency to Mitrany's approach. Mitrany concentrated on international organization in public hands. However, if we examine contemporary communities, the point would seem to be that the examples of international organization with which most of us have a tangible relationship are not public global international governmental or non-governmental organizations such as the UN or the Red Cross, or regional transnational bodies such as the EU, but businesses operating internationally: from the packaging for the breakfast milk to the toothpaste brand we use last thing at night. Every day, whether as employees or even more so as consumers, we come into contact with some aspect of private international organization.

Therefore, the institutions of the EU are only one, institutional, approach to transnational solutions circumventing or overcoming the barriers of the nation-state. Further key players in circumventing the nation-state are the transnational business actors. Mitrany's original state-centric approach was all the more remarkable as he himself served on the board of the Anglo-Dutch-based transnational company Unilever 1944-1960 as political advisor.[37] Nonetheless, this was a failure of perception which was perpetuated in Haas' *Beyond the Nation State*. Haas' book also failed to consider transnational companies, even fleetingly, a state-centrism all the more remarkable because a case study of the ILO forms a major part of it.[38]

Accordingly we should remember that although the establishment of the institutions of the European Communities was an important prerequisite, it is not they themselves that have freed, according to Mitrany, "men's loyalties," once "penned up within the territorial confines of the exclusivist nation-state."[39] It is the freedom of the market, which the Communities' treaties have encouraged, which has done so instead. Even the originator of Aachen's esteemed Charlemagne prize, founded in 1950, the textiles industrialist Kurt Pfeiffer, foresaw that the annual award should recall "the great founder of occidental culture" by its presentation for service rendered for the promotion of "occidental unity and, as indispensable prior step, economic unity."[40]

Nonetheless, this brings a further handicap to prospects for the ultimate success of the European integration process. If Europe is attractive to its members or potential members only for economic reasons, then no matter how wealthy its individual parts may be, the potential harmful effects of competition and rivalry (which the European movement sought to circumvent) will continue to pose a threat to the Community in particular and the world in general. I would suggest that the capitalist form of economic organization risks becoming victim of its own success. Both practically based and theoretical studies come to this conclusion. The authors of a comparative study on the future of the car industry cite a Japanese union critique of attempts at ever greater performance and the obsession with competition leading to a fall off in quality of life.[41] Hans Jonas has surmised: "If nothing is achieved to the same extent as achievement itself, then we become prisoners of achievement."[42]

THE FUNCTIONAL RESPONSE TO EXCLUSION

In our analysis of various approaches to European integration so far, we have discussed the limitations of the process and the tendency to exclude sectors and groups. In this section, I will identify possible functional strategies in pursuit of greater provision of freedoms in societal conceptions, which might go some way towards eliminating tendencies to exclude.

The exclusion of the EU unemployed and poor has the same sum and substance as that applying to those beyond the Community fortress walls (or recalling Mitrany's Romanian origins, the castle-church walls) in the rest of Europe or other parts of the world. In Germany for example, there is no official publication on poverty levels. Reports are compiled by non-state welfare and social organizations.[43] Yet we could recall Mitrany's paper "A Working Peace System" published in 1943 outlining his belief that if people are given the opportunity to improve their social and economic circumstances "they will keep the peace."[44] His ideas thus have applications still in an EU of 18 million unemployed. I will discuss aspects of business' role in the negation *and* creation of social coherence in Part II.

We have already seen the validity of Mitrany's critique of European integration (and we might wonder at the official recognition throughout the Community of the memory of Monnet and Schuman expressed in names of buildings, streets and academic chairs, while Mitrany would seem to have been overlooked). It is a development of this strand that makes a reassessment of his original work an invaluable aid in the identification of mechanisms to further integration. Post-Cold War, neofunctionalist theories also have a further problem. As Paul Taylor wrote, "the neofunctionalist theories were developed mainly in order to increase our understanding of the processes whereby a regional *political* system might emerge as in the case of the European Community."[45]

However, as we are finding out, regional supranational systems are becoming outflanked by global processes. Nonetheless, this wider global perspective gives us an invaluable insight into correcting neofunctional analysis of European integration. For Stephen George, for example, the most convincing restatement of neofunctionalism came in a paper published by Jeppe Tranholm-Mikkelsen in 1991. Nonetheless, Tranholm-Mikkelsen argued that two factors, nationalism among the European public and diversity among states, tended to act as hindrances to the neofunctionalist approach and analysis of the European integration process. Additionally, Tranholm-Mikkelsen suggested that three further aspects could both foster or hinder the neofunctionalist integration process: Germany, the international security situation and increasing global interdependence.[46]

The two interrelated focuses of this book, Germany and the possibilities of postnational social coherence, give us important insights into how to correct these deficiencies in neofunctionalism. Furthermore, we can see that if George or Tranholm-Mikkelsen had referred to the writings of Mitrany, they could have remembered, as we have seen already, that functionalism without its neo prefix was intended to harness forces in society to overcome nationalism in a global rather than a regional form of organization. It thus behooves us (as well as them) not to forget the remarks of

Mitrany in our analysis: "All that one asks from political scientists who may be critical of the functional approach is that, on their part, they should in every instance watch closely for the 'relation of things.' "[47]

Accordingly, I would argue that we have to extend functionalism from the neo-functionalist approaches of European elites to grassroots level if we are to overcome nationalist chauvinism. Also I would argue that we will find more equitable solutions to global causes of and needs underlying migration only if they are applied to communities of migration as well as those of immigration. Ultimately therefore, we will aim to follow Mitrany's exhortation to see the "relation of things" extending worldwide, beyond the EU.[48]

Therefore, we should investigate alternative means of exploiting global interdependence to ensure that diversity between states and individuals is not used as a means of perpetuating division of wealth but as a potential source of the creation of wealth and well-being. The functional strategies identified in this chapter can form the basis for our further discussion. With the benefit of the lessons outlined here, we should discard conceptions of common good or the primacy of competition – despite the validity that these may have within parts of the general process – in favor of a conception of *collective* good that encompasses transinstitutional and transnational approaches. Before this, however, in the final chapter of Part I, we should nonetheless identify how limitations to the European Union contribution to this greater collective goal may be best overcome. We will see that EU institutional approaches have problems of unwieldiness.

NOTES

1. See Andrew Moravcsik and Kalypso Nicolaïdis, 'Explaining the Treaty of Amsterdam: Interests, Influence, Institutions', in Begg, Peterson (eds.), *JCMS*, Vol. 37, no. 1, pp. 59-85 (p. 60).

2. The terms intergovernmental and realist have come to be used interchangeably, because as Heywood has pointed out succinctly on the realists, "the central assumption is that the state is the principal actor ... on the world stage, and, being sovereign, is able to act as an autonomous entity." See Andrew Heywood, *Politics* (London: Macmillan, 1997), p. 142.

3. See Richard Leaver, 'International Political Economy and the Changing World Order: Evolution or Involution?', pp. 130-141 (p. 134); and Richard Stubbs and Geoffrey Underhill, 'Global Trends, Regional Patterns', pp 331-335, in Stubbs and Underhill (eds.), *Political Economy and the Changing Global Order* (London: Macmillan, 1994).

4. For synopsis of multilevel governance, see George, pp. 54-56.

5. David Held, *Democracy and the Global Order: From the Modern State to Cosmopolitan Governance* (Cambridge: Polity Press, 1995), p. 24.

6. See Held, pp. 99-140 (p. 99).

7. Jean-Marie Guéhenno, *Le Fin de la Démocratie* [*Das Ende der Demokratie*] (Munich: Artemis & Winkler Verlag, 1994), pp. 165-166.

8. See Linklater's discussion of Foucault and Derrida's conception of political

frameworks, pp. 74, 196. Guéhenno's argument favoring post-state structures is firmly in the tradition of Foucault.

9. Anthony Giddens, *Beyond Left and Right* [*Jenseits von Links und Rechts*] (Frankfurt/Main: Suhrkamp 1997), pp. 1-11, 15-16.

10. Held, 'Democracy and the International Order', in Archibugi and Held (eds.), pp. 96-120 (p. 106).

11. Held, 'Democracy and the International Order', p. 110.

12. For opinion poll figures of those who believed that German unification would occur see Werner Weidenfeld and Karl-Rudolf Korte, 'Nation und Nationalbewußtsein' in Weidenfeld, Korte (eds.), *Handbuch zur deutschen Einheit* (Frankfurt/Main: Campus Verlag, 1996), pp. 494-500. Weidenfeld and Korte cite mid-eighties opinion polls in the FRG showing 70-80% figures in support of long-term goals of reunification; 8% believed that this was possible by the end of the century (p. 492). By implication, an overwhelming number, 92%, did not believe that unification was possible by the end of the century, this bulk of unimaginative opinion seemingly upholding the need for Held's vision. Nonetheless, I would argue that a better vision is required than his, one that empowers people rather than an abstract political system.

13. See Part II of my *Post-National Patriotism*.

14. In his discussion of the "limits of democratic political theory and international relations theory," Held notes that the only commentators who questioned the 'sovereignty' of state in the first half of the century as being Figgis and Laski. [See *Democracy and the Global Order: From the Modern State to Cosmopolitan Governance*, pp. 23-27.]

15. See Murray Forsyth, 'The Political Theory of Federalism: The Relevance of Classical Approaches', in Joachim Jens Hesse and Vincent Wright (eds.), *Federalizing Europe? The Costs, Benefits, and Preconditions of Federal Political Systems* (Oxford University Press, 1996), pp. 25-45 (pp. 25-26).

16. Forsyth, p. 27.

17. In his zeal for categorization Forsyth adduces the views of (among others) Christopher Tugendhat, Walter Hallstein and the Federal German constitutional court, to conclude, "the political theorist ... has no need to be restrained by the caution of the legal profession.... It may be true that the Community is not a 'state' or a 'federal state' but this does not prevent it from being a federal union, that is to say a permanent linking together of states to form a corporate entity with a distinct boundary vis-à-vis the outside world." See Forsyth, pp. 26-40 (pp. 39-40).

18. Forsyth, pp. 36-40.

19. See, for example, Theodora Kostakopoulou, 'Why a 'Community of Europeans' Could be a Community of Exclusion: A Reply to Howe' in Simon Bulmer and Andrew Scott (eds.), *JCMS*, Volume 35 no. 2 (Oxford: Blackwell, 1997), pp. 301-308; compare also views of J. Lodge, cited in Chapter 3.

20. On reserve currency rivalry see 'Euro wird mehr als ein Fünftel der Weltwährungsreserven ausmachen', *FAZ* 4.8.1998, p. 22; Martin and Schumann, p. 114.

21. See Leaver, pp. 135-136.

22. See Iain Begg and John Peterson, 'Editorial Statement', *JCMS*, Vol. 37, no. 1 (Oxford: Blackwell, 1999), pp. 1-12 (p. 3). Begg and Peterson cite the bananas dispute.

23. Dirk Herbermann, 'Flagschiff ohne Orientierung', *Die Zeit*, Nr. 42, 8.10.1998, p. 55.

24. Mitrany, 'Regional Pacts: Their Uses and Dangers,' in his *The Functional The-*

ory of Politics, pp. 151-159 (pp. 152-153).

25. For notion of Europe as a geographical expression but not as an "idea," see Dolf Sternberger, 'Komponenten der geistigen Gestalt Europas', in his *Verfassungspatriotismus Schriften X* (Frankfurt/Main: Insel Verlag, 1990), pp. 39-54.

26. See, for example, Werner Weidenfeld and Joseph Janning, 'Europa vor der Vollendung', *FAZ*, 3.7.1998, p. 8. Weidenfeld and Janning discuss prospects of 'Das große Europa' and 'Weltmachtfaktor Euro'.

27. See Paul Taylor's introduction to Mittrany's *The Functional Theory of Politics*, p. x; also Mitrany, p. 141.

28. David Mitrany, *International Affairs*, xxiv, 1948, cited by Ernst Haas, *Beyond the Nation State* (Stanford University Press, 1964), p. 7.

29. George, p. 195.

30. Mitrany, 'Nationality and Nationalism', pp, 137-145 (pp. 142-143).

31. For example, he wrote, "a new philosophy for a world society must ... begin by asking that we renounce the pagan worship of political frontiers as the source of our public law and morals." See 'The Progress of International Government', in his *The Functional Theory of Politics*, pp. 85-104 (pp. 100-101); see also the chapter title "Through Functional Action to International Society," of his 1941 paper 'Territorial, Ideological, or Functional International Organisation?', also in his *The Functional Theory of Politics*, pp. 105-122.

32. Mitrany, 'Retrospect and Prospect', in his *The Functional Theory of Politics*, pp. 239-266 (pp. 263-264).

33. See Bhikhu Parekh's argument, "cultural diversity ... is a collective good" in his paper 'Cultural Diversity and Liberal Democracy', in David Beetham (ed.), *Defining and Measuring Democracy* (London: Sage, 1994), pp. 199-221 (p. 208).

34. See Charles Taylor, 'The Politics of Recognition', in *Multiculturalism and 'The Politics of Recognition'*, with commentary by Amy Gutmann (ed.) et al. (Princeton University Press, 1992), pp. 25-73. Especially: "my discovering my own identity doesn't mean that I work it out in isolation, but I negotiate it through dialogue, partly overt, partly internal with others." (p. 34). See also Phillips, *Post-National Patriotism*, Chapter 16, where I discuss ideas about the negotiation and recognition of cultural diversity at local community level.

35. Haas, p. 47.

36. Kohler-Koch in Kriele (ed.), p. 83.

37. Mitrany, *The Functional Theory of Politics*, p. 31.

38. Haas.

39. Quoted in Haas, p. 9. The relevant passage in full: "When men's loyalties are penned up within the territorial confines of the exclusivist nation-state, there is little hope of working for the general welfare. However, these loyalties, once freed from the shackles of national insecurity and allowed to identify with humanity at large will achieve the true common good."

40. Georg-Paul Hefty, 'Auf den Fundamenten der Kaiserpfalz,' *FAZ Bilder und Zeiten*, 11.5.1996.

41. See Horst Neumann and Dirk Nolte, 'Protektionismus in der Automobilindustrie', *WSI Mitteilungen* 5/1993, 299-302 (p. 300) who cite from a study by the Japanese counterpart of IG Metall, JA/IMF-JC, that concludes: "If competition becomes a goal in itself, and people start to compete at every conceivable cost, then competition becomes a

monster, which can destroy life, society, and even the economy."

42. Jonas, p. 32.

43. Richard Hauser, 'Das empirische Bild der Armut in der Bundesrepublik – ein Überblick', in *Aus Politik und Zeitgeschichte* B31-32/95 28.7.1995, pp. 3-13 (p. 3). In 1998, the EU Commission threatened to take the Federal Republic to the European Court because poorly paid employees from other EU states were denied full social security payments available to German colleagues to help support their families. See 'Auseinandersetzung um deutsche Sozialhilfe für EU-Arbeitnehmer', *FAZ*, 30.7.1998, p. 12.

44. Cited by P. Taylor, in Mitrany, *The Functional Theory of Politics*, p. xi.

45. P. Taylor, p. xiii.

46. J. Tranholm-Mikkelsen, 'Neofunctionalism: Obstinate or Obsolete? A Reappraisal in the Light of the New Dynamism of the EC', *Millenium*, 20 1991, pp. 1-22 cited in George, pp. 49-50.

47. Mitrany, *The Functional Theory of Politics*, p. 37.

48. I pursue ideas concerning functionalism at grassroots level in greater detail in my *Post-National Patriotism*, Chapter 3.

7

Parameters and Limits of Democracy in Europe

In the preceding chapter, I argued that democracy within the EU and our understanding of democratic mechanisms could not be linked solely to existing institutional conceptions of democracy. EU structural modifications cannot in themselves simplify the complexities of the interdependencies in our contemporary world of which they are part. However, it would be beneficial were they to contain a clear constitutional statement of principles as an initial point of guidance to facilitate our responses to problems that we encounter in our everyday lives. These principles could serve as initial guidance pointers to better respond to economic interdependence within Europe and Europe's interdependence with the world beyond. Accordingly, following this chapter, and its consideration of the current limitations on democracy and social coherence in the EU, I will argue in Part II that the "closer cooperation" amendment to the European Union Treaty at Amsterdam may contain an important mechanism which could provide the basis of the establishment of benchmarks of social coherence within multilateral frameworks. Additionally, I will argue that an increase in understanding achieved through dialogue within and between multilateral frameworks can utilize the complexity of EU structures as only a part of a greater democratic process fostering heterogeneity, benefiting the collective good.

In examining the history of Western European integration, we have seen that thus far the mechanism which has proved most effective in overcoming division between nation-states is not institutional, but rather the interdependence of an increasingly transnational economy. Following the failure, with the French National Assembly's rejection of the EDC, of the avowedly institutional impetus to integration, Western Europe came to rely on the market as the main path to further integration. Nonetheless, it may be that considerable remaining political and social differences in the Community could spill over into tensions and resentments during the infant years of the greatest institutional "success" achieved by the Community yet, the ECB-administered EMU, which could be seen by many as servicing the needs of the market, but not necessarily the needs of community.

We can see that the success of emphasizing the market has led to problems with the institutional approach to European integration in other sectors. The market demands speed. However; social and political reflection can deflect and hinder the needs of business. As I have already noted in Chapter 3, the "democracy deficit" of the EU has frequently been discussed. But the fundamental dilemma standing in the way of its elimination is that it may impinge on the need for quick decision making and economic efficiency, which, we have seen, has been the motor thus far towards integration.[1]

Furthermore, outside the EU, market barriers are being progressively eliminated too. Restraints on world trade, legacies of prewar recession, were eliminated gradually from a level of average 40% level of import duty in 1947 to under 5% in 1995 under the General Agreement on Tariffs and Trade (GATT) negotiations.[2] GATT's successor, the WTO, in existence since January 1995, now oversees the progressive removal of trade barriers as agreed at the Treaty of Marrakech in April 1994. It also arbitrates on problems of national specificities of distribution and health regulation, which may also infringe upon aspects of trade.[3]

In this chapter now, I will describe, first, the nature of the European Union Treaty, second, the Commission, third, the European Parliament, and fourth, the European Council and Council of Ministers. With this evidence, at the end of this chapter, we will be able to reach some initial conclusions about the limitations of the European integration process.

THE EUROPEAN UNION TREATY

In our examination of the limits to democracy and social coherence in the EU, let us first examine how these are constricted by the Treaty framework. At Maastricht, the Council extended the Community element (with substantial transfers of states' sovereignty) and complemented it with the establishment of two further columns on intergovernmental cooperation, these being in the second column, Common Foreign and Security Policy (CFSP), and in the third, Justice and Home Affairs. We have seen, in Chapter 5, that the Treaty of European Union was clear in setting out the EMU provisions. However, the clarity did not extend to the other provisions of the Treaty.

The first column of the Treaty structure was named European Community. It contained the provisions on EMU, customs union and internal market along with further additional new or amended measures, including consumer protection, education, health, research and environment, trans-European networks, social policy and Union citizenship. In the first column also, extended powers of the EP were agreed, and the Committee of the Regions was set up. The latter provides a forum for representatives from local authorities, municipalities and self-governing regions. Under the Treaty, the Council and Commission must seek advice from the Committee on education and training, cultural affairs, health, trans-European networks and structural and regional policy.[4]

Lobbying for a social counterweight to the single market resulted in an advancement of the 1989 Social Charter at Maastricht to an incorporation and expansion of its provisions in the Social Chapter. At the insistence of the UK government, which refused to sign it, the Social Chapter was kept separate from the main Treaty, but following a change of governing party the Chapter was incorporated in the first column of the European Union Treaty at the Amsterdam summit in June 1997. The Social Chapter was made possible by agreement on 31 October 1991 between ETUC, UNICE (Union of Industrial and Employers' Confederations of Europe) and CEEP (the European Public Employers Federation), to carry out social dialogue at the European level.[5] Until then UNICE had insisted upon the non-binding nature of the talks (begun at the instigation of the Commission in January 1985), but ultimately the employers' readiness to sign the agreement was influenced by the belief that consensual partnership was better than confrontation. The recognition of the need for consensus rather than confrontation between the social partners is the most important aspect of the Social Chapter. Nevertheless, the Commission's first suggestion that legislation provide for the setting up of European works councils was rejected firmly by UNICE.[6] But, as Wolfgang Platzer surmises, the experience of history shows that labor law legislation only follows everyday industrial reality.[7] Volkswagen (VW) agreed with unions to set up a European works council in February 1992. In addition, the UK was neither an initial signatory to either the Social Charter or the Social Protocol of Maastricht, but a British-based company, United Biscuits, decided in 1994 to ignore the British opt-out, then still in force, and to include British employees on its European works council.[8]

The second column of the EU treaty contained provisions on a future CFSP; the third column on cooperation on Justice and Home Affairs. At Amsterdam, this model was slightly modified: limited practical provisions concerning visas, asylum and immigration were transferred from the third column to the Community column. It was agreed also to create the post of High Representative of the CFSP.[9]

European Council meetings since then have also been unable to arrive at consensus on aspects of political union. Equally little progress has been achieved in reconciling diverse nation-state welfare provisions in a unitary Community system. This failure contrasts with the origins of the Community integration process. We have seen that, originally, the institutionalization of coal and steel production under the ECSC was a product of its times, incorporating a desire in many quarters to see an end of capitalism. Nonetheless, as a result of its successful supranational regulation appropriate to then social and political needs, it has perhaps caused an error in perception of a need for a repetition of the social and political regulation in other sectors on the part of a similar European high authority. This has permeated views critical of the social and political components of the most recent treaties of Maastricht and Amsterdam. Some have seen the need for social regulation as a counterbalance to the powers of the global market and increasing wealth disparity within states and between states. Hans-Peter Martin and Harald Schumann, for example, have seen globalization as a trap and an attack on democracy and prosperity.[10] But social and political needs, along with economic opportunities in post-Cold War Europe, are vastly different to those of 1951.

Moreover, as Beate Kohler-Koch has pointed out, the EU does not function hierarchically,[11] and it seems to me therefore that to overcome the symptoms of Eurosclerosis which remain in social and political spheres of Community organization, perhaps most damagingly in the relationship of the European elites to the European populations, we should investigate active exploitation of the possibilities of extrastructural and innerstructural organization, which may later endow existing structures of the EU with new perspectives, simplifications and greater relevance. I will go into these ideas in the first chapter of Part II, "Closer Cooperation and the Transnational Development of Social Coherence." At this point however, as a prerequisite to this, let us continue with our consideration of existing EU limits to the development of social coherence.

In the run-up to Maastricht, Helmut Kohl declared that he would not return from the summit without agreement on political union. However, he seemingly only secured agreement from his fellow Council members to augment complexity in the Treaty system, which, as we have seen in this section, as well as a Community element (with substantial transfers of states' sovereignty) now contained two further columns on intergovernmental cooperation. Accordingly, the Treaty was seen as a failure in the respect that the Federal government seemed to gain little concrete return for its preparedness to enter EMU. We have already seen also that European integration was a matter of "high politics" in Germany. Thus there was considerable disappointment that perceived parallels between the Federal German model and prospects for future European Community development had not been developed further.[12] Then SPD leader Björn Engholm claimed that Kohl had failed on the central question of democracy in the EC.[13] For one *Handelsblatt* commentator, agreement to give the EP the power of codecision with the Council (see the section "The European Parliament" below) was a "straightforward euphemism. The concurrent loss of power of the national parliaments and continuing effective powerlessness of the European Parliament is a grave construction error."[14] Moreover, these views were echoed by a broad spectrum of business leaders. A BDI spokesman expressly contrasted the clarity of the EMU plan with that of the political union. "While a solid binding time table for the Economic and Currency union was established, a political deepening was only achieved in piecemeal terms."[15]

THE COMMISSION

The lack of democratic legitimacy in the Community for many was clear in regard to the workings of the Commission. The Commission has the right to originate legislation. However, the only legitimacy of the Commission, containing politicians failed or discredited at the national level, persons whom *The Economist* has labeled "politicians past their best" – Neil Kinnock, Edith Cresson, Leon Brittan to name but three – is that its members are nominated by the Council.[16]

Nonetheless, despite member governments' complicity in this state of affairs, this has not prevented them from making the Commission a frequent object of criticism, arguing against its concentration of power, and that the citizens of Europe are against the development of a European superstate.[17] Thus, on one hand, at Maastricht, the Council members agreed that the Commission's right to initiate policy proposals for consideration by the Council be extended to Common Foreign and Security Policy and Cooperation in Justice and Home Affairs.[18] Yet, realizing that their own hegemony in this area would be impinged, the Council members decided at Amsterdam to attach the newly created post of the High Representative of CFSP to itself and not to the Commission.[19]

Moreover, despite criticism concerning the fraud and mismanagement of the

Commission's administration of the EU budget, most financial losses incurred in misappropriations in Community expenditure occur once funds pass to member states.[20] Perhaps in view of the position of the Commission and individual commissioners as whipping boys and girls of European organization in the Community, we can recall Mitrany's criticism of the regional approach to supranational organization: "whatever man's professions, his practice rarely excels the law he accepts."[21] In respect of the Commission, its dependence on the Council means that members of the latter may make an ass of it whenever the occasion suits. It is in respect to the Commission that Watson's comparison of the EU to the Holy Roman Empire as "a sponge, useful to all and dangerous to none," is most appropriate and also most enlightening.[22] The "all" of Watson's statement in respect to the Commission can be applied to all member state governments, also all interest groups; but not to all of the EU's citizens, or even a substantial majority.[23]

The Commission that took office in January 1995 had 20 members. In early 1999, facing corruption allegations which had prompted the EP to seriously threaten to use its power to veto the Commission for the first time, President Jacques Santer agreed to an audit to block a censure vote. The individual targets of parliamentarians' approbation on the Commission were protected by the Parliament's reluctance to make use of its power to reject the whole of the Commission, the only procedural means available to it to force resignation of individuals. Santer agreed to respect the findings of the report, prepared by five civil servants from member states appointed by Parliament. The damning report, which found that "it is becoming difficult to find anybody ... who has even the slightest sense of responsibility," prompted Santer and all his colleagues to resign (before they attempted to come back into office immediately, thereby providing further evidence for the report's findings). Parliament's negative response to Santer's belief, that the Commission could continue to serve in an extended interim capacity, played a role in the Council's swift meeting to appoint Romano Prodi as the new president of the Commission.[24]

Under the terms of the Amsterdam Treaty, from May 1999 the new President Prodi has added powers of executive compared with his predecessors. The president of the Commission may decide which portfolios are assigned to individual Commissioners. Prodi was chosen as Santer's successor, because Council wanted a stronger profile EU head. He has indicated that he will expect a stronger inclination of all Commissioners to accept individual responsibility.[25] But Council had no desire for a strong Commission in policy terms, only in operational terms of managing the budget, and managing antitrust legislation and international trade talks.[26]

THE EUROPEAN PARLIAMENT

Based on beginnings in the SEA, the Treaty of European Union at Maastricht and its amendment at Amsterdam have progressively extended more power to the EP. The degree of power available to the Parliament depends on the area under consideration. Parliament's powers can be broken down from lowest to highest into four categories: Consultation, Cooperation, Codecision and Assent/Dissent.[27]

The Parliament has consultation rights only on EU treaties with third states or international organizations, CFSP and fixing of agriculture prices (i.e., in the case of the latter, a policy area covering the lion's share of the EU budget).

The Parliament is accorded the power of cooperation with the Council of Ministers in areas of environment, transport employment training, social funds, trans-European networks and EMU: If Parliament changes or rejects laws passed by Council, the Council must then pass them on second reading unanimously for them to become law.

The Parliament has rights of codecision in areas of internal market, education, public health, consumer affairs and culture. A parliamentary committee meets with members of Council to prepare legislation, in advance of debate of actual legislation in Council and EP; during subsequent legislation process, in cases where Parliament demands changes to text passed by Council, then a committee is formed including members of Commission to find a compromise. The compromise must then be approved by a majority in both EP and Council of Ministers.

Finally rejection/assent: the Parliament may reject or approve Council of Ministers' decisions on enlargement or association with non-member states; goals of structural funds; EU budget. In the case of the budget, therefore, we can see that only by vetoing the Community process as a whole could the Parliament give voice to opposition on aspects of the CAP. With a two-thirds majority it can force the Commissioners to resign. Under Article 158 of the Maastricht Treaty the EP was given only power of Consultation on the appointment of the president of the Commission and new commissioners, but in the light of Jacques Santer's acquiescence in submitting himself and his fellow commissioners to EP hearings and vote on their appointment in 1994-95,[28] the parliamentary power in this aspect became de facto assent/rejection. We can see also that in obtaining assent from Parliament, the commissioners lessen their legitimacy dependence on Council (or indeed non-state interest sectors). The Parliament's role in the demise of the Commission in March 1999, as discussed above, can also on balance be evaluated as positive: although Parliament drew back from an outright censure vote in January, the refusal of individual commissioners to resign following the audit report publication is bound to add to pressure for the future individual accountability of commissioners.

As a consequence of the complexity of the procedures I have just summarized, and the disappointment of many that the EU is expanding without seemingly becoming more accountable to its citizens, the tendency in some prointegrationist observers is mounting frustration. Peter Glotz, for example, in the light of these developments has viewed the future of the EU as a technocratic project without cultural ideas, adding in despair: "The differences in mentality lie very deep."[29] Indeed regarding the specialization of debate as reflected in EP procedure, Julie Smith notes that "since proposals are complicated, it is frequently only members of the relevant committees who understand them and attend the plenary sessions."[30]

On the other hand, the tendency remains to call for greater powers for the EP. Jürgen Habermas went so far as to conclude that the only brake to German predominance over Europe (without stating what he meant by German predominance) is more democracy for Brussels. Federal Europe, he wrote, had to build on the historically and culturally unique heritage of each nation for Europeans to be in the position to control the processes of the single market.[31] However, as we may understand by factors considered in Chapter 12 "The Multilateral Practices of Lobbying and the Privatization of Democracy," it seems more likely that greater powers for the EP would not necessarily lead to more democracy, only a shift in focus of lobbying organizations from state to supranational level.

Shirley Williams has also argued that more parliamentary democracy is necessary at the European level, arguing, no doubt correctly however, that the EP would only supplant its national counterparts as a locus for public and media attention were it to gain tax-raising powers.[32] But the fundamental barrier to an EP and government functioning relevantly to voters' needs is the sheer scale and potential unmanageability of such a body, especially with the prospect of the Community extending eastwards in line with the declared desires of member and non-member governments alike. Under the terms of the Amsterdam Treaty, the Council decided on an upper limit of 700 MEPs to serve the EP. However the figure would seem to be chosen as a number conveniently accommodating the next wave of accessions to the EU without having to address fundamental questions of relevant and democratic structure.[33] Where would the EU's Eastern border be located? Could it ultimately include Russia? Will Turkey ever become more than an associate member? We should recall Mitrany's critique that the creation of supranational states will only recreate rivalries present between nation-states on a greater, potentially more catastrophic scale.[34]

National parliaments lack the resources and expertise to question developments on a European scale. Denmark's *Folketing* is the only national Parliament able adequately to scrutinize and directly influence the decisions made at the European level by various incarnations of the Council of Ministers and the European council at over 100 annual meetings. The *Folketing*'s Market Committee meets at the same time as Council meetings and mandates the participating minister according to the issue for discussion. However, if all national parliaments were to do this it would lead to a total blockade on decision making.[35]

We have already noted in Chapter 3 on the SEA that national parliaments see the EP as a potential rival power center. The EP itself would seem to be infected by similar insecurities in respect to the 222-member Committee of the Regions, set up under the terms of Maastricht, and which has met since March 1994. Instead of viewing the Committee of the Regions as an ally in the extension of democracy in the EU, the EP has seen it as a rival. This may stem in part from the fact that individual MEPs have problems in arriving at alternative definitions of their utility commensurate with unfulfilled aspirations of many of them to supplant the traditions of nation-state legislature. We could also link this suggestion to the failure of MEPs to improve their status within their respective political parties, whose activity remains firmly focussed on member-state legislature elections. To confuse things further, the EP has its *own* parallel parliamentary committee, "Regional Affairs and Regional Policy." Thus in Martin Westlake's judgement the new body (the Committee of the Regions) is a potential "rival to parliament itself," and consequently the EP argued in a November 1993 resolution that "the Committee of the Regions must not become an assembly participating in the drawing up of Community legislation as part of a bicameral system." The EP's suggested draft constitution of February 1994 foresaw no more than an advisory role for the Committee.[36]

THE COUNCIL OF MINISTERS

In view of the sheer problem that the mass of interests and issues tends to debilitate the coordination of EP work, can we see the Council of Ministers as a body better placed to be a more efficient form of legislature of Community issues?[37] Currently, as long as the Parliament only has codecision rights at best, having only an advisory role on some issues (e.g., as in the instance of its advice concerning the Committee of the Regions, that other EU bodies only have an advisory role), the meetings of the Council are a more important seat of EU legislature. Ministers are legitimate democratic representatives as members of elected member state governments. However, were the Council of Ministers to be the future source of European governance, then similar problems of mass would also occur as faced by national and European parliaments. The problem of overview is perhaps the worst, as shown by former FRG Chancellor Schmidt's critique of the interface of state and Community procedures:

The number of hundreds (!) of national ministers or their representatives in the Councils of Ministers must be reduced; after all the Treaty of Rome talks only of "the" Council of Ministers, that means one single body. None of the 12 national heads of government has control any more over what his ministers or their bureaucrats are doing in the many Councils of Ministers.[38]

Moreover, since the above was written, the number of member states has already increased to 15. Schmidt simplifies also: on one hand, he fails to take account of the coordination of the sheer mass of interest groups with similar aims or the reconciliation of competing organizations;[39] on the other a reduction in the number of Councils of Ministers would impair specialist scrutiny and debate. William Wallace commented also on the difficulty for those on power of maintaining an overview. However he also notes a caveat to be made on the need for specialist scrutiny:

The technical nature of most of the dossiers engrosses those involved in them and discourages political oversight ... in most instances the dossier, after its brief moment of prime ministerial purview, is recaptured by the experts and the representatives of affected interests, and grinds on toward agreement within the compartmentalized field of intergovernmental business in which it started.[40]

Thus we can see that the founders' neofunctional approach to European Union has for many resulted in a growing detachment from its citizens, the purported reason for its existence. Discussing the role of the Council, one commentator has defined legitimacy as "the ability of an institution or system to articulate the interests and provide for the needs of a particular group, and to fulfil these two functions with authority ... at a reasonable speed."[41] This would seem to be more a definition of effectiveness than legitimacy. Be that as it may, the legitimacy of Council decisions is apparent when they are passed unanimously, and quickly. But in cases of lasting impasses, as in the linked issues of agricultural reform and the date of EU accession of Eastern European states, the legitimacy quotient drops. Moreover, with the introduction of majority voting principles on the advent of the single market, and their extension under the Maastricht and Amsterdam treaties, this democratic legitimacy

becomes questionable were decisions taken that override the policy of a democrati-
cally elected government of a member state.

PROSPECTS FOR FUTURE EU INSTITUTIONAL REPRESENTATIVE
DEMOCRACY

Having assessed the limitations of the EU institutional process and having
sketched out some of their procedural and structural intricacies, we might now draw
some tentative conclusions concerning the current situation and prospects for the
Community's future development.

The Community's reliance on (and success with) heterogeneous perspectives
has resulted in problems of vertical and horizontal coalescence. In terms of horizontal
coalescence, we have already noted the debate between financial and political circles
about the meaning of the Treaty wording concerning orientations in external exchange rate policy. We can see further evidence for this in the vertical as well as
horizontal obfuscation caused by the term "subsidiarity."[42] As William Wallace has
pointed out, subsidiarity came into Community use and legislation (Article 3 b of the
Maastricht Treaty) due to two pressures, which have resulted in two diametrically
opposed interpretations of its meaning. On one hand, it was conceived principally by
the British government as means of servicing its stated aim of preserving the sovereignty of the Westminster legislature. On the other hand, it was conceived by the
German government as conveying a federal conception. Thus, it reflected both British
government opposition to the use and hence propagation of "federal" principles, as
well as German Länder pressure to maintain federal principles, to redress the effects
of Community legislation on the balance of power between themselves and the Federal government in Bonn.[43]

I would argue that both conceptions are compatible with the other as long as one
is able to recognize the validity of the other, and as long as proponents of both traditions recognize the limitations contingent upon their own beliefs, when both societies
of which they are part are dependent on the other. As things stand however, the term
"subsidiarity" and its incorporation in the Treaty, while reflecting two very different
political cultures, does little to reconcile the two in the long term. Thus as discussed
by Wolfram Hilz, the two very different UK and FRG conceptions of the term can-
celled each other out in respect to what both interpreted as *closeness to citizens* or
legislative efficiency. Instead, the principle of subsidiarity as incorporated in article
five of the European Community Treaty of Amsterdam, only forces the Commission
to give detailed account to member states' governments of the necessity of Community measures. This neither encourages legislative efficiency nor necessarily the proposal of legislation to improve the lives of European citizens.[44]

Moreover, when such negotiation processes produce Treaty wordings of this
kind, which only reflect back one side's belief upon itself, rather than serving as a
transparent window of mutual understanding, this has a further consequence: state
governments' involvement in decision-making frameworks at the EU level may
paradoxically lead to greater freedom of action from domestic interests in their home
states.[45] We may see evidence for this tendency in European politics as a whole in the
criticism in Germany that the federal *Länder* as polities are actually losing power, a
fact disguised by the power of the *Land* governments to blockade Federal policy in

the *Bundesrat*. Power is concentrated in the person of the state premier, thus dubbed "margrave."[46] We could make the comparison on the European scale. Member states' parliaments have not so much lost power to institutions of the EU, but to their heads of government, would-be margraves marking out their respective fiefdoms.

Within the complex construct of the EU/EC treaties, we can perhaps see that the legacy of over 40 years of negotiation and compromise conducted in the various official community languages has led to the tendency of choosing to construct parallel worlds according to member states' governments' interpretations of community. These may or may not reflect the plurality of communities within the Community. The Community has not become community with a small "c." Article one of the Treaty on European Union states that the task of the Union is to provide for the coherence and solidarity in relationships between member states as well as between their peoples. Article two also states similarly that the task of the Community should be to encourage the social unity and solidarity between members. However, both these articles are partly based upon the false premise contained in paragraph three, article six, that the Union respects the national identity (*sic: singular*) of its member states.[47]

I discuss the falseness of the premise of a single national identity for each member state elsewhere.[48] For now, however, we can see that debate concerning the manifold array of possible individual and collective goals has resulted in opponents and proponents of different approaches to integration arguing about suitable descriptive labels for the Community: EU, Federation, Confederation, International Organization, Community, Union and so on. These arguments do not necessarily entail a mutual recognition for the validity of individual or group perspectives within this collective. None of these terms or descriptions is wholly appropriate or applicable, but this complexity has not been addressed and challenged by referring to it openly as such. The lack of transparency extends to the negotiated Community name for itself (selves). The complex treaty construct of the European Communities lead to the questions: is it EEC? EC? EU? ECSC? EURATOM? How many of these still exist? The answer to my last question is "all," bar the EEC. This was officially renamed the EC, the first of the three constituent columns of the EU treaty agreed at Maastricht. Under the Amsterdam amendments, the Union Treaty refers to the EC element as the Treaty on the Foundation of the European Community.[49]

The complexity of the naming process is a further dissuading factor to ordinary citizens from becoming EU-, or for that matter, EC-friendly. Were a business or a sovereign state to act in such a way towards its goals and identities it would attract ridicule. In this respect, we can usefully compare the EU with a polynational forebear in Europe. We can recall the example of the Austro-Hungarian empire and its dual description of its institutions and office bearers alternately as *kaiserlich-königlich* and *kaiserlich und königlich*. Robert Musil poked fun at the disappeared state: "it required a mysterious science to be able to know for certain as to which institutions and persons were to be named k.k., und which k.u.k."[50]

The complexity of decision-making processes in Europe and the impenetrability of the results of these decisions make a social, economic, ecological and democratic cost use analysis increasingly difficult.[51] Nonetheless, as proponents of federal Europe, who see its development as almost certain, have themselves acknowledged, a federal Europe is "a more costly form of government than many convinced federalists are prepared to concede."[52] Furthermore, there are no democratic control mechanisms of European Council meetings. Availability of information on them is not comprehensive, and if Council meetings are to be seen as one part of a nascent European legislature, public access to them is far poorer in comparison with national parliaments (for example, Council discussions are not televised). Moreover, nobody has proposed that a meeting of a *shadow* European Council body might be a useful forum for outlining criticisms of European policy, concurrently, or in the immediate aftermath of *actual* Council meetings (perhaps the attractiveness of this proposal will increase as a result of the success of the center-right parties in opposition to the overwhelmingly center-left member state governments in the 1999 EP elections).

Thus, in the absence of a state-level channel for scrutiny of Community procedures, national politicians, especially those in opposition, are confronted frequently with invidious choices. On one hand, they may choose to reject outright national government policy which aims towards further integration. On the other hand, they may concur, but not necessarily because of any substantial knowledge or depth of support for the issue at hand, but much more based on the pursuance of European ideals rather than ensuring practicalities of community. This results in lack of direction and inner-party strife, which is a potentially grave hindrance to effective opposition at the state level, and certainly not constructive to the good governance of states or of the Community. It has also prevented the effective formulation of transnational alternatives by opposition parties. In Germany, for example, the then Federal opposition SPD leadership offered no reasonable alternative in European terms to the EMU plan, only exploiting popular opposition to abandoning the D-mark. In the immediate aftermath of Maastricht, Oskar Lafontaine outlined his opposition to the common currency by stating:

An economic and currency union, where a single unified central bank controls monetary policy, at the same time as varying wages, social and financial policy are implemented in the individual member states will lead to similar catastrophic conditions as in the hasty German-German monetary union, where economic sense was left behind.[53]

Perhaps Lafontaine's views were influenced by the bruising to his ego inflicted by his poor result as chancellor candidate in the 1990 FRG election. They were certainly articulated at a time when he could point to the wisdom of his Cassandran warnings during that campaign concerning the costs of German currency union. However, his views were stifled by others in the party leadership, and the SPD later voted with the government on the Maastricht Treaty.[54] Lafontaine was later to resign from the SPD-led FRG government in 1999, having articulated similar views during his short burlesque as finance minister.

Thus far we have viewed democracy in the EU in terms of conventional sociopolitical parameters of the nation-state. In these terms, there are parallels between state constitutions and the Treaty provisions and parallels between Council(s) and Commission on one hand and member governments. But the unwieldiness of the EU components in these parallels would invite considerable doubt whether the parallels will ever meet neatly at some point on a distant common European horizon. We have seen within conventional sociopolitical parameters also, that the EP's codecision with the Council as agreed at Maastricht, and amended at Amsterdam, is not an adequate counterweight to the powers lost by state legislatures. Nor would the EP power of codecision seem to be a legitimated expansion of community opportunity and influence of comparable scope made available to business following the advent of the single market. In the debate following Maastricht, many hoped that the Treaty's equivocations in face of demands for more democracy would be corrected in the so-called Maastricht II summit, originally to be held in 1996, but postponed pending Labour's accession to office in the UK, along with the hope of more favorable economic conditions in the rest of Europe, in France and Germany in particular. However within parameters of representative democracy, the Amsterdam Council meeting in June 1997 was seen as not having achieved very much.[55]

Hopes that the new UK Labour government would put an end to the British obstinacy at Council meetings were unfulfilled because of new obstacles. Others, notably Germany, were less reluctant to press for reform.[56] Kohl's increasing reserve in pushing for EU political reform in his last years in power, especially in the period from the Amsterdam summit to the 1998 Federal elections, can be traced to increasing *Länder* resistance; we could see some of the latter perhaps filling the nationalist vacuum left by the tendency of the Federal government to proclaim pursuit of post-national goals.[57]

Thus far, by this section's review of future prospects, we have also seen much evidence for the argument that the EU has been subsumed by the functionalist means and not the ends of unity as envisioned by the founders. Indeed there is much to be said for the view of William Wallace who has argued that the limits of European integration can only be extended by augmenting now traditional mechanisms: "By qualitative and structural change, not by the gradual processes of multilateral rule-making and regime-building within an increasingly opaque and complex treaty-based framework."[58]

But we would do well to remember that any body politic contains all sorts of specialist parts for different tasks, and it may be that multilateral structures are the best means of coping with the demands of a multipolar world. We have seen that even were the member states able to agree upon a clarified federal structure, it would also face considerable problems, not least of which would be how those states excluded would react to its presence. Nonetheless, EU institutions need to be coordinated better with member state institutions if the needs of Europe's primary community of interest, its citizens, are to be better served. We may see this as attuning what could be defined as more distant and passive organs of sense, our transnational ears and eyes, with the needs of blind and deaf national mouths of EU citizens, which otherwise might become progressively more mute through lack of recognition and participation. Thus, an agreement on a set of basic principles of citizens' rights would be useful. During the 1999 German presidency of the Council, FRG Justice Minister Herta Däubler-Gmelin proposed such a document to her counterparts, but was on record as stating that such a charter of basic rights would encounter "a gamut of awkward legal and political issues" before it became reality.[59]

Beyond this, however, I would argue that now we could have reached a position where we can conceive of both an enlargement and opening of the EU framework which permits more freedom to build in space and clarity. We should investigate the possibilities of extrastructural (i.e. outside existing EU structures) as well as inner-structural organization, which may later bestow new perspectives, simplifications and greater relevance to existing EU structures. Let me clarify in the first chapter of the next part of the book what I mean by this by first studying one aspect of the Treaty of Amsterdam.

NOTES

1. Merkel, *FAZ*, 24.4.1996, p. 12. Merkel identifies three areas of democratic deficit: a European level separation of powers, executive control, and the liaison structures of social and political interests.

2. See Robert Pearce, Marina Papanastassio, 'European Markets and the Strategic Roles of Multinational Enterprise Subsidiaries in the UK', in *JCMS*, Vol. 35 no. 2, June 1997, pp. 244-266; Herbermann; Mrusek, *FAZ*, 9.5.1998, p. 15.

3. See Günter Renner, 'Außenbeziehungen der Europäischen Union', Bundeszentrale für politische Bildung (ed.), *Informationen zur Politischen Bildung 213 Europäische Union* (Bonn: March 1995), pp. 44-47.

4. See Westlake, pp. 49-50; 'Europäische Union', *Informationen zur Politischen Bildung* 213, pp. 18, 36.

5. See Wolfgang Platzer, *Lernprozeß Europa* (Bonn: Dietz, 1993), pp. 85-87. The offical name of the CEEP in English is actually the rather long-winded "European Centre of Enterprises with Public Participation and of Enterprises of General Economic Interest." See http://www.ceep.org.

6. Birgit Cramon Daiber, 'Wer A sagt, muß auch B sagen: Über die Notwendigkeit sozialpolitischer Regelungen in der Europäischen Union. Eine Art Erlebnisbericht aus der politischen Praxis',in Dietz et al. (eds.), pp. 107-121 (p. 109).

7. Platzer, *Gewerkschaftspolitik ohne Grenzen*, p. 158.

8. Letter by John Monks General Secretary of British TUC, 'Employees enjoy the flavour of Biscuits', *The Independent*, letters page, 11.11.1994; Monks expressed the hope that now widely established employee information bodies could be developed into councils with consultation rights.

9. Moravcsik, Nicolaïdis, p. 78.

10. See the title of their book: Hans-Peter Martin, Harald Schumann, *Die Globalisierungsfalle: Der Angriff auf Demokratie und Wohlstand.* In this book, I discuss globalization the section 'Business Location and Global Points' in Chapter 9.

11. Beate Kohler-Koch, 'Organized (*sic*) Interests in European Integration: The Evolution of a New Type of Governance', in Wallace, Young (eds.), pp. 42-68 (p. 53).

12. See Gerhard Lehmbruch, 'German Federalism and the Challenge of Unification', in Hesse, Wright (eds.), pp. 169-203 (p. 196).

13. *FAZ*, 12.12.1991, p. 2.

14. Rainer Nahrendorf, 'Konstruktionsfehler', *Handelsblatt*, 12.12.1991, p. 2.

15. 'Wirtschaft reagiert auf Maastricht mit Skepsis', *Frankfurter Rundschau*, 12.12.1991, p. 7; also 'Zufriedenheit und Skepsis nach Maastricht', *FAZ*, 12.12.1991, p. 16.

16. See 'Charlemagne: Europe's next Commissioners', *The Economist*, 27.3.1999, p. 36.

17. For example, see 'Sind die Strukturen der EU-Kommision noch angemessen? Kohl und Chirac schreiben an Premierminister Blair/ Der Bundeskanzler kritisiert Einmischungsversuche', *FAZ*, 9.6.1998, p. 1.

18. Finn Laursen, 'The Role of The Commission', in Andersen, Eliassen (eds.), pp 119-141 (p. 131).

19. See Youri Devuyst, 'The Community Method after Amsterdam', in Iain Begg, John Peterson (eds.) *JCMS*, Vol. 37 no. 1 (Oxford: Blackwell, 1999), pp. 109-120, p. 114.

20. 'Recommissioning Europe', *The Economist*, 30.1.1999, pp. 27-28.

21. Mitrany, p. 155.

22. Watson also usefully cites a passage from James Sheehan's *German History 1770-1866* (Oxford University Press, 1989), "The Reich came from a historical world in which nationality had no political meaning, and states did not command total sovereignty. Unlike nations and states, the Reich did not insist on pre-eminent authority and unquestioning allegiance. Its goal was not to clarify and dominate but rather to order and balance fragmented institutions and multiple loyalties." See Watson, p. 23.

23. How much the Commission has become a prisoner of the law that it accepts is shown by President Prodi's designation of a new department, 'Citizens of Europe' as the specific remit of the Commission vice-president from 1999. The unfortunate implication is that the other commissioners have no direct remit to serve Europe's citizens. See ' "Liste der künftigen EU-Kommissare bis Mitte Juli" ', *FAZ*, 4.6.1999, p. 5.

24. See 'Crisis in Brussels: Europe has to scratch its head', *The Economist*, 20.3.1999, pp. 19-20, 29.

25. See for example his remarks as Commission President Designate at the Cologne European summit: "from every member of my future team I expect the readiness to resign should I see myself forced to suggest such a step to him." Prodi also expressed disquiet at the Council that only one of those short listed for his new Commission was a woman. The 1995 Commission had five women members. 'Europäische Union stärkt ihre militärische Rolle', *Frankfurter Rundschau*, 4.6.1999, p. 1.

26. See 'The Challenge awaiting Romano Prodi', *The Economist*, 3.4.1999, pp. 23-24.

27. Summary of EP powers from: Bundeszentrale für politische Bildung (ed.) 'Europäische Union', *Informationen zur Politischen Bildung 213* (Bonn: March 1995) p. 17; Westlake, pp. 134-163; Julie Smith, *Voice of the People: The European Parliament in the 1990s* (London: The Royal Institute of International Affairs, 1995), pp. 98-100. Despite the book's title, reflecting, although not questioning, the EP's overbearing aspiration to serve a single common good, we can see that Smith gives an indication of the complexity of the EU process (rather than a confession of her limited analytical or arithmetical abilities) by stating that (in the first Treaty column) "The legislative process in the EC is complex, with *at least* [my italics] eight different procedures" (p. 79).

28. See Julie Smith, pp. 74-75.

29. Peter Glotz, 'Europäische Visionen' *NG/FH*, 7/96, pp. 592-594 (p. 593, p. 592).

30. Julie Smith, p. 81.

31. See Jürgen Habemas, *Vergangenheit als Zukunft* (Munich: Piper, 1993), pp. 202-203.

32. Williams, p. 166.

33. In June 1994, 567 MEPs were elected. Now with 15 EU members, there are 626 MEPs.

34. See also the views of Peter Glotz, 'Editorial', *NG/FH* 7/92, p. 579: "The idea that 25 nation-states from the Atlantic to the Ukrainian border can be accommodated in a state overseen by a European Parliament is well-intentioned pan-European dilettantism."

35. Wolfgang Merkel, *FAZ*, 24.4.1996, p. 12.

36. See Westlake p. 49-50.

37. The term 'Council of Ministers' has come to mean meetings constituted by ministers of member states with specialist portfolios: finance, justice, transport etc.. Meetings constituted by heads of governments are actually known under the term 'The European Council'.

38. Helmut Schmidt, Handeln für Deutschland (Reinbek: Rororo, 1994), p. 216.

39. Kohler Koch (1992), p. 112.

40. William Wallace, *Regional Integration: The West European Experience* (Washington D.C.: The Brookings Institution, 1994), p. 72.

41. Fiona Hayes-Renshaw, 'The Role of the Council', in Svein Andersen, Kjell Eliassen, *The European Union: How Democratic is it?* (London: Sage, 1996), pp. 143-161.

42. See Lodge, pp. 192-193.

43. William Wallace, *Regional integration*, pp. 77-78.

44. See Wolfram Hilz, 'Bedeutung und Instrumentalisierung des Subsidaritätoprinzips für den europäischen Integrationsprozeß', in *Aus Politik und Zeitgeschichte* B21-22/99, 21. 5.1999, pp. 28-38.

45. Kohler-Koch, in Wallace and Young (eds.), p. 61.

46. See views of Hans Herbert von Arnim in Astrid Hölscher, '"Gut bezahlte Bedeutungslosigkeit" über Reformbedarf und –fähigkeit der Bundesländer', *Frankfurter Rundschau*, 24.3.1999, p. 6.

47. See Daniel-Erasmus Khan (ed.), *Vertrag über die Europäische Union mit sämtlichen Protokollen und Erklärungen. Vertrag zur Gründung der Europäischen Gemeinschaft (EG-Vertrag) in den Fassungen von Maastricht und Amsterdam* (Munich: Deutscher Taschenbuch Verlag, 1998), p. 237 (Union treaty article one); p. 239 (Union treaty article six); p. 260 (EC treaty article two).

48. See my *Post-National Patriotism*, Chapters 2 and 3.

49. For example, article two of the Union treaty, setting out the Union's goals, referring to article five of the EC treaty. See Khan (ed.), p. 237-238 (Union treaty article two), p. 262 (EC treaty article five).

50. Robert Musil, *Mann ohne Eigenschaften I* (Reinbek: Rororo, 1978), p. 33.

51. Merckel, *FAZ*, 24.4.1996, p. 12.

52. See conclusions of Hesse, Wright, 'Federalizing Europe: The Path to Adjustment', in Hesse, Wright (eds.), pp. 376-400 (p. 392, p. 396). Although I hope I made it plain in Chapter 6 that I would not argue against federalism on grounds of cost alone, it seems to me to be unlikely that the citizens of Europe would have any material or democratic gain from federal structures, and those outside the EU would not gain at all.

53. Lafontaine's comments were made in a paper (containing the conveniently round number of 10 theses) titled "Regarding the future tasks of German politics." Note that the paper's title gives no indication of a post-national perspective. See: 'Lafontaine empfielt der SPD die Ablehnung der Verträge von Maastricht', *FAZ*, 6.3.1992, p. 2.

54. Gunter Hofmann, 'Haltet den Oskar!', *Die Zeit*, Nr. 12, 13.3.1992, p. 5.

55. See Eberhard Wisdorff, '"Ohne Glanz" Kommentar', *Handelsblatt*, 18.6.97, p.

2; Andreas Oldag, 'Der Gipfel der Reförmchen', *Süddeutsche Zeitung*, 18.6.97, p. 4.

56. The German government vetoed a significant extension of Council qualified majority voting (QMV) on financial and social policy because of *Länder* opposition but favored its introduction on CFSP; the French government favored the former, but rejected the latter. See Moravcsik, Nicolaïdis, p. 77; Devuyst, p. 114.

57. See Uwe Leonardy, 'The Political Dimension, German Practice, and the European Perspective' in Hesse, Wright (eds.), pp. 73-100, Especially (p. 89): "The German *Länder* ... being part of a functioning federal system, will not agree to be sacrificed for the sake of European Federalism." See also Thomas Hanke, Christian Wernicke, 'Die neue Angst vor Europa', *Die Zeit*, Nr. 26, 18.6.1998, p. 3.

58. William Wallace, *Regional integration*, p. 86.

59. See 'Bonn will europäische Grundrechte-Charta', *Das Parlament*, Nr. 16 7.5.1999, p. 18.

Part II

Chances of Community: Transnational and Transinstitutional Parameters for Greater Social Coherence

As we saw in the last chapter of Part I, the geographical and political limitation of the scope of the EU has problems in our interdependent world. It may therefore be helpful to emphasize a transinstitutional as well as a transnational approach that provides us with the chance of overcoming these. This will be the emphasis of Part II. In Chapter 8, I will develop ideas concerning transinstitutional as well as transnational approaches with reference to recent developments in the EU, emphasizing that cooperation and dialogue across and within multilateral frameworks could establish benchmarks of social coherence. In Chapter 9, I will expand these arguments by a consideration of the global span of business. In the two subsequent chapters, I will examine the specific examples of DaimlerChrysler, Siemens and BMW. In Chapter 12, having assembled a foundation of knowledge stemming from German-based business contexts, I will examine prospects of extending democratic processes by taking advantage of the world-wide scope brought by the means and practices of private firms active globally. Based on these findings, as an interim conclusion to the subject matter of this book, I will conduct a brief summing up in Chapter 13

8

Closer Cooperation and the Transnational Development of Social Coherence

As we saw in Chapter 7, the EP has different powers depending on the sector of legislation under discussion. Under traditional understandings of liberal representative democracy in nation-states, it would seem to be a bit strange to have a shifting scale of power depending on the issue under consideration. We have already noted also that the legitimacy of the Council decision-making process is subject to increasing question when neither unanimous nor speedy. With these aspects in mind, federalists look towards more powers being given to the EP. However, the conceptions of federalists remain within hierarchical sociopolitical parameters of the sovereignty of the nation-state transferred to supranational level.

Hence, I would return to the point I made in my discussion in Chapter 5, "EMU and the Establishment of Greater Interdependence," concerning *influence*. In interdependent society, we have a measure of government over ourselves and a measure of government over others. Neither is complete. Thus I would agree with the argument of Svein Andersen and Tom Burns that the EU is an example of post-parliamentary governance. They suggest that modern government is "multi-polar with the interpenetration of state agencies and agents of civil society.... The complex differentiation of society is reflected in the differentiation and complexity of governance, the differentiation of representation, the differentiation of systems of knowledge and expertise, and the spectrum of values and lifestyles of ordinary citizens."[1]

CLOSER COOPERATION IN THE TREATY OF AMSTERDAM

This theoretical analysis is echoed in the formulation of the European Union Treaty at Amsterdam. In the course of this chapter, I will argue that the Treaty's provision for "closer cooperation" may contain an important mechanism, which could provide the basis of the establishment of benchmarks of social coherence within multilateral frameworks. The institution of the EU is only one of these. I would like to pursue the line suggested by Eric Philippart and Geoffrey Edwards that "Amsterdam and closer co-operation might be seen as one step in the direction of 'multi-perspectival polity'."[2] I would suggest that closer cooperation provides a potentially vital contributory force to overcome social and political diversity within the EU *and* beyond. Moreover, I will argue that the concept of closer cooperation is more likely to bring a levelling up rather than a leveling down of social standards.

Under the Treaty, to prevent disintegration of the EU as an entity, closer cooperation inside the EU must involve at least a majority of states. The concept and procedure were responses to debate leading up to the Amsterdam summit on the need for variable geometry and greater flexibility in the Community, although the term "flexibility" was removed from the final text of the Treaty signed in October 1997.[3] Three types of closer cooperation are outlined in the Treaty. These are:

- A general system of rules under certain preconditions
- Closer cooperation in particular fields
- Case by case through opt out.

At Amsterdam, in addition to the first (EC) column, closer cooperation was agreed on police and judicial cooperation, but it was not forthcoming on CFSP. In terms of procedure, member states interested in areas of closer cooperation may put the proposal to the Commission, which puts a proposal or (regarding matters of police and judicial cooperation) presents its opinion to the pertinent Council of Ministers. Council decides on the proposal by qualified majority voting (QMV). This triggering process is subject to a veto if one member state presents "important and stated reasons of national policy." This veto can then be overcome only by a unanimous vote of the European Council.[4]

We can see that closer cooperation is a contractual reflection of what had already become the practical reality within the EU, and in the world beyond, namely the desire or need to opt out of or opt into relationships in different sectors of organization. In the EU, this had been the case with the UK opting out of the Social Charter and Social Chapter in 1989 and 1991, respectively, and along with Denmark choosing not to join EMU on inauguration. On the other hand, the exclusion of Greece and Sweden has in no way been accompanied by the suggestion that they would be banished to perpetual rejection from EMU. Also, at the June 1999 Council meeting, a possible collective EU military capacity was discussed, where member states that were non-NATO members would be exempted from participation.[5]

MULTIPOLAR CLOSER COOPERATION TRANSCENDING THE EU

Across Europe as a whole, states have had the freedom not only to form the strictly consultative Council of Europe, but to opt in increasingly larger numbers over the last half century for various more closely aligned bodies in different sectors with overlapping memberships.[6] Different bodies related to different sectors have not led to disaggregation as discussed by Philippart and Edwards,[7] but to increasing overlap. For example, although closer cooperation was not forthcoming on CFSP at Amsterdam, in the post-Cold War era it is worth noting that only two members of the preeminent security body for Europe, NATO, have not expressed an interest in joining the EU: USA and Canada.[8] But these states, along with Japan, are members of the OECD, whose annual report is debated every year by the parliamentary assembly of the Council of Europe. All the European members of NATO are linked in some way to the EU in a framework of relationships.[9] Meanwhile Iceland and Norway are party to the Schengen Treaty's abolition of border controls.[10]

We can see the tendency to overlap within member states too. In the United Kingdom, Scottish MPs at the UK Parliament have a say in English affairs, which many English MPs perceive as an injustice, because they have no say over the area of Scottish affairs now under the remit of Scotland's new Parliament. Nonetheless, English MPs can influence the level of taxation in Scotland, and in greater number than their Scottish counterparts influence British security and foreign policy (although concurrent with the inauguration of Scotland's new parliament, all the UK government ministers responsible for these sectors were Scottish).

The tendency would appear to be that the partiality of states to form relationships in some sectors but not others would not seem to have led to disintegration in interstate relationships but quite the reverse. Links in one sector would appear to have fostered the establishment of links in others at a later juncture. The original six members of the ECSC and EEC have become the 15 of the EU. None has left the Council of Europe formed before it. Members of the European Free Trade Association (EFTA) with the exception of Switzerland formed the European Economic Area (EEA) with the EU in 1994. The United Kingdom signed up to the Social Chapter of the EU treaty in 1997. It seems almost certain that the "non-Euroland" members of the EU will join EMU at a later stage. In this respect, we can perhaps see the most positive aspect of the process in the run-up to the euro is that which one EU insider judged as the phenomenon of benchmarking and peer review.[11] No one likes to be bottom of the class, or left out. When one group sees another group doing something without it, very often it may see its future participation and cooperation with the other group as desirable.

BENCHMARKING AND CLOSER SOCIAL COOPERATION

Heidrun Abromeit has argued that flexible cooperation could bring a system of mass referenda on opting in to levels of decision making.[12] However, while I would agree that such an extension of democracy is fine in principle, I cannot see that such a system would generate any more popular support for transnational organization in Europe or beyond than is present under the current status quo.[13] On the other hand, perceptions of the success of transnational measures bringing about a greater measure of social security – in the sense of achieving substantial unemployment cuts and securing good quality workplaces – would make transnational cooperation more popular. Accordingly, having acquainted ourselves in this chapter so far with the principle of closer cooperation, along with the concept of benchmarking, let us try in this section to connect both of these to potential everyday needs and practices of society.

In this respect, I would see closer cooperation as the optimal means of overcoming social and political differentials in the Community, present in ever greater measure since the six became the 15, and potentially greater with the prospect of further expansion to the east. This would not lead to exclusion of those not participating but their inclusion at a later date. We can see that there is the potential for a number of EU member states agreeing on a number of measures that may offset the social effects of the single market and EMU. A number of member states with a high level of existing social provision could form a core group around which the majority for closer cooperation could be found: Austria, Denmark, Germany, Finland, Sweden and The Netherlands. Bearing in mind the likelihood that France, for example, would not wish to find itself excluded from such a group, for reasons of national prestige alone, it seems likely that the French government would act to join in also. That would leave only one other member state required to form the necessary majority for closer cooperation on social provisions. Even in the case of France, agreement reached in its metal industry in 1998 to introduce a 35-hour working week in the year 2000 is an indication that national divergences within EU industrial sectors are diminishing. This puts French workers on a par with their German counterparts. We could even say that in the light of the five weeks' annual holiday allowance available to French metalworkers compared to the six enjoyed by their counterparts in German industry, France is only a week behind Germany.[14]

We can link the ideas of benchmarking and closer cooperation with the realization in the Community, officially recognized also by the Council agreement in the Amsterdam Treaty, that employment is "a matter of common concern." The Council further called upon the EU to "work towards developing a coordinating strategy for employment." This agreement, although very much made in the Community tradition of restricting activity on social and employment policy to symbolic statements, can be seen as a declaration of intent and evolved from the work of the European Employment Initiative (EEI).[15] The initiative was set up by European Socialist Party leaders in 1993 (with the involvement of the President of the European Commission Delors), and its practical expression was a committee chaired by former Swedish Finance Minister Allan Larsson that produced a report published in spring 1994 titled "Put Europe to Work."[16] We can extrapolate two points relevant to our discussion here. First, we can see that the report and later the agreement by the Council was the result of closer cooperation activity both independent of EU structures and transcending them. Sweden was not yet an EU member, either at the launch of the EEI or on the completion of the Larsson report. Furthermore, Karl Johannsson describes how the work of the EEI, and concluding report, were based upon points already discussed in a forum of Nordic Social Democrats and trade unions also chaired by Larsson, SAMAK.[17]

Second, we can treasure Johannsson's description of Larsson as "an outstanding policy entrepreneur,"[18] to recall that a decade before, another Swede, the chairman of Volvo, had played a leading role in the adoption of the single market plan. Many have seen the formulation of the single market as fostering a move in Western Europe towards free-market capitalism, decamping from previous clear commitments to social responsibility towards perfidious neoliberal perceptions of the global market. Nonetheless we can see the coincidence of members of the Swedish elite favoring transnational cooperation in both economic and social fields as a persuasive indication that there is no shadowy big business conspiracy to bring about the end of welfare-state provisions in Europe, as much as this possibility lurks in the imaginations of some on Europe's left wing. Neither Volvo nor Swedish industry as a whole is noted for deregulated free-market practices but form an integral part of the wider tradition in Sweden of setting world-wide benchmarks in social provision and humanitarian practices.[19]

Even though the advent of free flows of capital means that provision of social coherence in national terms is increasingly irrelevant, inappropriate and certainly insufficient, social provision of community and global capitalism need not be seen as competing opposites.[20] Indeed, we can see that other companies involved in those early discussions on the single market – AEG, Siemens, Philips, Robert Bosch, – also have a long tradition of provision for the wider community, and not just their shareholders.[21]

Thus we can see that employers would not necessarily be ill disposed to the declaration on employment being enacted in terms of a measure of closer cooperation. I would argue that closer cooperation on social measures from such a starting point could see a leveling up of the whole Community, and, given the benchmark function of the EU for the rest of Europe, for states outside its borders also. Business organization transcends political boundaries. The ERT chairman at its formation was a Swede, although Sweden was at the time outside the Community. Current ERT chairman is Helmut Maucher, the head of the Swiss-based transnational Nestlé, the largest food company in the world (74,660 million Swiss francs consolidated sales, 1999). Maucher is a German citizen, and also president of the International Chamber of Commerce.[22]

In this light, I would argue that the concept of social benchmarking would be a much more effective response to the powers of world markets than the introduction of a global framework of democratic legislation, as suggested by Held, "which specifies the principles and objectives of cosmopolitan democratic law."[23] While no doubt well intentioned, such a measure could be instrumentalized by many and could be seen as belonging to the same genus as the Soviet system, indeed also condemned by Held, as having failed because of its "arrogant and misplaced presumption of knowledge" about popular needs.[24]

As evidence for my suggestion of benchmarking, I would point out that there was no leveling down of criteria for EMU entry, but a substantial common rise in financial stringency. Nor should the stability and growth pact of EMU members be seen as a barrier to extended social provision for the Community: the presence of financial stability in Germany, for example, has actually fostered and not debilitated social provision in society. Nor would I see the case I made in Part I, concerning the overwhelmingly economic reasons underlying steps to closer European integration, standing in the way of my suggestion. In Chapter 9, we will see that there are also compelling economic motivations for taking such steps, not just some sense of well-meaning utilitarianism. As I will outline also in the next chapter, in the section "The Global Business Application of the German Consensus Model," employees' labor rights and pay levels can be safeguarded even although locations with lower wage levels and safeguards may be theoretically available to transnational employers elsewhere.

The concept of closer cooperation could be the necessary step towards member states agreeing programs to combat European unemployment, which could be more effective than symbolic declarations.[25] No solution to economic problems has been agreed thus far that avoids an attack on existing welfare provisions, because working and social conditions vary more across Europe than those variances present within member states, indeed including those present between Western and Eastern Germany following German unification. Moreover, in Germany, the miracle solution of the unified nation-state has been found wanting in the attempt to find uniform Federal solutions to divergent economic problems.

Furthermore, throughout the Community, the single market has resulted in growing heterogeneity within states, increasing pressures to cut back on measures of state intervention. Even in traditionally economically weak regions in Europe, divergences are emerging. The Republic of Ireland, for example, has seen a massive leap in GDP per capita performance during the early nineties. Under the prevailing parameters of economic efficiency therefore, Ireland is seen as a success. But this has mainly been as a result of strong growth in the financial services and high technology sectors in the Dublin metropolitan area. The rest of the country still suffers from what the European Commission terms euphemistically as a "labour surplus."[26]

OVERCOMING OBSTACLES TO CLOSER SOCIAL COOPERATION

Thus closer cooperation is an imperative to offset unemployment and a means of correcting supranational approaches which have served largely thus far to strengthen the economic orthodoxy that capitalists' wealth is the due reward for the risk attendant upon each investment decision. As stated by the late Alfred Herrhausen, if the capitalist makes the wrong decision, he loses his existence as a capitalist: "With the loss of his capital, his company, he ceases to be a production factor ... his economic function disappears, not absolutely and in general, but for those individually affected, totally." Meanwhile, Herrhausen argued that when an employee loses his job: "[he] loses ... indeed ... his place of work, but not his place of work as such, and certainly not his existence as a worker."[27] However Herrhausen's perspective, that a worker remains a worker, whether he loses his job or not, is given the lie by levels of unemployment even higher in Europe than during his lifetime. On the other hand, the capitalist has accrued further rewards for investing his resources at considerably less risk, and not enough incentives to use it to benefit communities' employment sectors. Herrhausen's perspective, which is shared by many less well able than he was to articulate them, is not drawn from a sense of community, but from the abstract sense of purpose stemming from the mobility of the international businessman. Unless the sometimes conflicting demands of social community and economic mobility can be reconciled, then the deviation of official EU objectives from the needs of significant numbers of Europeans' lives will continue. The consequence is that significant sectors of the population will remain confronted with awkward choices between belonging to out-of-work (disfunctioning) communities or seeking employment elsewhere, raising the risk of diminishment of community, both old and new. If these are the only choices available, the chasm between economic inclusion and political exclusion will not be overcome.

Although there may be a growing recognition of the need for more than just economic policies in Europe, this realization has for the most part been handicapped by the traditions and mechanisms established under the original Treaty of Rome. As authors of a study of the European integration process have observed, "In so far as public discussion about the topic of Europe occurs at all, it is confined in large measure to the economic sector."[28] Indeed we can see that since Maastricht, the Social

Chapter has come a poor third, in terms of discussion, to EMU or political union.

Jelle Visser has identified the almost universal decline throughout Europe in union membership, and hence pressure group strength, in percentage of total workforce during the eighties. He sees this as a factor acting against extension of social legislation at the European level. He traces the decline in union membership not only to high unemployment levels, but also just as much to the creation of new jobs in advanced technology sectors. Nevertheless, he points out that the high social and economic costs of European societies supporting high jobless totals are leading to consequent higher state deficits. Higher deficits are bringing increasing pressures for deregulation and lower wage settlements, core issues of union representation. Unions trace their legitimacy to the industrial society, to an era of full employment where organized labor could justifiably present itself as pursuing the aspirations of the whole of society. They cannot do so now. While high unemployment levels persist, unions' power and legitimacy will continue to erode unless they find a way of contributing to a feasible and creative policy towards full employment.[29]

Although the percentage of employees organized in unions in Germany remains way above the international average documented by the ILO (at 30% compared with an estimated 12%), German unions have recorded a 17% drop in membership in the ten-year period 1988-98.[30]

While the then L I UC President Ernst Breit stated in January 1989 that the goals of standardization of wages and European-wide social dialogue remained at the fore-front of European policies, his aspirations are colored by the same utopian ideals which were to be discredited shortly afterwards by the collapse of state socialism.[31] These goals are unfeasible within an undifferentiated institutional framework. In society at large, in contrast, the scale of differentials and mass of participants involved is too great. We can see that the undifferentiated approach of EU organization so far has failed to give social issues a relevant useful universal institutional forum, unlike economic or financial affairs. The demands of finance place a premium on efficiency at the expense of time, which has so harmed the efficacy of the articulation of social concerns.

MULTIPOLAR DIALOGUE AND CLOSER COOPERATION

Thus given these factors, before turning to the next chapter's consideration of "The Global Location of Business Inside and Outside the EU," I would argue that pursuing dialogue via differentiated channels of closer cooperation could be one means of overcoming the problems of diversity. By this means we can perhaps see the beginnings of a process of fulfilling hitherto potentially divisive social needs, needs which have debilitated attempts thus far for European integration to be accomplished as a societal process, not simply as an economic and monetary union. We can see integration as a multisocietal process, within, across and beyond EU borders, in Europe and world-wide.

In addition to the mechanism of closer cooperation, therefore, I would argue that growing dialogue between multilateral frameworks pursuing closer social cooperation could turn the complexity of EU structures into a democratic process of elaboration of heterogeneity, benefiting the collective good. We could see this development bringing about a whole array of diverse but interlinked perspectives, which can help all the parties to exchange information on needs and aspirations. Recalling my discussion of Mitrany and the collective good in Chapter 6, I would suggest that such dialogical processes may not only help find out more about the others' point of view, but may also help ascertain one's own positions more precisely.

In the face of differing cultural backgrounds, political organization, standards of living and the like, there are frequent calls for a Europe of diversity; *discordia concurs* as an expression of the Continent's fundamental unity.[32] But what exactly could unity in diversity mean in practical terms? Walter Hornstein and Gerd Mutz have suggested that these calls ignore the huge transnational connections of economic developments, modernization processes and cultural transformations going on within communities throughout Europe.[33] I will address these issues in the companion volume to this book by outlining a conception of post-national patriotism. At this juncture, however, we can see that multilateral frameworks as forums for maximizing dialogue are our best chance of responding to diversity in a multipolar world.[34]

There is nothing new in this idea, but when many would see the future in rigid and hierarchical federal structures, or worse still, in a retreat to fundamentalist national positions, its restatement is an important part of moving the discussion to greener pastures. The idea of politics as a conversation has been propounded often. Giddens cites the work of Richard Rorty and Hans Georg Gadamer, before quoting from Michael Oakeshott's view that the understanding of our civilization can be seen as a conversation between a diversity of human activities articulated in their own manner and language. Oakeshott thought that this diversity can be best called a conversation not because it depends on contention and negation but the building blocks of conversation: the recognition of the other and mutual obligation.[35] But we can trace such thoughts echoing farther back than the lecture halls of the London School of Economics. Two centuries ago Heinrich von Kleist wrote: "*l'appétit vient en mangeant*. Language is ... not like a bridle, acting like a brake on the wheel of the mind, but like a second wheel on the same axle, running in parallel with it."[36]

In other words, the greater the dialogue, the greater prospect of success in the integration process. Ideas that are developed in isolation in answer to problems resulting from globalization cannot be expressed properly. A Europe burgeoning from a multiplicity of different languages and cultures used for communication *can* develop a greater sense of community. I mean these remarks in terms of language and culture to also apply to specialist interest and production sectors as well as in the linguistic and ethnic sense.

I will follow up these remarks in Chapter 12 by outlining a possible reconception of approaches to lobbying. As we shall see immediately in the next chapter, however, dialogue in transnational businesses is a global process of communication not only with other companies and customers, but within companies too. The location of decision making within a firm may not necessarily be the location of production. This has significant ramifications for not only national institutional conceptions of political organization, but supranational conceptions too. A significant irony is that Philips has employees seconded to the European Commission. Like all other European-based electronics firms, however, Philips makes its CD players outside Europe, whereas several Japanese firms have production locations inside the Community. Yet the European Commission views Philips as an indigenous European firm, not so its

Japanese competitors, who have no employees seconded to it.[37]

Thus, the decisions of both transnational companies based in the EU and those based outside, but producing inside Community borders, can bring about a large variance of contradictory conclusions about the future of social coherence. A discussion of these is the focus of the next chapter.

NOTES

1. Andersen and Burns, in Andersen and Eliassen (eds.), p. 228.

2. Eric Philippart and Geoffrey Edwards, 'The Provisions on Closer Co-operation in the Treaty of Amsterdam: The Politics of Flexibility in the European Union', in Begg and Peterson (eds.), *JCMS*, Vol. 37 no. 1 (Oxford: Blackwell, 1999), pp. 87-108 (pp. 105-106).

3. Philippart and Edwards, p. 89.

4. See Philippart and Edwards, pp. 89-100.

5. See *Frankfurter Rundschau*, 4.6.1999, p. 1.

6. In December 1993, the EP passed a resolution recognizing that the Maastricht Treaty's provision of intergovernmental cooperation on Justice and Home Affairs would lead to an overlap in EU and Council of Europe activity, and recognized the role of the older body as a democratic "ante-chamber" for prospective EU membership. See Westlake, pp. 69-70.

7. See Philippart and Edwards, p. 94.

8. See Westlake, p. 69.

9. The other two non-EU NATO members, Iceland and Norway are both members of the Nordic Council in existence since 1951, and the EEA, in force since January 1994. Austria, Sweden and Finland, all members of EEA, the latter two also of the Nordic Council, joined the EU in January 1995. Sweden is neither a member of NATO nor (as yet) a member of EMU. Neither Austria nor Finland are members of NATO but are members of EMU, and others.

10. Philippart and Edwards, p. 93.

11. See Begg and Peterson, 'Editorial Statement', p. 8; Devuyst, in Begg and Peterson (eds.), p. 116.

12. See Heidrun Abromeit, 'Ein Vorschlag zur Demoktratisierung des Europäischen Entscheidungssystems', in Vorstand der Deutschen Vereinigung für politische Wissenschaft (ed.), *PVS* March 1998 (Opladen: Westdeutscher Verlag, 1998), pp. 80-90.

13. For example, the Union of European Federalists fell far short of their rather modest aim to collect 1 million signatures (less than half a percent of the EU population) in a petition "for a European Constitution" in the year running up to European Parliament elections on 13 June 1999. See Bruno Kaufmann, 'Mehr Demokratie wagen', *Die Zeit*, Nr. 23, 2.6.1999, p. 10.

14. On French metal tariff agreement, initially unsigned by two unions – CGT and CFDT – because agreement contained no guarantee of further job creation, see '35 Stunden in Frankreichs Metallindustrie', *FAZ*, 30.7.1998, pp. 11-12.

15. The setting up of the EEI coincided with the publication of the Commission white paper *Growth, Competition and Employment*. As an example see Kommission der Europäischen Gemeinschaften, *Wachstum, Wettbewerbsfähigkeit, Beschäftigung.*

Herausforderungen der Gegenwart und Wege ins 21. Jahrhundert. Weißbuch (Bulletin der Europäischen Gemeinschaften, Beilage 6/93).

16. On Larsson report see Karl Magnus Johansson, 'Tracing the employment title in the Amsterdam treaty: uncovering transnational coalitions and political parties and trade unions lobbying together' in Jeremy Richardson (ed.), *Journal of European Public Policy* Vol. 5 no. 1 1999, pp. 85-101.

17. Johansson, p. 90.

18. Johansson, p. 97.

19. For the suggestion that Sweden's EU application was made for industrial strategy reasons, see Nils Morten Udgaard, 'The Nordic Countries', in Weidenfeld and Janning (eds.), pp. 175-182.

20. Sweden abandoned close state control of capital flows in the mid-eighties, which resulted in an outflow rather than inflow of capital investment. See Ramesh Mishra, 'The Welfare of Nations', in Robert Boyer and Daniel Drache (eds.), *States against Markets: The Limits of Globalization* (London: Routledge, 1996), pp. 316-333 (p. 324).

21. Robert Bosch GmbH is actually owned by a foundation for social and humanitarian purposes set up by the company's founder. AEG was subsequently taken over by Daimler-Benz, and is now largely defunct due to closure and resale of its former constituent parts.

22. See Maria Green Cowles, 'Organising Industrial Coalitions: A Challenge for the Future?' in Wallace and Young (eds.), pp. 116-140; http://www. nestle.com/investor_relations/index.html. Many may be skeptical about the likelihood of such companies as Nestlé, not noted for past displays of international social conscience, taking tangible steps to provide material support for greater social standards. But I would argue that there is a growing recognition in such companies of the need for them to play a wider social role, perhaps partially motivated as a response to such skepticism.

23. See Held, *Democracy and the Global Order*, pp. 251-266 (p. 255).

24. Held, p. 248.

25. As an example, see Kommission der Europäischen Gemeinschaften, *Wachstum, Wettbewerbsfähigkeit, Beschäftigung.*

26. See John Murray Brown, 'Europe's new "miracle" recovery', Financial Times Survey Ireland, *Financial Times*, 24.6.1996, p. III; also 'In Irland wächst die Wirtschaft wie in keinem anderen OECD-Land', *FAZ*, 13.7.98, p. 20. In 1997, although the economy boomed, unemployment in Ireland averaged 10.2%, albeit down from 11.5% in 1996.

27. Herrhausen, 'Wirtschaftliche Grundmuster', in *Denken – Ordnen – Gestalten*, pp. 113-119 (p. 114).

28. Walter Hornstein and Gerd Mutz, *Die europäische Einigung als gesellschaftlicher Prozeß: soziale Problemlagen, Partizipation und kulturelle Transformation* (Baden Baden: Nomos Verlagsgesellschaften 1993), p. 23.

29. Visser, in Hyman and Ferner (eds.), p. 102.

30. Rainer Hank, 'Gewerkschaften in der Globalisierung', *FAZ*, 30.4.1998, p. 17.

31. Platzer, *Gewerkschaftspolitik ohne Grenzen*, p. 173.

32. Theodor Schneider, *Nationalismus und Nationalstaat* (Göttingen: Vandenhoeck und Ruprecht, 1991), p. 376.

33. Hornstein and Mutz, p. 21.

34. I prefer the term "framework" to "network" because it suggests more freedom than the snags of a net.

35. Michael Oakeshott 'Rationalism in politics', in *Rationalism in Politics and Other Essays* (London: Methuen, 1962), p. 304, cited in Giddens, *Beyond Left and Right*, p. 30.

36. Heinrich von Kleist, 'Über die allmähliche Verfertigung der Gedanken beim Reden', *Werke in einem Band* (Munich: Carl Hanser Verlag, 1966), pp. 810-814.

37. See Alan Cawson, 'Big Firms as Political Actors: Corporate power and the Governance of the European Consumer Electronics Industry', in Wallace and Young (eds.), pp. 185-205 (pp. 198-200). Companies' investment in Eastern Germany also benefited from staff secondment to a public body. See Chapter 7 of my *Post-National Patriotism*.

9

The Global Location of Business Inside and Outside the EU: Possibilities for Community

In this chapter, I will tie two themes together that spread beyond the politics and geographical reach of the EU: the global span of business, and post-national community. There are two interlinked questions: what are the social consequences for European society (in non-EU and EU states alike) of the trend towards companies no longer operating in national markets? What are the social and political consequences for companies increasingly unrestricted by national borders, and therefore with a vested interest in the accentuation of post-nationally based employee and client allegiances?

Let us begin to answer these questions in this chapter. First, an examination of transnational firms operating inside and outside the EU will lead us to be skeptical about the aptness of national and state centered conceptions of organization and identity. The second section will reveal how further analysis will benefit greatly from our focus on Germany. We will be able to examine underlying social and political reasons for companies, still described under the increasingly misnomeric label "German," and principally agents of the economic needs of community, nevertheless having the potential to have a crucial social benchmarking input on global business policies inside and outside the EU. I will make this link in the third section. I will follow this suggestion with a brief discussion of globalization in the fourth section, which will lead to a discussion of possible conflict between variable and fixed points in global economic participation. In the final section of this chapter, I will be able to suggest that German business' system of codetermination may be a suitable model for the reconciliation of differing economic needs world-wide. In the two chapters following this one (10 and 11), I will adduce examples from German-based companies as empirical evidence for my arguments.

In this chapter we shall see that we must distance ourselves increasingly from solely geographically based conceptions of organization and identity. I will argue nonetheless that companies are dependent on positive client conceptions of the vendor's place and standing in the community to succeed in transnational and local marketplaces.

THE DIVERGENCE OF INTEREST BETWEEN TRANSNATIONAL BUSINESS AND COMMUNITY

In this section we will examine how it is increasingly difficult to discern how business interacts with the geographical community and therefore how increasingly difficult it is to see how to reconcile the needs of business with the geographical community.

We have already seen how the focus on the single market and EMU has served to obscure the effects on the EU's relations with the world beyond its borders. However, the evolution of Community homogeneity will serve to focus on even greater elements of heterogeneity in terms of culture and economic needs beyond its borders. The differences in cultures and economic need between the Community and the world at large are greater than have ever been present between Western European communities or indeed in Europe as a whole.

The advent of the single market has had considerable effects on extra-EU economies, as well as the economy of the EU itself, by virtue of transnational enterprise (TNE) activities.[1] Broadly speaking, TNEs have exploited the creation of the single market in different ways, according to whether the company base is located inside or outside the Community. Some of those based inside the EU have managed to position themselves to use the broader base of the single market as a platform for the expansion of their extra-EU global operations. Meanwhile for non-Community-based TNEs, the possibility of inner-EU expansion from one state to the other is simplified, and hence facilitated, by the single market superseding individual national markets. These intermeshing trends of investment are growing: According to official EU figures, companies based in the Community invested 91 billion ecu in non-EU states in 1997, circa 73% more than the previous year (an interesting comparison of scale is that the proposed EU Commission budget for 1998 was a similar level: DM 171 billion). The largest capital exporter was the UK with 33 billion ecu, followed by Germany with just under 15 billion. Capital investment into the EU in the same period from companies based outside the Community amounted to 42 billion ecu, up by just over 50% on the previous year, over half going to the UK (just under 23 billion ecu). Only 703 million ecu were invested in Germany in the same period.[2]

The low level of the latter figure could be adduced as evidence of foreign manufacturers' agreement with some German employers' claims that Germany is an undesirable location for investment because of an overregulated and expensive labor market. On the other hand, as we shall discuss further in this chapter, such claims may be self-fulfilling. If German business figures say that Germany is a poor choice then it will be seen by their peers abroad as being so and therefore will be.

The trend to greater capital investment flows in general however would suggest that TNE activity straddling borders will make any response by EU institutions based solely on territorial limits as outdated as the national states the Community was meant to supplant. The Commission policy on company amalgamations acknowledges this. The competition directorate checks all cases of fusions involving companies with a global turnover of 5 billion ecu/euro and a turnover within the internal market of 250 million ecu/euro. Whether or not the companies' headquarters are located inside or outside the EU is not a consideration, as was demonstrated with the Commission questioning the Boeing takeover of McDonnell Douglas, which ultimately raised the former firm's turnover by $5.8 billion to $18 billion.[3]

Nonetheless, geographically based conceptions of organization and identity remain publicly appealing, or at the very least, publicly maintained. An indication of the difficulty of surmounting the discrepancy between geographically based popular perception and global business reality was given, for example, by the contradictory statement of then FRG Foreign Minister Klaus Kinkel about Boeing's takeover of McDonnell Douglas. He described the move as an "industrial and economic policy declaration of war against Europe" and then contradicted the transnational organizational precepts of Airbus and German government aspirations to European unity by stating in relation to Airbus, "I see myself as head salesman of the nation."[4]

We may conclude this section therefore by remarking that such discrepancies as the example of Kinkel's statement about Boeing show us that the task of pinpointing, or even arriving at a rough estimation of the transnational interrelationship between interdependent individual and collective societal perspectives, is even more problematic than that noted within national parameters by Friedrich List over a century ago.[5] More recently, even in the more narrowly drawn parameters of business culture, Mark Casson has admitted that in view of considerable heterogeneity within national boundaries, it would be naïve to expect to observe a quantifiably discernible impact on a national economy's performance depending on the nature of national business culture. But he emphasizes its "significant impact" where it reduces the latter's transactions costs.[6]

THE COALITION OF INTERESTS BETWEEN BUSINESS AND COMMUNITY IN GERMANY

With the reservations concluding the previous section in mind, I will argue here that a focus on companies based in Germany, on firms still known prevalently both to Germans and non-Germans alike in public and private discussion by the designation "the German firm, [*Standard Co AG*]," can uncover evidence for seeing that input from German-based firms into the global reach of business could play a substantial role in the extension of social coherence across Europe, and beyond.

The three interlinked aspects that would lead me to this tentative conclusion are:
1.   Germany's reputation as a location of premium manufacturing quality based on the historical tradition of the marketing trademark stamp "Made in Germany."
2.   The post-Second World War German model of industrial consensus based on powers of employee codetermination.
3.   The association of businesses in Germany both with the industrial foundation of the Nazi crimes against humanity, and subsequent measures towards the Federal German state's subsequent rehabilitation of the idea of "Germany" in the international community.

The linkage between these three aspects is complex. But if we now make an initial attempt towards understanding them, we may on balance be optimistic about the likelihood of an extension of post-national social coherence across Europe, and beyond.

The three words "Made in Germany" stand for durable product quality, but this is thrown into question, as has been pointed out in the case of Mercedes, if the company's production is no longer located in Germany.[7] If products made by the firm's subsidiary company fail to live up to consumers' expectations, then the likelihood that people will pay a premium price for more expensive high-quality product from Germany itself will also fall. Hoechst AG and its American subsidiary Celanese, for example, were forced to offer householders $850 million compensation because of the delivery of defective plastic fuel pipes. The pipes were produced in the USA. However, the publicity concerning poor quality product was associated with the German company.[8] (Hoechst's expensive experience of defective pipes is also illustrative of problems of parent company lack of quality control with the advent of increasingly diffuse global investment.)

Thus we should question the relevance and bearing of the national parameter set by the nineteenth century term "Made in Germany" in regard to companies whose operations have growing commercial and social implications in the whole of Europe and the world beyond. Indeed, in the light of high-profile marketing of brands as well as the increasing trend towards decentralized production, Georg Blume and Siegmar Mosdorf's suggestion regarding future development is increasingly present reality: "In future, the label 'Made in Germany' is not the key aspect, but the label 'Made by BMW, by Bosch or by Siemens' – wherever these firms' products are made in the world."[9]

Nonetheless, though we should question the accuracy and relevance of the term "Made in Germany," so successful has this marketing tool been that companies, still in a position to profit from it, are unlikely to divest themselves from association with it. It seems unlikely that customers would be more inclined to buy a product with the label "Made in the EU." The experience of the UK Bovine Spongiform Encephalopathy beef scandal demonstrates that in many cases, customers prefer more specific knowledge of a product's origin. Thus, there are powerful residual reasons connected with branding for customers continuing to believe that these companies are German and for firms to indulge them in these beliefs although they may be in many cases be misplaced. Customers may, for example, buy an Audi sports coupe made in Hungary, or a Porsche made in Finland. The "new Beetle" is made in Mexico. (In Germany, VW also markets this car under the English brand name. It is perhaps the international success of the "Beetle," particularly in America, rather than the success of the *Käfer* in German-speaking countries which was instrumental in VW deciding to launch the new retro-product.)[10]

But the increasingly historical tradition of "Made in Germany" is linked also to non-Germans' perceptions of Germany as a whole, and remaining non-German prejudices about Germany stemming from the Nazi legacy. Here we would come to powerful reasons for German-based companies to divorce themselves from the national association. Indeed, as we saw in Chapter 2, German business as well as government pursued steps to Western integration and European unity to facilitate both internal and external rehabilitation from the stigma of the Nazi era. Although the support of the business sector for the political goals of the Federal Republic provided the crucial material foundation in the development of post-war Europe, as we saw with the example of the Ahlen manifesto (see Chapter 2), capitalism's association with the war had compromised its position among the population as a whole in Germany. It was furthermore on the defensive against the threat from the Soviet zone.

Therefore, a precondition of capitalism's post-Second World War rehabilitation among the German population at large, also a precondition of the substantial material wealth later created as a result of the Federal Republic's economic miracle, was the advent of industrial consensus based on powers of employee codetermination. The achievement of employee codetermination gave employees not only democratic rights, but responsibilities in the workplace. It can also be said to have played a key role in the economic success which not only brought about a share of economic wealth for all, but also a renewed deeper sense of social worth of Germans about themselves as an identifiable group within international society.

Although in increasing measure part of interdependent transnational business since 1945, with the advent of employee codetermination structures strengthening the relationships between employer and employee, German-based companies additionally have become more a part of the imagined community of Germans than ever before.[11] Furthermore, many German companies have a greater historical continuity than the Federal Republic, and through loss and confiscation of foreign assets in two world wars became even more associated with national community by force of collective circumstance and individual biographical experiences of firm personnel.[12]

Thus, businesses based in Germany were prominent in German society's responses to racism in 1992-93 and, faced by claims for compensation from victims of Nazi forced labor policies and their dependents, joined in 1998 to set up the "German Companies' Foundation Initiative: Remembrance, Responsibility, Future."[13]

Many companies may indeed represent a longer-term continuity than the Federal Republic. On the other hand, their structures and organizations may have just as little in common with their forebears known under similar or the same company and brand names in the marketplace 60 years ago as modern liberal democratic Germany has in common with the *Reich*.[14] The highest profile example of this change, which also raises questions about the future of business drawing upon a nationally based industrial culture, is the fusion of Daimler-Benz with the US corporation Chrysler in 1998. As one *FAZ* leader column saw it, it indeed belongs "to the most exciting plans in the history of German companies."[15] Even before this fusion, however, the practices and business orientation branded under the company's three-pointed star had become radically different. I will discuss the example of DaimlerChrysler in greater detail in Chapter 10.

Furthermore, within the broader societal context of Germany as a whole, we can make a further suggestion pertaining to narrower aspects of business culture. Casson has suggested that managers may be inclined "to promote loyalty to the firm at the expense of loyalty to other groups, such as the family or local community. If moral commitment to these groups is anyway very low, this tactic may be quite successful."[16] Thus we may be able to surmise that in the Federal Republic as a whole, the advent of codetermination on one hand and the proscription of attachment to the national group on the other may have combined to increase the strength of employee loyalty to the firm. Thus, it may be that a business culture has developed of a higher level of employee loyalty in companies based in Germany compared with counterparts elsewhere. I will discuss this point further in respect to Daimler-Benz's fusion with Chrysler.

Thus in Germany, as in other Western industrial nation-state societies, we may see rational economic arguments for shedding nationally based conceptions of identity. Furthermore, we may see deeper underlying social and political values for doing so than elsewhere in Europe. These values are, as we shall see in the remainder of the book, reflected also in company organization and policy and the actions and statements of individuals within companies. On the other hand, we should not forget that both individual company representatives and companies, with their particular emphasis on the primacy of economic goals, influence the actions and direction of society as a whole. Nevertheless, where this economic activity is world-wide, I would argue that the degree of responsibility sensed by the individual businessman or company is a reflection of the underlying social and political values of their society of origin, and its perception of itself in the world. Here, we may see that this relationship is expressly acknowledged by German-based companies. We can see this reflected for example in a section of Siemens' 1987 "Guidelines for Executives" titled "Social and Societal Responsibility":

The company must not only assert itself in economic and technical competition but also in respect to developments in societal policy. ... Participation in business associations and organizations as well as the acceptance of honorary posts and indeed political involvement on the basis of our constitution are important contributions to the maintenance of a free societal order.[17]

Meanwhile, the media conglomerate Bertelsmann, in addition to guidelines for upper management, also has a company constitution, in existence since 1972, signed by the heads of the firm's works council, supervisory and management boards, clearly stating the firm's advocacy of a free, democratic and social order. Not only does the company maintain the need for a market economy to ensure the fulfillment of these precepts, but it maintains also the need for "a societal order with social duties, in which owners of large productive wealth recognize their status contingent upon trustees' obligations to the general public."[18]

In addition to the examples of Siemens and Bertelsmann, Hans Lenk and Matthias Maring list similar expressions of social and political intent on the part of BASF, Bayer, BMW, Hoechst and VW. Bayer AG's upper management principles (1988) contain the section "Responsibility towards society and the environment," pledging to contribute to the solutions to "regional and supraregional societal problems." By way of comparison, USA-based IBM's 1990 business principles also included in the Lenk and Maring volume are a reflection of a different culture's conception of business. IBM accentuates individuals and organization and is patriarchal in tone, furthermore discouraging employees to take responsibility; for example, "If you have ... questions, please turn to your superior or the IBM legal division." As opposed to German-based firms, IBM's business principles ignore the firm's role in society. In fact the word "society" is not mentioned.[19]

Thus, those who have seen the role of large companies in Germany as having much in common with the corporatist role of private organizations in support of the state in other Western European states see their role too narrowly. I would argue that large companies in Germany are much more than forces that support the state.[20] They are forces that provide keystone support to *society* as a whole, facilitating the habitual articulation and exercise of a wide range of social values, practices and structures. Accordingly, where existing values, practices and structures are deemed to be threatened, it befalls customers of these companies to ask whether or not the pledges to societal order made by corporations are being fulfilled. Therefore, I would agree with Crouch in his emphasis that corporatism and pluralism need not be rivals, but in the light of diminishing importance of nation-states, I would not only wish to investigate how "tightly and centrally organized structures" facilitate pluralism in society as a whole as Crouch describes, but also how pluralism can be facilitated within these structures to extend social coherence within companies.[21]

If the location of production is no longer "Made in Germany," can we find answers to the questions on consequences this has if the location of decision still remains so? In the light of our discussion in this section so far, we should hope to find the answers, both in respect to German-based companies, and to sites of investment in non-German locations of production. While the demarcation regarding "Made in Germany" is increasing blurred, I would argue that the significant size of major companies such as DaimlerChrysler, Siemens and VW will ensure that the future forms of industrial organization and employment policies of firms based in Germany will have key importance for future political, economic and social developments, not only in the EU but in the world beyond also. Let us now make this link.

TOWARDS A MUTUAL RECOGNITION OF THE POLITICAL AND SOCIAL RESPONSIBILITIES OF BUSINESS?

We have examined profound political and social reasons for companies based in Germany having a significant role, not just in economic development in geographical regions of their activity, but in political and social spheres too. However these reasons are complex. Also the goals of political and social activity of all companies are necessarily subordinated to their economic goals. Thus we may speculate that German business potential to play a wider global role in political and social development has not received due recognition, either by commentators or German business figures.

For example, according to Sharam Chubin, "[German foreign trade] policy is largely unregulated by government which in any case sees its interest as the same as the large corporations with which it enjoys an all too cosy relationship."[22] Chubin believes also that the German government will have to "emancipate itself ... from the embrace of "big business" and start on the road to educating the public on what constitutes German interests other than those narrowly defined as economic, or those that only affect the homeland directly and tangibly."[23]

But what exactly are German or European interests outside of those expressed in purely economic terms? "European" like "national" business interest implies a geographical location, but as we saw in Chapter 8, in the section "Multipolar Dialogue and Closer Cooperation," by considering the example of Philips' close association with the Commission, this does not necessarily entail a coalescence with production location.

Furthermore, we may doubt whether it is the sole responsibility of German government to educate "the public on what constitutes German interests." In one sense, this is such a widely framed task that it would require a wider dialogue throughout

German society than epistemic action on the part of government, and would certainly greatly benefit from the input of German business. On the other hand, within this wider context, it is an impossibly narrowly framed task: how does one define German interests, as distinct from French, European or US interests? Clearly therefore, global debate is required about social and political values. It would be a misguided perspective to expect to find a definitive answer. I would argue that the wider goal of such a debate is to foster the process of dialogue itself.

Even a short examination of the comments of a few business figures in Germany shows us that we should not expect to find any definitive answer, even within the narrow context of German business, which constitutes the focus of a significant part of this work. On a 1998 trade visit to the People's Republic of China, for example, President of the BDI Hans-Olaf Henkel defended Economics Minister Gunther Rexrodt against criticism within the latter's party about his ministerial record and stature. Henkel stated that such domestic in fighting damaged the reputation of Germany as a business location. He contrasted the critics' behavior with Rexrodt, who according to Henkel, was working successfully for "the interests of German business."[24]

But was German business or the German economy as a whole at issue here? Henkel uses the word "*Wirtschaft*," and this word can mean both in English. Henkel is a noted proponent of radical neoliberalism. Thus we can presume that in view of his position as head of the big business lobby, and his former position with IBM, which (as we saw earlier in the previous section) makes no reference to society as such, Henkel meant a narrower interpretation of "*deutsche Wirtschaft*" than the wider national economic interest.

Eighteen months before, VW board member Martin Posth, speaking at the second Chinese-German Economic Congress in Beijing, taking place during the official state visit of Federal President Roman Herzog, had claimed that business commitment in China was a means of contributing to political reforms. "Here we are communicating our ideas of market economy and freedom on a daily basis."[25]

In our examination of the possibilities for political and social development of business, it is important to focus on Posth's use of the word "we." Does he mean VW, German business, European business or a wider Western political agenda? His use of the word freedom would indicate the latter, but as we shall see in Chapter 12, the development of the Community political process in the eighties meant that the mutual lack of understanding of often diverse needs of employers and employed resulted in divisions that still have to be overcome in the establishment of greater social coherence in Europe.

To sum up the points made in this chapter so far: the national adjective, for example in the term "German business," implies that the enterprise originally stood for a national interest either intentionally (the best examples of this being VW or (privatized) utilities throughout Europe), or by coincidence of territorial overlap of organizational antecedents. The same could be said for "European business." However if we bear in mind the multidimensional forces pressing inside and outside on every company in the international marketplace, interfacing with manifold and frequently contradictory forces present at inner- and intercommunity level, then we can see that such terms are not helpful. We would be better identifying other qualities in individual businesses operating world-wide that help us understand their nature a little better. Having done so, we will be able to analyze prospects of fostering greater social coherence in the world-wide community of business activity, between (potential) employers, (potential) employees and (potential) customers.

BUSINESS LOCATION AND GLOBAL POINTS

Before we consider the actions of individual companies, in this section we should consider the concept of "globalization" briefly to help us understand how global and local, geographical and non-geographical parameters pertaining to business location interact. This will help us see how transnational companies could act as interest mediators between different functional and geographical communities worldwide.

Globalization is a term used in contradictory ways, because it applies to various functional, technical and nation-state systems, groups and individuals. I have already acknowledged Giddens' understanding of the phenomenon in the Introduction, and I would agree with his definition that globalization is "action at distance." It is "not ... primarily ... an economic phenomenon."[26]

Recalling my remarks in the second section of the Introduction, regarding uncertainty, that this was also present before the end of the Cold War, the same goes for globalization. Aspects of globalization were also present before 1989, and in fact played a role in the creation and perpetuation of the Cold War as well as its end. However, only upon the elimination of state-socialist red stains on the map have we been especially conscious of one aspect of globalization, namely the power and interdependence of global economic forces. Despite the attraction of this contemporary focus, the level of manufactured goods exported as a percentage of GDP was actually at its highest in Western economies (including Japan) in 1913.[27] Perhaps we can see therefore that for many in the West, it was turbulence in the international order that has resulted in an intensification of fears regarding the power of economic forces. Moreover, with regard to circa 18 million people unemployed in the EU, and also quantitatively increasing abject poverty in the developing world, there may be good reason for these fears. Nonetheless, with an intensified awareness of such problems, globalization does not necessarily mean an erosion of solidarity: rather more it can be seen as leading to an increasing differentiation of solidarity.[28]

Roland Robertson discusses the growing use of the term globalization in the academic community from the early to mid-eighties. He sees it as referring to "compression" and our "intensification of consciousness of the world as whole." He discusses the point also that the notion has been substantially influenced by the term "global village," introduced in Marshall McLuhan's *Explorations in Communication* (1960). However, Robertson also draws our attention to the fact that for all the news-media's acknowledgements of a global community, media reporting, organization and subject matter are still expressions of diverse nation-state systems: "Such realities are far from the communal connotations which some have read into McLuhan's imagery."[29]

Furthermore, bearing in mind Robertson's point about the continuance of diverse systems in states, on the basis of the evidence we have assessed already, we should also consider the diversity of functional systems as potential obstacles to transnational communality. As I will discuss in greater detail in the next section, business location is not just that of the avowedly geographically fixed parameter of production, but of innately geographically mobile parameters of trade, investment and insurance. The first decision to be taken in the economic global market process, is the decision on where to invest, which, as I will argue in the next section, is never entirely objective.

Norbert Walter of Deutsche Bank, for example, has argued that "world financial markets have become a classic example for the world being a global village."[30] Walter's point regarding the financial sector acknowledges that for growing numbers of affluent people, geographical location is becoming increasingly irrelevant in economic, social and cultural terms. The concentration of greater material wealth has been made possible as economic activity becomes increasingly "dematerialized."[31] For the affluent, globalization brings the option of what Bernd Guggenberger has termed "participation without presence."[32]

Nonetheless, changes in the nature of individuals' and groups' relationship to geographical location are widely differentiated according to economic function. We may surmise that teleaction brought by advances in telecommunication and information technology has enabled economic participation world-wide for some functional communities that are independent of the constraints of geographical location. In terms of functional communities, I am thinking in particular of bankers, insurance and commodity brokers. Meanwhile, transnational enterprises are able to centrally control and coordinate production processes world-wide. Sony head Akio Morita dubbed this possibility "global localization."[33]

Others, passive participants in the changes brought by the diminishment in meaning of geographical distance, whose economic participation may still be dependent on geographical location, might benefit. However, they may not. Thus, with different groups placing varying importance upon geographical location as a precept of economic participation, there is attendant potential for conflict of interest.

Indeed it may be that traditional conceptions of group identity, developed ultimately under geographically limited structures of nation-state, might actually be reinforced because of actual or perceived interference upon these conceptions by functional financial communities (e.g. bankers or commodity brokers) acting without reference to geographical location. Despite or because of increasing involvement with the global economy, there are many who continue to find value in traditional conceptions, but who see their continued existence within geographically defined community threatened, with opportunities of social and economic participation diminished. Globalization may therefore be a potential cause of xenophobia. Due to the Asian financial crisis in 1997-98, for example, Malaysian Prime Minister Bin Mohamed Mahathir claimed that the currency turmoil was caused by foreign currency speculators, whom he termed "conspirators." Mahathir ignored the lack of foreign currency held by Malaysian banks as a factor contributing to the crisis, and made scapegoats of immigrants working illegally in Malaysia, ordering their forcible repatriation, and of his deputy Prime Minister Anwar Ibraham, who had advocated neoliberal policies. Ibraham was fired and tried for corruption and sodomy.[34]

The geographical community's formerly unchallenged main frame of reference was the nation-state. But we are seeing that this is changing. Moreover, economic activity in Europe or North America conducted by Sony or Toyota may be described as Japanese business, although most of those employed by these firms would not define themselves as Japanese or have any other tangible connection with Japan. Thus, here it may be useful for further analysis to define geographical community. I would define a geographical community as one where the opportunity for economic activity, whether of individual employee or employer, is dependent not only on proximity to a given geographical location, but dependent also on the sense and articulation of shared group identity. Both proximity and shared identity are required to diminish differences between otherwise diverse individuals. These differences could otherwise stunt business activity. Thus, as we shall see in the next section, all businesses have an interest in the maintenance of geographical community.

With this definition in mind, we can go forward to analyze how potential conflict may be resolved between different groups placing varying importance upon geographical location. We should try to find a more useful formulation than global village or global community. Both of these terms have senses of geographical distance, no matter how small, and therefore would seem to imply an actual linkage with geographical location. However, this claim is spurious in the case of global financial market activity. Instead, I would suggest a term that could account for the complex interrelationships between geographical community, market capital and the needs of transnational business: global points.

I see this term accounting usefully for different kinds of points of access to participation by individuals and groups in the global economy. These different kinds of points form complex and diffuse constellations of power and influence.[35] Global points contain no sense of geographical distance and no sense of geographical community. Nonetheless membership of a geographical community may indeed be a necessary prerequisite for effective participation in the global economy. Therefore geographical community may constitute a global point.

Furthermore, as the boundaries of geographical community are subjected to increasing complexity and contestation, with consequences for the articulation of opinion,[36] my term "global point" serves as a reminder that the term "point of view" implies a link with geographical location also. However, if point of view is formed within functional community independently either to the geographical location where it is articulated, or in respect to the geographical location to which it applies, how might a potential resulting conflict of interest be resolved with the minimum negative consequences to either interested party?

I would argue that transnational manufacturing businesses may provide the mediating link between geographically detached points of economic participation and those that depend upon membership of a geographical community. Transnational manufacturing businesses are global and local. Although they may be located worldwide, they are not entirely detached from geographical location. Both production and sales are dependent on geographical location. Transnational businesses may further provide a link between reconciling the needs of the developed world, where most are based, and the needs of the lesser developed world, where many have production subsidiaries.

In the remainder of this chapter, let us link this argument with the analysis made in the previous three sections and turn to investigate how German-based business may provide a leading role in finding solutions to the conflict between geographical community and functional community that may extend rather than diminish social coherence.

THE GLOBAL BUSINESS APPLICATION OF THE GERMAN CONSENSUS MODEL

In this section, after dismissing the view that consensus capitalism diminishes economic performance, I will suggest that German business practices of codetermination may be a suitable model for the reconciliation of differing economic needs of geographical community and functional communities operating without geographical links. Thus, in the next chapter, by the study of the DaimlerChrysler amalgamation process, we will be able to begin an examination of the practical prospects of the principles of codetermination in German-based companies being extended from the national to the international arena.

Erich Weede finds that "pure capitalism" offers the better prospects for economic growth and global development in general than the German consensus model. He argues also that globalization will have two major consequences. First, that it will lead to downward pressures on the wages of less qualified parts of the workforce in richer states. Second, he believes nonetheless that this will lead to increasing chances for their counterparts in poorer states, thereby strengthening democratic structures in less affluent regions. I would disagree with him. As Weede himself acknowledges, his judgement is precarious if based solely on the empirical economic evidence he offers in support of his argument. He cites mid-nineties figures for growth and unemployment showing slightly better performance in the UK and US economies, more free market in character, than that of more social market Germany. However as Weede acknowledges, the weaker economic performance of Germany is counterbalanced by the stronger performances during the same period of the similarly run social market economies of Sweden and The Netherlands.[37]

Weede's deployment of economic data further overlooks three factors entirely. First, he disregards the consistently strong economic performance of the Federal Republic since its foundation. Second, unlike Germany, neither the UK nor US economies has borne the consequences of unification with a former Eastern bloc state. The undertaking of German unification has been fraught with economic difficulties. Third, his economic figures are related to the developed Western world, which would seem to rather disqualify them from supporting his argument that "pure capitalism" rather than the German consensus model offers the best prospects for the growth of the global economy.

In broad agreement with Weede's arguments, however, some representatives of large business interests in Germany have claimed that the continuance of companies opting to locate existing or new production in Germany is endangered by the consensus model of capitalism. They argue that in the light of the global choice of decision making available to businesses, overregulation and too high levels of workforce pay make Germany's consensus model uncompetitive.[38] BDI President Henkel argued in autumn 1995 that high levels of pay in the German market led to higher levels of investment capital being invested instead in the creation of jobs abroad. Jobs were thus becoming Germany's greatest export. Martin and Schumann have cited this and other views akin to it as "the location lie(s)."[39]

Martin and Schumann's view is supported less polemically by both business and academic observers. The head of Siemens, Heinrich von Pierer, has maintained that sweeping condemnations concerning location ignore reality and that "painting things in black and white is unpleasant and not very helpful."[40] In propounding this, Pierer is very much in the tradition of his predecessor, Karlheinz Kaske.[41]

Robert Bosch GmbH has published what perhaps can be best described as a handbook on the design and location of new factories, intended for contracting companies and community political administrative figures. The criteria for choice of new location are outlined: geographical characteristics of the prospective site; economic and industrial structure; labor market; cultural aspects (whether the area is an attractive place for company employees to live); transport; locational costs, including taxes payable on the site; linked to this also the possibility of subsidy; the size of the investment required; power supply; difficulties of obtaining planning permission. We can see therefore that the labor market factor is only one of ten factors. Furthermore, wage costs are only a secondary consideration in terms of the labor market. Here, Bosch advises, "in terms of the employment market, the most important decisive criteria are population density, demographic structure, general education levels, and especially, industrial training standards."[42]

Meanwhile, academics Boyer and Drache have highlighted that 85% of foreign investment occurs exclusively between the trio of North America, Europe and Japan – that is, within regions where labor costs are similar.[43] Buckley and Artisien have pointed out that the wide choice of production locations brought by the scope of transnational activity open to companies with requisite resources means that they are able to carry out production rationalization processes of cost reduction, increasing overall efficiency and potential for economic growth. However, reducing labor costs is not necessarily the principle source of reductions in outlay. Buckley and Artisien quote from an *Economist* 23 August 1986 high tech supplement that labor accounts for only 5-15% of total outlay. Much greater cost control is possible by reducing material costs. Stock inventories, for example, account for typically 30% of material costs. Thus in view of mechanization and automation also they identify what they term "locational inertia" mitigating against "a wholesale shift of manufacturing industry from North to South."[44]

The growing distribution of high skills, innovation and expertise throughout Europe also plays a role in the increasing choice of production location for TNEs.[45] In high technology sectors, however, the continuing location of the lion's share in the EU of spending on research and development in Germany, France and the UK will act as a powerful incentive for companies to continue to see these states as attractive production locations.[46]

Furthermore, although the above point would indicate that there are reasons underlying business location policy which are rationally held, we must also take account of the relationship between subjective point of view and objective global context. I would argue therefore that there can be no such thing as the free market. A market free of community is no market at all, merely an inventory of costs and assets. If we specifically consider the theory of companies rather than the general theory of markets, we may emphasize that the private firm is also a community, and also part of a greater community of sectoral expertise. In a new foreword to her theoretical work on the firm, Edith Penrose has dismissed economic analysis based simply on a firm/market dichotomy, and upholds the view that "the firm in reality is not an island in a sea of market transactions, but itself part of a network consisting of rivals in direct competition, of suppliers of goods and services ... as well as of consumers, be they individuals, organizations, other firms or even governments."[47] She notes also the increasing tendency during the eighties and nineties of increasing fuzziness in administrative boundaries between firms, increasingly cooperating with each other in networked alliances.[48]

Emotional ties as well as infrastructure are crucial. But, despite the innate subjectivity of these, there is also an underlying rationale to the importance of emotional ties. Companies' survival in competition depends on the emphasis on cooperation and teamwork as a primary requirement. We can thus identify a potential problem for companies if society as a whole becomes increasingly differentiated and individualistic, and hence a vested interest on the part of private firms in the retention of social coherence. The head of personnel development with VW has complained that young trainees arrive at the company very self-oriented, having received no education at school in how to work in teams. But as he points out: "The world has become highly complex, and levels of knowledge have multiplied. Therefore we can only use the best engineer if he can work together with others."[49]

Thus on a wider scale, a measure of teamwork is required between company and community also, to strengthen the coherence of the company within the community as a whole. And if we recall that customers do not necessarily leave a given company on grounds of cost, but are far more likely to stay with a company because they have come to trust those they are dealing with, we can see that the same holds true with companies also. Companies, as customers of the community, do not leave communities on grounds of cost alone either. Thus, employer arguments during protracted rounds of industrial collective bargaining, in Germany and other affluent regions in the world, that unless costs are cut, production will have to move elsewhere, are not as paramount as they would have their employees believe. Accordingly, we can see there is an interdependence between business and community.

At this point, I would emphasize strongly that I concur with Giddens' argument against sweeping demonizations of business in reaction to its considerable power and ability to transfer large capital sums world-wide. Nonetheless, I would put a question mark on his following argument that the influence of globalization tends to stop the building of monopolies or oligopolies that had been present at the national level.[50] Giddens supports his argument by citing an *Economist* article from 17 April 1993, "The fall of big business" which reported big businesses shedding levels of middle management and forming autonomous decision-making centers instead to better compete with smaller local rivals.[51] My research would seem to only partially bear out Giddens' point. Some companies seek to make themselves more attractive to investment by extending the autonomy of leading workers. Attendant decentralization of decision making entails less power residing in the decision; consequently company shareholders' confidence rises that their investment is less at risk. The tandem tendency towards economies of scale and the growth in company size is resulting therefore in the interests of capital becoming diffuse. However, to encourage mutual interdependence rather than headquarters' dependence on autonomous centers, companies have introduced share option and investment plans for their own managers. For example the hugely successful media company Bertelsmann AG (business year 1998/99: turnover DM 26 billion) encourages its own sector/area managers to invest sums from 25,000 to 2 million marks in their own parts of the company.[52] Such provisions make defections to rivals or declarations of independence from managers already operating with a high degree of autonomy less likely.

But there is a greater differential picture. We can say that there would equally appear to be quite a widespread trend towards mass concentration in all sectors of industry: raw materials, manufacturing, telecommunications, and banking being much-publicized examples. In this context, Giddens himself points out that social change tends to occur dialectically, a movement in one direction causing the opposite reaction by another.[53] Thus, the wide diversity of personnel, functional and sectoral interests would seem to preclude any observer from judging whether generally any one firm's development world-wide can influence a change in another in a similar or opposite direction. With the passage of time, we may yet be able to judge that companies will be able to build monopolies at the transnational level just as much as at the state level.

Furthermore, there is another aspect that poses a danger to social coherence that we must consider. Within processes of decentralization, there may be increasing competition *within* private companies. Companies create teams to compete against other teams elsewhere in the company. The generated competitive vitality fosters the survival of the company as a whole. Team members prove their value to a specific team and the company in general by constantly seeking to forge new alliances with members of rival teams elsewhere. The loyalty of the individual to his peers is thereby constantly sacrificed to the benefit of self as well as company: a member of a series of dynamic teams ensures his or her continued employment. The holding company furthermore creates subsidiaries regularly working on the same projects, but utilizing differentials in expertise levels and approaches. This stretches the safety net of access points to catch potential customers in contact with the company, whose interest is in finding solutions to their needs rather than understanding the means by which this solution is developed.[54]

Thus, this increased decentralization and deregulation in business is not necessarily more democratic. Far from it – it often means more competition within companies and further pressures to conform to perfidious practices. But we should investigate ways in which businesses can become more democratic, taking account of geographical communities' interests. Related to this, we should also investigate how we may overcome negative perceptions of the term "solidarity." Weede, for example, in favoring pure as opposed to consensus-based capitalism, does not view the term solidarity as a positive term. He notes that such solidarity, as "Collective action by groups ... may aim to damage outsiders."[55]

But the presence of bonds within groups need not necessarily be accompanied by barriers against those who are not part of the group. With a study over the next two chapters of the examples of DaimlerChrysler and Siemens, we will see presently how such barriers may be overcome.

FACTORS FAVORING THE TRANSNATIONAL APPLICATION OF GERMAN CONSENSUS CAPITALISM

Before that, however, to sum up the conclusions of this chapter: for companies based in Germany and acting increasingly internationally, there are powerful persuasive economic and political factors, not only to retain the social consensus form of operation in Germany, but to extend it to their operations world-wide.

Employee codetermination can help reduce business culture transaction costs in companies operating transnationally across heterogeneous markets world-wide. Such operations will inevitably depend on reconciling different approaches and needs present in heterogeneous workforces. Codetermination's encouragement of employees to work self-sufficiently and to take responsibility for day-to-day tasks is of increasing importance in companies increasingly dependent on adjusting production techniques to marketing new products in a dynamic marketplace.[56] In this respect there are parallels between codetermination and lean production. As Blume and Mosdorf have pointed out, Japanese-based companies' original success with techniques of lean production was not so much dependent on automated production techniques but the integration of the workforce via cooperation in working groups and the elimination of hierarchies.[57] It may be that these parallels could meet on some future horizon, for example, in the event of a merger between DaimlerChrysler and Mitsubishi Motors. DaimlerChrysler took a 34% stake in Mitsubishi's car division in 2000.[58]

The relationship between company and market is not simply that of a single entity acting within a given framework. The company can innovate and change the market framework, and it cooperates with others to construct new frameworks.[59] Accordingly, there may be a case for seeing not only new frameworks in terms of market but in terms of political organization too. I will return to this thought in Chapter 12.

In political terms, I would argue that were employers in Germany to depart from the post-Second World War model of social consensus, they could risk a level of social and industrial strife that could precipitate crucial lasting damage to the reputation of individual companies still associated in great measure with the concept of "Made in Germany" but striving currently towards an international production base so that they may compete globally.

Furthermore, in view of the dynamic of business towards transnational organization, I would argue that it is in the interests of individual companies to extend this regime of social consensus to their operations world-wide as a means of fostering employee and customer loyalty internationally, and also to lobby for this regime of social consensus to be extended to competitor companies based outside Germany. There is evidence that some business figures in Germany may already be inclined to lobby for an extension of social consensus.[60] On the basis of the arguments considered here, this would arguably be much more a means of drawing attention to one's own "good" practices than resulting in non-German competitors being exposed to higher production costs. As we have seen in this chapter, it seems unlikely that codetermination is a cause of higher production costs. Conversely, in the light of this aspect, it might very well be that German-based companies would be better off keeping the lid on the methods of codetermination to continue to secure competitive leads over Anglo-Saxon competitors.

Indeed, codetermination has helped make German companies among the most successful in the world, and marketing strategies could also make much of its ethical appeal to customers. To misquote an old Audi advertising slogan: *Vorsprung durch Dialog?*[61] Extending my point made in Chapter 8 regarding closer cooperation and benchmarking, I would argue that codetermination could be extended progressively from individual states via the EU to the world beyond. There would seem to be economic arguments in its favor, valuable bargaining chips when ethical considerations come into play.[62] We may also see that opinion poll evidence, showing extensive public support throughout Europe for the extension of codetermination and local democracy, provides additional, political backing.[63] As we shall see by an examination of individual companies in the next two chapters, there are already indicators favoring the increasing extension of codetermination. Finally, I would argue that if companies based in Germany are seen to be associated with a commitment to more codetermination in company organization world-wide, then this could go a long way to redressing perceptions that German business remains inextricably linked with Germany's Nazi nemesis.[64]

At the beginning of this chapter I asked what the social and political consequences could be for companies unrestricted by national borders, and therefore with a vested interest in the accentuation of post-nationally based employee and client allegiances. I have suggested that we can see there is a complex of values in German business organization that could bring about an extension of social coherence transnationally. Thus, in addition to my arguments at the outset of this book that a study of Germany was crucial to the future of Europe, we can see that within this framework, the study of German companies is crucial to an examination of future social coherence too. Accordingly, let us now turn next to an examination of the global and community interests of DaimlerChrysler, Siemens and BMW.

NOTES

1. TNEs are more often than not referred to as multinational enterprises or companies (MNEs). For example, see Pearce and Papanastassio; Held, pp. 127 ff. But in the context of the issues studied in this work, the latter terms are usually misnomers when applied to such companies. The top management of TNEs is indeed cosmopolitan, but the composition of boards of directors tends to contain an overwhelming majority, usually men, stemming from the nation-state where the company is based. Thus, such companies cannot be described as "post-national" either, and the term "global firm" is also inappropriate.

2. Source of figures on capital investment: 'EU-Direktinvestitionen im Jahr 1997', *FAZ*, 7.8.1998, p. 22; proposed EU budget in: 'EU-Ausgaben sollen um 3,4 Prozent wachsen', *FAZ*, 30.4.1998, p. 19.

3. 'Brüssel wartet noch auf die Anmeldung', *FAZ*, 7.5.1998, p. 24; 'Antiquiert und chaotisch', *Die Zeit*, Nr. 51, 10.12.1998, p. 26.

4. See 'Ein kleiner Airbus für jeden Außenminister', *FAZ*, 25.5.1998, p. 19. Kinkel would be able to find justification for his role as chief salesman of the nation because of

DASA's stake in Airbus. But it would only be a partial justification. At the time, DASA, the German-based subsidiary of DaimlerChrysler, which we could describe within geographical parameters as a German and US-based firm, held a 37.9% stake in Airbus, on a parity with the French-state-owned Aerospatiale. British Aerospace held 20% and the Spanish state owned CASA 4.2%. In 1999, DASA announced an agreement with the Spanish government that it take over CASA. The Spanish government stated, however, that it intended to retain circa 11.5-13.5% of CASA shares. See 'Spanien will Luftfahrtunternehmen Casa an die Dasa verkaufen', *FAZ*, 12.6.1999, p. 17.

5. In Chapter 4 of his *Das nationale System* List wrote: "It is difficult to say whether material forces affect the powers of understanding more, or whether the powers of understanding affect material forces more, or whether societal forces affect individual powers or whether the latter affect the former more. What however is certain is that both interact enormously with each other." Cited in Friedrich Bülow, *Friedrch List: Ein Volkswirt kämpft für Deutschlands Einheit* (Göttingen: Musterschmidt-Verlag, 1959), p. 93.

6. See Mark Casson, *The Economics of Business Culture: Game Theory, Transaction Costs, and Economic Performance* (Oxford: Clarendon Press, 1991), p. 225. In terms of business culture, transaction costs refer to diverging habits of conduct of business, which may lead to saving or squandering of resources. These transaction costs should not be confused with those I referred to purely in terms of monetary transactions in Chapter 5, "EMU and the Establishment of Greater Interdependence."

7. See Michael Heller, 'Made by Mercedes', *FAZ*, 5.2.1993, p. 17, particularly: "Despite spectacular plans abroad, it should not be forgotten that Mercedes has profited enormously from its anchorage in Germany."

8. Volker Wörl, 'Made in Germany – Was sonst?' *Süddeutsche Zeitung*; 5/6.8.95, p. 23.

9. Georg Blume and Siegmar Mosdorf, 'Unternehmenskultur des 21. Jahrhunderts', in *FH/NG* 12/1993, pp. 1096-1103 (p. 1098).

10. See 'Volkswagen plant, ein neues Werk in Nordamerika zu errichten', *FAZ*, 23.2.1998, p. 21; 'Im Motorenwerk Györ laufen die ersten Autos vom Band', *FAZ*, 26.5.1998, p. 25.

11. For use of imagined community in this sense, see Benedict Anderson, Die Erfindung der Nation: zur Karriere eines folgenreichen Konzepts, [Imagined Communities: Reflections on the Origins and Spread of Nationalism] (Frankfurt/Main: Campus Verlag, 1988). Anderson points out that nations are an imagined political community. I discuss these ideas in greater length in relation to Germany in Chapter 1 of my *Post-National Patriotism*.

12. For the scope and effects of Siemens' resulting losses, reflected in the title alone, see Georg Siemens, *History of the House of Siemens; Volume II The Era of World Wars* (Freiburg/Munich: Karl Alber, 1957).

13. See 'Schacher um ein Versöhnungswerk', *Süddeutsche Zeitung*, 22/23/24.5.1999, p. 2. Also see contributors' awareness of the continued high interest and relevance of research on the Nazi era in Lothar Gall and Manfred Pohl (eds.), *Unternehmen im Nationalsozialismus* (Munich: Beck, 1998).

14. Could we say, for example, that "fanta," introduced in Germany during the war to replace Coca-Cola (withdrawn from the market for political reasons), is a Nazi softdrink brand? To answer yes would be preposterous. On the changing nature of the firm,

see Edith Penrose, *The Theory of the Growth of the Firm* (Oxford University Press, 1995), pp. 13-14. See also my graphical models, Chapter 11, this volume.

15. Jürgen Dunsch, 'Der Schmelztiegel Daimler-Chrysler', *FAZ*, 19.9.1998, p. 13.

16. Casson, pp. 234-235.

17. 'Siemens AG: Leitsätze für Führungskräfte (1987)', in Hans Lenk and Matthias Maring (eds.), *Wirtschaft und Ethik* (Stuttgart: Philipp Reclam jun., 1992), pp. 387-391 (pp. 390-391).

18. See Reinhard Mohn, *Erfolg durch Partnerschaft: Eine Unternehmensstrategie für den Menschen* (Berlin: Siedler Verlag, 1986), pp. 145-149 (p. 147); also http://www.bertelsmann.de/facts/essentials/essentials.cfm.

19. See Lenk and Maring, pp. 362-385.

20. For discussion of corporatism and 'Staatsträgende Kräfte' see Colin Crouch, *Industrial Relations and European State Traditions* (Oxford: Clarendon Press, 1993), pp. 6-12, p. 231.

21. Crouch, p. 231.

22. Sharam Chubin, 'Introduction', in Chubin (ed.), *Germany and the Middle East* (London: Pinter, 1992), p. 5.

23. Chubin, pp. 9-10.

24. 'Henkel: Rexrodt arbeitet erfolgreich für die Wirtschaft', *FAZ*, 30.4.1998, p. 19.

25. 'China gewinnt als Zukunftsmarkt an Interesse', *FAZ*, 22.11.1996, p. 19.

26. Giddens, *Beyond Left and Right*, p. 4.

27. See Paul Bairoch, 'Globalization myths and Realities: One century of external trade and foreign investment', in Boyer and Drache (eds.), pp. 173-210. For discussion of high levels of pre-1914 economic integration, see also Elmar Rieger and Stephan Leibfried, 'Die sozialpolitischen Grenzen der Globalisierung', in *PVS* 38 1997 Heft 4, pp. 771-796.

28. See Franz-Xaver Kaufmann, 'Globalisierung und Gesellschaft', in *Aus Politik und Zeitgeschichte* B18/98 24.4.1998, pp. 3-10.

29. Roland Robertson, *Globalization: Social Theory and Global Culture* (London: Sage, 1992), pp. 8-9.

30 Walter in (eds.), p. 45.

31. This term stems from D. Quah. See Nicholas Barr, *The Economics of the Welfare State*, 3rd ed. (Oxford University Press, 1998), pp. 12, 411.

32. See Bernd Guggenberger, 'Unterwegs im Nirgendwo', *Die Zeit*, 11.11.1994, pp. 43-44. I prefer Guggenberger's term, because it emphasizes *activity* brought by globalization more accurately than Beck's term "the presence of the absent," which would seem to falsely imply passivity. See Ulrich Beck, 'Wie wird Demokratie im Zeitalter der Globalisierung möglich?' in Beck (ed.), *Politik der Globalisierung* (Frankfurt/Main: Suhrkamp, 1998), pp. 7-65, p. 12.

33. See Blume and Mosdorf, p. 1098.

34. See Helmut Wagner, 'The "Invisible Hands": Who paid the bill and who made a bargain in the Asian financial meltdown?' in Yon Kwang Park (ed.), *The Journal of East Asian Affairs* Vol XII, no. 2, (Seoul, 1998), pp. 599-619 (p. 608); Howard Lentner, 'Implications of the Economic Crisis for East Asian Foreign Policies', in Yon Kwang Park (ed.), *The Journal of East Asian Affairs* Vol XIII, no. 1 (Seoul, 1999), pp. 1-32.

35. On diffusion of power, see Guéhenno, *Das Ende der Demokratie*, pp. 28-29.

36. See consideration of functionalism in Chapter 6. Also Hauke Brunkhorst, *De-*

mokratie und Differenz (Frankfurt/Main: Fischer Verlag, 1994), p. 26.

37. See Erich Weede, 'Arbeit und Wachstum in den westlichen Industriegesell-schaften', in Dieter Blumenwitz et al. (eds.), *Zeitschrift für Politik* Heft 1 März 1999 (Cologne: Carl Heymanns Verlag, 1999), pp. 30-49. Economic figures (from *The Economist*) cited by Weede are for 1997 (1996 figure in parenthesis) UK unemployment rate 5.1% (6.9%), USA 4.6 (5.3%), France 12.4% (12.5%), Germany 11.8% (10.7%), The Netherlands 5.2% (6.5%), Sweden 6.5% (7.9%).

38. See, for example, the views of Herrhausen on location regarding Germany in: 'Produktionsstandort Bundesrepublik in Gefahr', *Denken – Ordnen – Gestalten*, pp. 239-254 (p. 239).

39. See Martin and Schumann, pp. 212-220.

40. Heinrich von Pierer, 'Die deutsche Debatte', in Weidenfeld (ed.), *International-ale Politik*, Nr. 5, May 1998, pp. 1-6 (p. 6).

41. See Kaske's remarks: "Complaining is a part of business ... but complaining too much ... ruins business. *Made in Germany* does not become any more attractive by it," in 'Einäugiger König', *Wirtschaftswoche*, Nr. 53, 24.12.1992, p. 36.

42. See Hermann Franzke (ed.), *Industriebau Bosch: Standorte Bauten Technik* (Basle: Birkhäuser, 1991), pp. 16-19. Reasons for the inadequacy of former production locations are given as: the need to dispense with diversified locations; lack of room for expansion; handicaps imposed by legislation; logistical needs of client firms; outdated production facilities; wage levels; currency exchange rates. (pp. 14-16).

43. Boyer and Drache (eds.), 'Introduction', in *States against Markets*, pp. 1-27 (p. 2).

44. See Peter Buckley and Patrick Artisien, *North-South Direct Investment in the European Communities: The Employment Impact of Direct Investment by British, French and German Multinationals in Greece, Portugal and Spain* (London: Macmillan, 1987), p. 23, pp. 150-152. See also results of 1997 study, which found that companies in Ger-many moving production abroad principally to cut labor costs were disappointed that financial savings were lower than expected, product quality lower, and labor forces out-side of Germany were less able to react quickly to order gluts. In: 'Die Standortver-lagerungen haben viele Unternehmen enttäuscht', *FAZ* 4.6.1998, p. 20.

45. See conclusions of questionnaire survey of 190 companies in Pearce and Pa-panastassio.

46. See Jürgen Turek, 'Global Competitiveness and Emerging Technologies: Europe in the World Economy', in Weidenfeld and Janning (eds.), pp 65-81 (pp. 67-68). OECD definition of high technology production is where Research and Development costs are at least 8.5% of production price.

47. See Penrose, 'Foreword to the third edition' (pp. ix-xxi [p. xvi]), where she ac-knowledges the ideas of G.B. Richardson presented in his article 'The Organisation of Industry', *Economic Journal*, Vol. 82, 1972.

48. Penrose, pp. xix-xx.

49. Sylvia and Martin Greiffenhagen, *Deutschland: ein schwieriges Vaterland* (Munich: Paul List Verlag, 1993), p. 352.

50. Giddens, *Beyond Left and Right*, p. 89.

51. Giddens, *Beyond Left and Right*, pp. 121-123.

52. 'Beteiligung der Führungskräfte', *Handelsblatt*, 27/28.11.1992, p. 7; 'Bertels-mann kauft die amerikanische Verlagsgruppe Random House', *FAZ*, 24.3.1998, p. 21;

Bertelsmann Geschäftsbericht 1998-99.

53. Giddens, *Beyond Left and Right*, p. 122.

54. Paragraph based on author conversations with employees at Debis and Deutsche Telekom. It should be noted however that in the main, I have eliminated the option of interviews as a means of researching this book as being too subjective an approach than warranted by its general scope. The employees' views reported in this paragraph were given to me in a private capacity as students of English during language lessons, when I myself was not seen as acting as a researcher but as their teacher.

55. Weede, p. 34.

56. See Gerhard Schröder speech to 1998 conference of central committee of international metal workers unions: ' "Ich will das einmal rein ökonomisch begründen" ' *FAZ*, 29.5.1998, p. 19.

57. See Blume and Mosdorf, p. 1101.

58. In return for its investment in debt-troubled Mitsubishi, DaimlerChrysler management hoped that closer cooperation between the two would benefit from the Japanese-based firm's knowhow in small car production. See Dietmar Lamparter, 'Jedem seinen Japaner', *Die Zeit*, Nr. 14, 30.3.2000, p. 37; 'Daimler steigt bei Mitsubishi-Motors ein', *FAZ*, 29.3.2000, p. 13.

59. See Penrose, pp. xviii-xx on the growth of interfirm networking, especially in technological fields.

60. See remarks of Daimler Director Manfred Gentz that sector wage agreements would have more sense extended from German *Land* to the European level: 'Mehr Geld für Reiche', *Die Zeit*, Nr. 25, 10.6.1998, p. 30.

61. For many years, the UK advertising slogan for Audi cars, also spoken on TV in a dry, restrained English accent, was *"Vorsprung durch Technik."* Few people seemed to know exactly what the phrase meant, but the enigmatic, albeit controlled, nature of the slogan undoubtedly helped sell the company's claim to its target audience, that its cars enjoyed their advantage (*Vorsprung*) over the competition due to technology.

62. Like everything in business, there is a price on ethics, and their deployment can be useful in negotiations. See Lenk and Maring, 'Wirtschaftsethik – ein Widerspruch in sich selbst?' in Lenk, Maring, pp. 7-30 (p. 26).

63. See replies of poll respondents that "Ensuring that there is more codetermination in the workplace and in municipal politics" is an important goal:

(Figures expressed as percentage)	Strongly left	Moderately left	Center	Moderately right	Strongly right
Western Germany	54	48	27	17	16
The Netherlands	82	61	43	32	47
United Kingdom	67	54	41	22	11
France	60	35	32	21	22
Spain	50	41	33	26	25
Italy	49	47	31	33	22

Source: Elisabeth Noelle-Neumann, 'Die Luft der Freiheit weht', *FAZ*, 24.6.1998, p. 5.

64. This last point is discussed in greater detail in Chapter 14 of my *Post-National Patriotism*.

DaimlerChrysler and the Transnational Extension of Social Coherence

During the course of this and the next chapter, to evince empirical evidence for my theoretical arguments of the previous chapter, I will focus on two of the three largest companies based (or now partly based) in Germany: DaimlerChrysler, formerly Daimler-Benz, and Siemens. A fourth company, BMW, itself the potential takeover target of VW, the second largest German-based company, as well as other larger vehicle manufacturers,[1] also forms part of the discussion (in Chapter 11), because its ill-fated takeover of the UK-based Rover group in 1994 can be compared usefully with Siemens' investment policy.

Daimler, Siemens and BMW are the most suitable examples of firms for our focus, because a study of these companies' activities gives us intriguing indications concerning the potential for transnational and transinstitutional extension of social coherence from Germany. As we shall see in this chapter, it may be that Daimler's proclaimed pursuit of "shareholder value" and expansion of its transnational location of decision making and operations – that is incorporating American business culture perspectives – could actually not only serve the maintenance of codetermination in Germany, but also its extension world-wide. Moreover, the seeming move away from perceptions of the existence of common firm and German community interest could prove to be a conducive environment for the extension of levels of social coherence present within firms in Germany to the transnational arena.

On the other hand, as we shall see in Chapter 11, Siemens' defensive attachment to German-based contexts for the conduct of business has resulted in transnational markets' mistrust, which endangers social coherence within the company itself and in the communities of its operation. Meanwhile, despite the disastrous financial failure of BMW's investment in Rover, the episode nonetheless could be an important positive step towards the establishment of greater post-national industrial consensus across Europe.

A study of these companies' fusion and investment activities will reveal divergent trends. However, we will come to an overall conclusion that there is a considerable likelihood that industrial consensus and codetermination, along with long-term investment behavior prevalent in Germany, will be sufficiently resilient to withstand the demands of the more deregulated short-term behavior of the global markets.

DAIMLER-BENZ AND DISREGARD FOR SOCIAL COHERENCE

In this section, we will see how the apparent disregard of Daimler-Benz for social coherence made the company more attractive to market capital, and was the prelude to the announcement of the company's merger with Chrysler.

Despite its image at home and abroad as a "German" company, Daimler-Benz gave an extremely significant indication of its transnational aspirations by the presentation of its company figures according to American but not German accounting practices commencing with its half yearly report in 1996. In presenting its raison d'être, its profit and loss by this means, the company went even further than its bankers Deutsche Bank, which utilized international accounting standards.[2] As well as being listed on the New York Stock Exchange from 1993, before the merger with Chrysler, circa 14% of Daimler-Benz shares were held by Kuwait, the second biggest shareholding after that of the Deutsche Bank with 24.6%.[3]

Like Daimler, many other German-based TNEs are increasingly seeking capital investment at the New York Stock Exchange.[4] In 1995 American investors held foreign shares valued at almost $500 billion, a level which was predicted to double by the end of the century. By comparison, at the end of 1995, the market value of all German PLCs was estimated at $550 billion.[5]

We have already noted that the view from the financial markets is the perception that they constitute a global village. Where US investment behavior is the village benchmark, this has knock-on effects on stock market and individual investor perceptions in Europe, which I will discuss in the next chapter, with a consideration of Siemens. North American investors expect high levels of capital, and increasingly Europe-based firms must match these demands. Seen in these terms, Daimler's capital return is progressively more attractive to investors: for 1997 a return of 10.2 % was almost double the 1996 figure of 5.8%. The firm's goal of 12% by 1999 was reached in 1998. Dividend paid per share in 1997 increased by 45% on 1996 (DM 1.10 to 1.60). Operating profit doubled to over DM 4.3 billion. On the other hand, although these figures were in keeping with Chairman Jürgen Schrempp's declarations of "shareholder value," and made the company popular once more with shareholders, it enabled Daimler to increase its workforce once more by 10,000 to 300,068.[6] This would not have been possible had the company's disastrous year of 1995 been repeated (for the only time in company history, no dividend was paid to shareholders).

Thus, like other TNEs based in Germany, Daimler's interests, intentions and firm culture may increasingly bear less relation to a German, let alone a European context. This extends from the top down. Schrempp, company head since 1995, has claimed that he has little in common with Germany and lets it be known that he longs for his ranch on the South African veldt. As he searched for investment partners world-wide, Schrempp said that he was a world citizen first, German second. He also stated that his primary responsibility was to shareholders, whom he set above fellow employees. In a *Spiegel* interview he let it be known where his priorities lay: "I don't really have much in common with Germany anyway.... It's going to get worse here as well, the big bang has got to come."[7]

Nevertheless, despite the aggressive tone of these remarks, in a consideration of the activity of the company since the beginning of Schrempp's tenure, we can see that policy action depends on geographical community-based conceptions as well as functional conception. Shedding the troubled German AEG subsidiary proved to be a costly process of splitting its operations into parts to be incorporated into other Daimler operations, sold or closed.[8] On the other hand, it proved to be easier for Daimler-Benz subsidiary DASA to shed its financially troubled Dutch ancillary, aero-manufacturer Fokker, as a non-German company in 1995-96. DASA boss Manfred Bischoff, in presenting his firm's rescue plan, stated that the future of the company's Dutch subsidiary was dependent on the readiness of The Netherlands' government to save its "own" aircraft industry. But DASA *owned* the majority of shares in Fokker. In the light of the jobs at stake, not to mention Fokker's status in Dutch society, it was clearly the aim of DASA management to pressure The Netherlands' government into providing the necessary DM 2 billion thought necessary to save the company. However, Dutch Economics Minister Hans Wijers rejected DASA's rescue plan, and DASA abandoned its involvement in Fokker.[9] Without DASA, Fokker registered bankrupt in March 1996, and final hopes for any future for the workforce and company were extinguished upon the collapse of talks with South Korean firm Samsung the following November.[10] (We can speculate that had Fokker been a French or British company, the nature of DASA's withdrawal would have been different, and perhaps its involvement would have never been permitted in the first place.)

At the time Daimler-Benz was a TNE stemming from an avowedly German tradition with an image both of itself and for its customers connected to this national context. However, as we have already seen, its aspirations extended beyond Europe. This proved to be spectacularly so with the announcement of the planned amalgamation with the US-based vehicle producer Chrysler in May 1998. In the next section we will examine the consequences for the social coherence of community and for the new company, which became the world's third largest automobile firm behind GM and Toyota.

FROM DAIMLER-BENZ TO DAIMLERCHRYSLER

In this section, we will see how during the DaimlerChrysler amalgamation process, management recognized the greater need for transnational employee cooperation to help transcend formerly divergent business cultures. This appeared to necessitate a lessening in the priority accorded to shareholder and market interests. Furthermore, we shall see that this need for cooperation will probably foster the transnational extension from Germany of employee codetermination.

This chapter is in large part sourced from reports on the merger in the *FAZ* business pages, which are edited by one of Germany's noted proponents of the free market, Hans Barbier. By an evaluation of these reports, we can acquire a base of empirical knowledge to give further foundation to the theoretical arguments I advanced in Chapter 9.

Since the merger's announcement, Schrempp seemingly has been less intent on wooing potential US investors, and more concerned with ensuring support from the German establishment and the wider community within Germany that have thus far been most closely associated with the company's success. Furthermore, the choice of name for the new company, one non-hyphenated word, indicating unity yet paying heed to sensibilities on all sides by retaining the upper case "C" of Chrysler, shows the paramount need to recognize different cultures as a means of optimizing cooperation at all company levels during the potentially very difficult fusion process.[11]

The ownership of the new DaimlerChrysler, valued on the stockmarket at the time of the merger as the world's third biggest firm overall (worth DM 141 billion behind General Electric and Toyota), is international. On its inception, Schrempp coheaded the firm with Chrysler chairman Robert Eaton. Some 57% of the shares were held by former Daimler-Benz shareholders, 43% by their Chrysler counterparts; 44% of the shareholding was estimated to be held in the USA, 37% in Germany, 7% in other parts of Europe and 12% in the rest of the world (much held by the state of Kuwait).[12]

Significantly, despite this stock-holding cosmopolitanism, the company is formed according to German company law, providing for employee and union representation on the supervisory board and works council. Both companies agreed during the fusion discussions that acceptance of the deal could be otherwise politically problematic in Germany.[13] Furthermore, there were political and financial considerations in regard to shareholders. German shareholders have more emotional ties to their shareholding than their US counterparts. Also, had the new company been non-German, Daimler-Benz's shareholders would have had financial reasons to oppose the fusion: they would have had to declare the difference in shares' face value and stock market value as taxable earnings.[14]

The factor of codetermination has implications for our consideration of the extension of social coherence, because of its facilitation of the representation of employee interests implicitly linked to a geographically fixed community, as a counterbalance to mobile capital interests. Nevertheless, we must consider the question, whose community is facilitated by codetermination? In respect to DaimlerChrysler we could see codetermination as a potential handicap to as well as promoter of links between the two company cultures. Let us examine therefore how codetermination may handicap and then promote links between the various communities affected by the merger.

Although perhaps less of a handicap to social coherence in the geographical community directly, codetermination was a potential obstacle to reconciling different company cultures at the beginning of the fusion process. The salaries of US board member managers were way above their Daimler German counterparts, and these concerns in Germany were aggravated by reports that leading Chrysler managers earned more in share option schemes as a result of the fusion than the cost of the actual fusion itself.[15] Accordingly, employee representatives on the supervisory board may be inclined to ask questions about the salaries of German managers raised to match their US counterparts, indeed for that matter, the higher salaries paid to US upper management.[16] Daimler-Benz's supervisory board had agreed in the past to an extraordinary payment (DM 600,000) to every director for his efforts at turning the company around during the company's record loss year 1995. But even this figure is still "peanuts" (to borrow supervisory board head Hilmar Kopper's notorious remarks made in his tenure at Deutsche Bank) in comparison to standard levels of remuneration expected by US board members.[17]

Salary differential was perhaps the most substantial factor also in some Daimler-Benz shareholders' skepticism following the announcement of the fusion. In May, Daimler-Benz also announced a share options plan to supplement its German-based managers' salaries. Under the scheme, one shareholder representative estimated that on the basis of the then current stock market price, leading managers would have earned an additional half a billion marks.[18] In giving further details of the proposed plan, Hilmar Kopper pointed out that questions of board contracts and personnel still had to be decided by the supervisory board.[19] Perhaps echoing an awareness of the sensitivities affecting the power balance on his supervisory board, following his company shareholders' overwhelming approval for the fusion, Schrempp claimed in an interview that "I'm no proponent of an overdimensional remuneration as can be partly found in the United States. Furthermore, in the second rank of executives, there is already hardly any difference in salaries between Daimler and Chrysler." Asked also where the new "World Corp." would have its headquarters in 2010, he answered "naturally in Stuttgart."[20]

The question of substantial raises in upper management salaries does not affect social coherence in communities directly, and in the respect that those in leading positions are given added incentives to keep the company in profit, the view could be advanced that this secures the future of jobs in the community. However, on the basis of adverse shareholder reaction to higher management salaries, it affects communities' perceptions concerning the merits, goals and virtues of the conduct of business. The remarks of Schrempp himself, cited in a previous paragraph, that salary levels in the USA for leading businessmen are "overdimensional" clearly reflect concerns among workforce and shareholders in Germany, which the new firm's board will have to take account of, no matter whether individual board members share these concerns or not.

BENEFITS OF DAIMLERCHRYSLER CODETERMINATION FOR TRANSNATIONAL SOCIAL COHERENCE?

In this section, I would like to address the possible benefits of codetermination for transnational social coherence arising from the DaimlerChrysler merger. I will argue that the possible extension of codetermination from Germany could promote transcommunity cooperation as well as cooperation within the company.

I would argue that the possibilities opened up by codetermination mean that employee representatives could exploit the use of opinion in Germany opposed to high salary differentials, not to veto these high management salaries directly – this could estrange American management from the codetermination model irrevocably – but to exert leverage in securing an improvement to social coherence elsewhere, both within the company and the wider geographical community. Here, we may recall subtleties of negotiation tactics which I discussed in Chapter 5. If employee representatives can pursue an avenue of explanation, showing credible linkages between different functional areas, they may be able to succeed in persuading management that the concept of exchange, giving up previous advantages, is not actually a sacrifice in real terms on the management's part. By pointing to the success of Daimler-Benz's operation in Germany where codetermination operates, employee representatives may be able to show management that employer advantage in having sole responsibility for the running of the company is in fact minimal.

In linking adverse reactions in Germany to higher US management salary levels to other aspects of firm organization, which are subject to question in an overt move from national to transnational parameters, employee representatives can pursue a strategy in negotiation of gaining management agreement on an extension of elements of employee codetermination to non-German-based parts of the company, principally in North America.

On the other hand, were clearly discernible demarcation lines to form between employer and employee representatives on the supervisory board, regarding salary levels for example, then both sides would find themselves resorting to tactics of extortion, threatening steps which may harm their own interests, and thereby threatening the merger's prospects for success. The employers could make plain to employee representatives that the prejudices of the 44% of the firm's shareholding held in the USA concerning the untenability of codetermination for the running of business would be confirmed. Conversely, a decision on the part of the employees' representatives to withhold their consent regarding higher salaries, although it could be over-ruled with the casting vote of the head of the supervisory board, would be politically and socially damaging to the company in Germany. The employee representatives could be perceived as standing in the way of flexible structures required in the global market.

Thus, I would argue that there may be compelling reasons on both sides for a development where a more pronounced hierarchical salary structure may be traded for agreement on a greater measure of world-wide representation *and* responsibility, by extending codetermination in Germany to the DaimlerChrysler workforce in North America and elsewhere in the world. In this respect, we can see that codetermination could promote transcommunity cooperation as well as cooperation within the company.

Nonetheless, as things stand currently, codetermination is currently a handicap to transnational social coherence within the company, as in other solely German-based TNEs. Although the DaimlerChrysler merger affects diversely situated company operations and wider communities world-wide, of the ten employee representatives on the new company's constituent supervisory board, nine are German. Only one, the head of the US automotive union, the United Automobile Aerospace and Agricultural Implement Workers of America (UAW), Steve Yokich, will represent North American employees (circa one-third of total workforce). Furthermore, there is no North American representation on the company works council. This remains a body representing solely German-based employees[21] (not all of these employees are German citizens).

The construction of both bodies shows the limitations of national labor law when applied to firms located globally. IG Metall head Klaus Zwickel has suggested that the German company law be changed to provide for the representation of workers abroad on works councils. Daimler has categorically rejected the extension of codetermination from Germany to the international arena.[22]

Notwithstanding this stance, if we consider benchmarking trends, as well as the potential for its negotiation, it seems difficult to envisage how Daimler can resist this step. Schrempp himself has praised codetermination as a method, which while slow-ing the decision-making process, makes the agreed policy more robust once taken.[23] He has also stated that Daimler requires a "an outstanding company image world-wide."[24] As Karin Benz-Overhage, IG Metall representative responsible for codeter-mination, has remarked, public perceptions of codetermination are shifting from a handicap to competition to an advantage for competition.[25]

Furthermore, German and American unions have agreed to coordinate the work of the German works councils with the UAW representation at Chrysler plants. Yo-kich's presence on the supervisory board is only courtesy of IG Metall agreeing to give up one of three positions available to union representatives on the board (the other seven are elected by Daimler employees in Germany).[26] Moreover, extending greater recognition to the North American workforce (the company also has produc-tion in Canada) would also be a means of demonstrating to the former Chrysler workforce that they are valued equally with their European counterparts.

However, this step would not only have to overcome prejudice in American management against codetermination. A change would also encounter prejudice on the German employee side too. This was shown by the opposition of Alfons Görge-manns, deputy head of the Daimler-Benz works council, to Yokich becoming the North American employees' representative on the supervisory board. Görgemanns stated that Yokich's position as US autoworkers' highest representative meant that he would be more interested in the welfare of Ford and General Motors, and not Daim-ler.[27] Here, I can develop the point I introduced in Chapter 9, in the section "The coalition of interests between business and community in Germany" further. There, I examined the strength of firm loyalty as having supplanted proscribed national bonds in Germany. We can interpret Görgemanns' remarks as echoing the irrationality commonly found in expressions of national prejudice.

Moreover, Görgemanns ignored the position of many representatives of IG Metall on the supervisory boards of many Daimler competitors. He further did not take into account that Chrysler workforces are unionized, as opposed to their counter-parts in Daimler's main US production plant in Tuscaloosa, Alabama.[28] While all Chrysler plants had access to full union representation, a UAW spokesman was re-ported as stating that the union was still trying to legitimize labor organization at Daimler in Alabama. Yokich, however, emphasized that he did not anticipate special difficulties in working with Daimler.[29]

Moreover, benchmarking with other companies may play a role in the extension of social coherence too. In the same month as the DaimlerChrysler fusion, in May 1998, VW announced its intention of setting up a world works council, consisting of its European works council (which we may recall was set up only six years before) together with workers' representatives from North and South America, South Africa and Asia. Some 80% of VW's 280,000 employees are organized in unions.[30] We can see evidence also for the suggestion I made earlier that a more pronounced hierarchi-cal salary structure may be traded for a measure of universal company representation *and* responsibility. In 1998, VW also foresaw the introduction of a share options scheme for employees.[31] In North America meanwhile, General Motors management and the UAW union might be better off concluding that a regulated partnership is a better form of industrial relations than the almost traditional mutual enmity. This resulted in a 54-day strike in 1998 that all but halted the firm's production in the USA. UAW/Ford relations are by comparison much better in the USA.[32] General Motors' ownership of Opel and its more recent acquisition of Saab in Europe could be a further avenue of opening up consensual approaches to the management of the parent company.

On the other hand, we can see a contradictory trend in another manufacturing sector: the pharmaceuticals company Hoechst Marion Roussell AG (HMR), founded in 1995 from the merger between Hoechst and US and French counterparts, has acted specifically to restrict any question that the German industrial practices of parent company Hoechst AG be extended to its international organization. The new TNE is headed by a small holding company with only 300 members presiding over 80 subsidiaries. Only companies with at least 2,000 employees are covered by German codetermination laws.[33] With the parent company Hoechst, the trend continued. The company announced in March 1999 that a further fusion, with French firm Rhône Poulenc, would take place under French company law, annual shareholders' meetings to take place in Strasbourg, not the company's traditional base Frankfurt/Main.[34] But perhaps the level of confidence in company management plays a role too. Hoechst has struggled for a number of years. Since the mid-nineties, VW has not. Moreover, as I discuss in the companion volume to this work, the partownership of VW by the *Land* Lower Saxony is a powerful means of influence on company policy on the part of VW's community of origin. I would argue that a more illuminating cross-sectoral comparison could be made were Hoechst's thriving fellow descendants of IG Farben, BASF or Bayer to undertake large-scale transnational fusions.[35]

In this chapter, we have been able to assess repercussions pertaining to only a small number of the global points affected by the DaimlerChrysler merger. We have not, for example, dealt with the reaction of other vehicle manufacturers to the merger, or the reaction of non-sector interests such as environmental groups. Nonetheless, we have been able to assess prospects for the maintenance of codetermination in German-based companies and its extension to sites of operation abroad. We have seen that codetermination could be used as a buffer, to absorb the potentially conflicting energies from the differing business cultures of two fomerly nationally-based TNEs, as DaimlerChrysler travels down the track of multinational merger. We have seen that the extension of codetermination could be a counterbalance in the short term to opposition in Germany to the introduction of the American business culture of high salaries into DaimlerChrysler structures. There is additional evidence that higher levels of salary are seemingly becoming the norm in other German-based TNEs, threatening vertical social coherence within the firm, and presaging a threat to horizontal social coherence across wider communities where the firm's activities are located. Siemens, the initial focus of the next chapter, has announced its intention to introduce a potentially lucrative share bonus scheme also. Even so, in regard to a continuance of higher salaries, in the longer term, German business culture perspectives, and in particular the continuance of codetermination, both stemming from the wider context of German community, will play a significant counterweight factor. Penrose suggests that this may be the future benchmarked track for the wide-gauged transnational train to follow:

The salaries of top executives will tend to get as high as the community will condone or as the conscience of the executives themselves will permit (and sometimes higher if the size of the remuneration can be concealed or "justified" by devices such as stock purchase options or other bonuses).[36]

Thus, with this proposal in mind, we may see that German managers may themselves be inclined not to award themselves the exorbitant salary levels common in US-based firms, either on grounds of conscience or because of benchmarking from the wider community.[37] For a transnational business, the wider community will in future progressively be the world.

But for the present, as we have already surmised in this chapter, in post-Second World War German business culture, the community identification within the firm has assumed a greater role in comparison to identification with the community at large outside the plant gates. This has perhaps helped to attune German business managers more closely with the needs of sectors with whom they otherwise would have had little in common in the wider national context. Within the context of a German-based firm, there are extensive legally instituted frameworks: the works council and the supervisory board. These contain symbolic as well as practically based powers for the expression and articulation of the community within the firm, and the salary level that will be condoned by this community. Indeed, we may speculate that Schrempp's proponence of the codetermination system is a result of the debt he has to the support given him by the employee representatives for his restructuring plan for Daimler-Benz in January 1997. Their support was crucial to the supervisory board approval to end the status of Mercedes-Benz as an independent PLC within the company structure, resulting in the resignation of Mercedes head Helmut Werner, his rival at the top of company management.[38]

However, the decisions of German business managers bearing on geographical community are not only drawn from the inner-company context: they themselves are part of other functional communities, which in turn interact and are affected by the actions and needs of other communities. The introduction of share bonus schemes has, judging by the favorable global market reactions, been condoned by the shareholding community. Let us now, in the next chapter, consider initially how Siemens' reluctance to recognize the needs of this community has in turn caused this community to withhold its trust from Siemens.

NOTES

    1. See, for example, 'Nervös', *Die Zeit*, Nr. 51, 10.12.1998, p. 39. Rumors have not abated since changes in the BMW boardroom in early 1999 and in March 2000. I examine aspects pertaining to VW in Chapter 8 of my *Post-National Patriotism*.

    2. 'Dividendenperspektive mit Steuergutschrift', *FAZ*, 12.4.1996, p. 18.

    3. Heinz Blüthmann and Hans Otto Eglau, 'Sein letzter Kampf', *Die Zeit*, Nr. 44, 28.10.1994, p. 25.

    4. BASF, for example, was set to become listed on The New York Stock Exchange in June 2000, to be better able to expand its US operation by offering shares instead of

cash for further acquisitions. We can speculate that this is the precursor also to a large-scale fusion with a US-based firm. See firm web pages, http://www.basf.de, Ulla Hofmann, 'Die Notierung an der Wall street verbilligt Akquisition der BASF', *FAZ*, 14.8.1998, p. 18. The rapidly expanding software firm SAP became the eighth German-based company to be listed on Wall Street in 1998. See ' "SAP wird das umsatzstärkste deutsche Wertpapier in Wall Street" ', *FAZ*, 1.8.1998, p. 18.

5. Benedikt Fehr, 'Der Zug nach Wall Street', *FAZ*, 22.11.1996, p. 17.

6. 'Daimler-Benz will den Umsatz in zehn Jahren verdoppeln', *FAZ*, 9.4.1998, p. 21; 'Daimler-Benz erreicht das Rendite-Ziel schon dieses Jahr', *FAZ*, 31.7.1998, p. 19; during the early nineties, 90,000 jobs were lost at Daimler-Benz through sell-offs and closures. See 'Arbeitsplatzsicherung', *FAZ*, 8.5.1998, p. 17.

7. Jürgen Leinemann, '"Wer bin denn schon ich?"' *Spiegel*, 21/96, 20.5.1996, pp. 114-126 (p. 123).

8. 'Daimler-Benz ist auf dem Weg zum globalen Automobilkonzern', *FAZ*, 4.8.1998, p. 17.

9. 'Spekulationen um Rettungsplan für Fokker,' *FAZ*, 28.9.1995, p. 28.

10. 'Endgültiges Aus für Flugzeugbauer Fokker,' *Neue Züricher Zeitung*, 29.11.1996, p. 9.

11. Both significance of company name for community and the longevity of this significance are shown by the post-DaimlerChrysler fusion workforce campaign in Daimler-Benz's Mannheim works to retain the name 'Benz', because of the historic connection of the city and works with Benz & Cie. AG. Benz had amalgamated with Daimler to form Daimler-Benz in 1926 (also, by coincidence, the year that Chrysler was founded following the amalgamation of three companies). As can be seen by the foot-notes here, however, the *FAZ* house style utilizes hyphenation, referring to 'Daimler-Chrysler'.

12. Share ownership figures in 'Daimler-Chrysler AG soll schon im November mit der Arbeit beginnen', *FAZ*, 18.7.1998, p. 21.

13. 'Schrempp schweigt, während Eaton auf Diskussion setzt', *FAZ*, 7.8.1998, p. 17.

14. 'Die Deutsche Bank spart viel Geld', *FAZ*, 12.5.1998, p. 25.

15. Following the end of the fusion process, Chrysler's leading 30 directors and managers were set to earn $395.8 million (DM 705 million) in cash and in share options, as opposed to consultancy fees and costs of the share exchange put at DM 550 million. See Heinz Blüthmann, 'Milliarden aus der Wundertüte', *Die Zeit*, Nr. 34, 13.8.1998, p. 19.

16. Chrysler Head Robert Eaton was estimated to have earned circa DM 20 million for 1997 compared with Schrempp's estimated DM 2-2.7 million. See 'Millionenschwere Differenzen bei Daimler-Chrysler-Spitzengehältern', *FAZ*, 10.8.1998, p. 15.

17. See 'Schrempp windet sich', *FAZ*, 22.6.1998, p. 13.

18. 'Wenger verliert auch Berufung gegen Daimler-Benz', *FAZ*, 13.8.1998, p. 16.

19. 'Neue Gehaltsstruktur bei Daimler-Chrysler', *FAZ*, 18.9.1998, p. 13.

20. '"Unser Vergütungsmodell wird weltweit zum Maßstab"', *FAZ*, 21.9.1998, p. 23.

21. In response, Daimler-Benz's director of strategy Eckhard Cordes stated: "We are creating a company that was not envisaged as such by the German legislators." Cited in *FAZ*, 18.7.1998, p. 21.

22. See 'Ein Gewerkschaftler aus Amerika bestimmt mit', *FAZ*, 29.5.1998, p. 23; 'Ein Sitz im Aufsichtsrat für die UAW', *FAZ*, 16.9. 1998, p. 22.

23. See Rainer Hank, 'In der Welt AG', *FAZ*, 22.7.1998, p. 13; also Schrempp's remarks: "[Codetermination] is actually in the final analysis a more constructive method of finding solutions than in other countries including the USA." See: 'Keine amerikanischen Spitzengehälter bei Daimler-Chrysler', *FAZ*, 22.6.1998, p. 25.

24. Christoph Hein, 'Daimler-Benz ist auf dem Weg zum globalen Automobilkonzern', *FAZ*, 4.8.1998, p. 17. Schrempp also stated that the company should promote the role of women employees, but an indication of quite how much has to be done in this respect is that in 1998, only one member of the combined supervisory and managing boards was a woman: Birgit Breuel, member of the former.

25. See 'IG Metall verlangt Mitbestimmungsnovelle', *FAZ*, 27.6.1998, p. 14.

26. Yokich originally called for North American employees to have four representatives on the supervisory board, which would be a more accurate reflection of the size of the region's workforce constituency; 74,000 of 121,000 Chrysler employees are UAW members. See 'IG Metall und UAW wollen bei Daimler Chrysler mitreden', *FAZ*, 26.5.1998, p. 22.

27. *FAZ*, 26.5.1998, p. 22.

28. ' "Bei uns läuft es ziemlich gut zur Zeit" ', *FAZ*, 12.5.1998, p. 25.

29. See 'Ein Sitz im Aufsichtsrat für die UAW', *FAZ*, 16.9. 1998, p. 22.

30. 'Volkswagen richtet Weltbetriebsrat ein', *FAZ*, 13.5.1998, p. 17.

31. Like its DaimlerChrysler counterpart, this scheme was also opposed in the courts by Ekkehard Wenger as infringing the rights of shareholders. See 'Aktienplan von VW für zulässig erklärt', *FAZ*, 30.7.1998, p. 14.

32. See 'Gewerkschaft und General Motors vereinbaren ein Ende des Streiks', *FAZ*, 30.6.1998, p. 14.

33. See Hank, *FAZ*, 22.7.1998, p. 13; on 1976 codetermination laws see Wolfgang Däubler, *Das Arbeitsrecht 1*, pp. 655ff, especially pp. 656-664 on firms' recourse to alternative organization forms with several "workforces," all numbering less than 2,000.

34. See Jutta Hoffritz, 'Robin Hood gesucht', *Die Zeit*, Nr. 20, 12.5.1999, p. 40.

35. Some believe that Bayer's recent lack of R&D success may lead it to spend a surplus estimated up to DM 40 billion on acquisitions. See Jutta Hoffritz, 'Bayer muß vorbeugen', *Die Zeit*, Nr. 10, 4.3.1999, pp. 19-20. On the relationship between VW and Lower Saxony, see Chapter 8 in my *Post-National Patriotism*.

36. Penrose, p. 28.

37. For this view see Jürgen Dunsch, 'Kritik an Aktienbezugsplänen zeigt Wirkung: Das Daimler-Modell findet kaum Nachahmer', in 'Die 100 größten Unternehmen', 40. Folge (*FAZ* supplement), 7.7.1998, p. B 5.

38. This was the view of a loose left-wing grouping in the company active under the banner "Mercedes-Benz Koordination." They cite the restructuring battle as one of the reasons for Schrempp's more consensual style from late 1996 onwards. See Mercedes Benz-Koordination/express-Redaktion (eds.), *Werktage werden schlechter. Die Auswirkungen der Unternehmenspolitik von Daimler Benz auf die Beschäftigten* (Offenbach: express, 1997), pp. 11-13.

11

Siemens, BMW and the Transnational Challenge to Social Coherence

In the previous chapter, we saw that the primary need for transnational employee cooperation in the DaimlerChrysler amalgamation process would appear to necessitate a downsizing in the comparative importance of the precept of shareholder value. We saw that under Jürgen Schrempp's management, the company's accentuation prior to the merger of functional financial conceptions, and its seeming disregard for community-based conceptions, has actually increased future prospects for an extension of social coherence in the communities of the company's transnational operation.

Initially, this chapter focuses upon the electronics and electrical engineering conglomerate, Siemens. By way of contrast to DaimlerChrysler, I am going to discuss indications of how two factors have served to endanger social coherence in the communities of Siemens' operation. First, Siemens' accentuation of codetermination and consensus with its employees, and second, market perceptions of the company's reluctance to make financial conceptions preeminent. Nonetheless, I would emphasize that this social coherence has been endangered not because the system of consensus capitalism is more flawed than pure capitalism. I would argue instead that social coherence in the communities of the company's operation has actually been endangered by the limitations of Siemens' application of these principles. We will see that though Siemens acknowledged its interdependence with its employees, the firm overlooked the necessity of its need – the inevitable consequence of its status as a conglomerate with a wide variety of interests – to recognize its interdependence with other firms also.

We will see that a mutual dependence between company and community will not protect either one of them when faced with global financial market pressures. Unless, that is, where both are part of a greater supporting network brought by other companies, or other communities (or preferably both of these). In finding this out, we will find reinforcement for my point in Chapter 5 concerning the need to understand and hence be able to exploit levels of interdependence.

In Chapter 5, I discussed the fruitlessness of perceptions of independence. As we have seen since then, in Chapter 9, Siemens has long recognized its interdependence with society. Crucially, however, as we shall see in the second section of this chapter, the company's position was weakened nonetheless by desires to retain its external independence in the marketplace. The firm was reluctant to recognize and exploit levels of interdependence with other companies to face off market pressures. We will see that the company's prior obstinate insistence on independence from other companies, which led it to subsidize its semiconductor business, led it into a position of dependence on market approval also and worse still, in a single instance, on the orders of a single company. This policy was fundamental in the disastrous end – for both company and community – of Siemens' short-lived investment in an advanced semiconductor plant at Wallsend in northern England.

In the third section of this chapter, we will examine further dangers to firm and state interdependence by considering the investment by BMW in the UK-based auto-company Rover, financially disastrous for both firm and community. Our study of the Wallsend episode and the BMW Rover crisis will serve to extend the empirical findings of Buckley and Artisien. They judged that government subsidies "are rarely sufficient – by themselves – to induce a change in location."[1] In this chapter, we will see that subsidy alone cannot induce a company to *stay* in one location either.

To help understand these points, to link them with the points we uncovered in the previous chapter referring to DaimlerChrysler, and with an eye too to the concluding findings of this book, I will conclude this chapter by means of a series of graphical models. While I would acknowledge that I myself tend to be circumspect about the usefulness of such depictions in analysis, in writing this chapter, I found that drawing them up helped my own understanding of the processes described in this book. Therefore, I have retained them. However, I fully appreciate that many readers throw their hands up in horror when faced with graphical models. If this is the case in respect to the individual currently perusing these lines, I would urge you to stick to the text.

SIEMENS AND THE FULFILMENT OF THE NEEDS OF FUNCTIONAL COMMUNITY

Let us turn first to Siemens' interdependence with community, and attempt to identify reasons underlying market capital's mistrust of the company during the nineties.

In this section, I will show how Siemens' accentuation of longer-term social functionality failed to fulfil the short-term needs of market capital during the late nineties. Here, as a prefatory remark before trying to find out why this should be, it is important to point out that market capital lacked confidence in Siemens despite the fact that the company remained in net profit: albeit down 12.7% on 1996, for 1997, the company still announced a surplus of DM 2.6 billion.[2]

Siemens is a company of international standing with a long history of worldwide manufacture and distribution of its products. It is a company that not only profited from the establishment of the flourishing world economy by the end of the nineteenth century, but by virtue of its manufacture of telegraph cables, was partly responsible for this growth also. The company's accentuation of the promotion of good relations with its workforce dates from this period and additionally has partial antecedence outside Germany.[3]

Nonetheless, we can trace company history since then, and its post-Second World War investment patterns, to see Siemens as a prime example for the point I made in the section "The coalition of interests between business and the community," in Chapter 9. There, I established the underlying context for German-based firms' close association with national community by force of collective circumstance and individual biographical experience. I made this point concerning the losses sustained as a result of two world wars. This is the case specifically with Siemens. As a result of the Second World War, the company was forced to move its headquarters from Berlin to Munich. After 1945, the company's foreign investment record was one of caution, borne from losing 40% of its assets in the First World War and 80% in the Second. Care in making foreign investment as late as the eighties extended also to sensitivities in mounting takeover bids for foreign companies. At the end of the eighties, for example, Siemens made a hostile takeover bid for the UK electronics firm Plessey, but only together with GEC.[4] Thus, only at the end of the business year in 1998 did Siemens once more find itself in a position of having more employees abroad than inside Germany, the first time since the nineteenth century.[5]

Siemens' position as a company with world-wide interests has led it to attempt to reposition itself in terms of company culture and practices. According to Günther Goth of the firm's Central Personnel Department (implicitly ignoring the international antecedents of his own company's international reputation): "The increasing globalization of Siemens demands an international comparability of all functions and a change to our firm culture."[6] The implication of this statement is that if all firm functions can be compared on an international basis, then this would lead to the elimination of higher salaries for firm employees in Germany in comparison with Siemens employees elsewhere. Since the beginning of the chairmanship of Heinrich von Pierer in 1992, the company has taken a number of steps to increase flexibility and initiative and eliminate hierarchical structures, in reaction to the demands of world-wide competition and capital markets. As a result, workforce productivity has seen annual increases of over 10%.[7]

But the steps did not lead to an upturn in company profits in the short term. Accordingly, market analysts did not upgrade Siemens' share-rating. Market pressures on the company continued, not least because capital returns remained lower than set targets. In 1994, Pierer announced that the company would increase its capital earnings to 15% by the year 2000.[8] Although this 15% figure is linked outside the company with the precept of shareholder value, the term "shareholder value" is avoided in Siemens. Instead, the preferred company term is the more widely applicable "increase in company value."[9]

We can speculate that had Siemens accentuated the stock-phrase of "shareholder value," the term most attractive to the markets, for the benefit of the outside audience of investors, but nevertheless continued to accentuate workforce consensus as its rallying call for its internal public, its employees, then this dual approach would have served to alleviate market pressures in substantial measure. However, the company's reluctance to do so meant that, as the company continued to face difficulties, the markets' mistrust continued.[10] In 1997, Pierer was increasingly coming under pressure, as earnings per share remained less than 3%.[11] By summer 1998, the revised

2000 target of 8.5% share return looked overambitious too.[12] Indeed, net income for 1998 was to decline to only DM 917 million before the firm bounced back to register a net income of DM 3,648 million for the 1999 financial year. [13]

Handicapped by low earnings per share, the company's share price failed to increase in line with the general stock market trend. Thus, Siemens' room for maneuver became more constrained by short-term financial considerations. In 1998, Siemens, with its DM 115 billion annual turnover and 416,000 employees, was worth less in stock market terms than the Software firm SAP with only 13,000 employees. Following Siemens' announcement in July 1998 of difficulties in its semiconductor business, the two leading global share-rating agencies, Standard & Poor's and Moody's, both queried Siemens' creditworthiness. Under continued market pressure, the company announced its intention in autumn 1998 to carry out a further drastic restructuring of its operation. The restructuring involved a sell-off of parts of the firm accounting for a turnover of DM 17 billion and including 60,000 of the workforce. These sales would however only be carried out upon the buyer giving assurances of retaining jobs.[14]

Outside Siemens, the head of the ERT and President of the International Chamber of Commerce, Helmut Maucher, also gave support to the company in a newspaper interview. He went out of his way to defend the then much publicized view of his ERT colleague Pierer, that an important consideration of business should be the creation and retention of jobs. The 10% fall in Siemens' share price which had followed publicity given to Pierer's remarks, was Maucher said, "total nonsense," and he himself had bought shares at the lower price. Maucher further emphasized the need, for example in cases of job losses as a consequence of the merger of companies, to state that resulting larger profits will be deployed to compensate in the social sector. Where his interviewers pointed out that such thinking was of no interest to potential company investors, Maucher replied that there was a need to overcome such short-term thinking. Intriguingly, as the head of Nestlé, the largest transnational food company in the world, (70 billion Swiss francs turnover, 1997) he judged:

This restriction now to supposed shareholder-interests is totally wrong. If I want to have long-term success, then I've got to consider all possible points of view: image, employees, churches, the unions ... If for that reason I make only 3.9 billion Swiss francs instead of 4 billion in a certain year, then that is a very clever decision. I gain credence internally.[15]

Meanwhile, within Siemens, in face of market pressures, interdependence between the workforce in Germany and management grew. Pierer received solid support from company works council head Alfons Graf for restructuring plans, and more flexible work practices. Graf, responding to the intention of IG Metall to hold protest days against these changes, stated that the sales of parts of the company meant neither a heightening nor a lessening of the threat of job losses.[16] Nonetheless, such manifestations of internal company consensus about sacrifices necessary in pursuit of goals of longer-term social functionality failed to fulfil the expectations of the markets. But this, we suggest, is not because management was not taking steps towards correcting previous inefficient performance. Rather, these steps were not seen as adequate because management was not seen to be encountering any substantial sign of employee opposition in taking them.

By way of contrast, during the first year of Schrempp's chairmanship, the Daimler-Benz share price climbed from 686 to 852 points. During this period, Schrempp was seen as encountering opposition. His public profile as a tough leader and willingness to risk confrontation – he overcame industrial unrest in protest at the company shedding 40,000 employees – was clearly enough to persuade the markets that Schrempp was the right man to overcome a company record loss of DM 5.7 billion under his predecessor Edzard Reuter. Even so, Schrempp had himself been greatly responsible for this record loss. As head of Daimler subsidiary DASA, he had been responsible for Daimler's acquisition of Fokker, calling it a "strategic decision." However, upon becoming head of the parent company, Schrempp acceded to shedding Fokker, writing off a further DM 2.3 billion.[17] Having ensured market support, Schrempp was better able to sound a more conciliatory note with the workforce in autumn 1996 when he needed to. Following a wave of unofficial strikes in protest at the board's decision to cut wages of sick workers by 20%, Schrempp negotiated a settlement with then works council head Karl Feuerstein revoking the board's cut. Furthermore, in a speech made to the Friedrich-Ebert Stiftung he announced that he would no longer emphasize "shareholder value," stating "I'm only shedding a negative expression, naturally without giving up the concept."[18]

In this section, we have seen that attempting to take steps to gain the trust of capital, Siemens moved hurriedly, taking a number of short-term restructuring measures. However, its attempts to do so while maximizing consensus with its workforce were seen as equivocation, and failed to convince the market.[19]

We may even see that the resulting uncertainty handicapping the firm's future development could lead to a consequent inclination to retreat to the redoubt of national community. One commentator has implied that the provinciality of Pierer, as head of Siemens, is symptomatic of the company's outlook. She notes the details of Pierer's curriculum vitae, almost exclusively located in Erlangen, Franconia. He was born, brought up, educated and became a leading Siemens manager in Erlangen, and continues to live there, a long-time town council member. Pierer himself says: "One needs a place where one can retreat to."[20]

However, we can see that in an interdependent world, this desire, however attractive, brings pressures on both community and company. Although both interact with the other, and are conducive to the vitality of the other, neither community nor company can ignore its market links with the outside world for long. An interdependence of Siemens with geographical community solely in Germany, long recognized in terms of company culture, is fundamentally unbalanced, as Siemens (and its employees) are active globally. We shall assess the reason for this imbalance, in the next section, a consideration of the case of Siemens' investment in Wallsend, England.

WALLSEND AND SIEMENS: THE NEED FOR INTERDEPENDENCE BETWEEN COMPANIES

To try to understand how firms may avoid the precarious position that Siemens found itself to be in, as described in the previous section, in this section I will assess the practical advantages of the trend towards growing interdependence between firms.

As we have seen, this is now an integral part of sociopolitical development in the world economy, particularly in high technology sectors (discussed in Chapter 9). However, here we will see that in attempting to retain a measure of independence from links with other firms, Siemens ignored the wisdom contained in its own guidelines to its upper management, to play a role in sociopolitical developments in society. A crucial part of current global sociopolitical development is the increase in levels of cooperation between transnational companies.

In this section, I will highlight this trend by discussing the example of Siemens' investment in Wallsend, northern England, where interdependence between companies was conspicuously absent. Accordingly, we will be able to draw the lesson from the episode, that interdependence between firms may be promoted as a means of strengthening social coherence.

To understand the need for interdependence between firms, I would recall my arguments concerning the underlying reasoning behind Siemens' close links to community in Germany in Chapter 9. There, I considered the historical context of the development of business culture closely associated with community in Germany. In the section "The Coalition of Interests between Business and Community in Germany," we noted that Siemens' guidelines laid emphasis on the need for the company's upper management to play a leading role in sociopolitical developments, acknowledging the firm's interdependence with community

We saw, however, that these guidelines were implicitly imbedded in the context of Germany only. However, we have noted that Siemens is a firm once more increasingly transcending states in its operations, and this is reflected in the policy goals and declarations of its leading management. Pierer declared the firm's intention to switch to US accounting standards from business year 1999/2000, in order to prepare the path to Wall Street registration and international purchase and cooperation agreements.[21] Then head of Siemens UK, Jürgen Gehrels joined Toyota boss Hiroshi Okuda in early 1997, in warning that Britain's continued non-participation in EMU would endanger future foreign investment to the UK.[22]

Thus, we can see that although made in the international context, these policy statements acknowledged the precepts contained in the company guidelines, namely the need to play a leading role in sociopolitical developments. However, we may see that a crucial reason for the imbalance between Siemens' close links with community on one hand and strained links with the markets on the other, was Siemens' previous reluctance to admit to a need for interdependence with other firms.

In 1998, as we have seen, Siemens was already under pressure from the markets due to its low share performance. Therefore, with the additional pressure of the bottom dropping out of the semiconductor market, the company was forced in dramatic fashion to abandon long-term planning strategy methods, and wrote off DM 3 billion by closing its semiconductor plant in Wallsend, Tyneside, in northern England. The plant, heavily subsidized by the British government, had only been officially opened a year before in 1997.[23] Crucially, however, the plant had not only been subsidized by the British government: Siemens itself had subsidized its chip production for many years. The company had formerly regarded losses in semiconductor production as an "insurance payment" for its market independence as a whole.[24]

However, the goal of market independence has proved to be an illusion, as shown by Siemens' problems with its share price. Furthermore, half of the Wallsend plant production had been scheduled over a ten year period for delivery to the Tai-wan-based firm Mosel Vitelic Inc. The downturn caused by the Asian economic crisis led Mosel Vitelic to cancel its contract, and Siemens was faced with overcapacity in microchip production and a 96% price collapse in the market. When production on Tyneside began, sale price per chip was £43. When the closure was announced it was 75p.[25]

Before the Asian crisis, Siemens had planned to build a chip design center on Tyneside, but the then head of Siemens UK, Jürgen Gehrels, had stated in January 1998 that its development was contingent on market developments.[26] Had the center been built, then the resulting high level of qualified personnel and technological infra-structure might have attracted further firms to the area, and a critical mass of invest-ment in the area might have been achieved.

John Zysman has concluded that European firms such as Siemens would be better advised to concentrate on sophisticated engineering applications of semicon-ductor technology. As he has pointed out also, Siemens is the sole remaining Euro-pean-based global competitor in the computer sector in general, but it remains "in the game" only by dint of being junior partner in alliances with IBM and Toshiba, and the supply of computer mainframes by Fujitsu.[27]

In the case of Wallsend, we can see that in attempting to retain a measure of in-dependence from links with other firms, Siemens ignored the wisdom contained in its own guidelines to its upper management, to play a leading role in sociopolitical de-velopments. The Wallsend experience would seem to be a lesson for Siemens to give up its aspirations to illusory independence once and for all. Indeed, in June 1999, Siemens announced the amalgamation of its computing division with Fujitsu.[28] This step followed the sale of its personal computer production plant in Augsburg to the Taiwanese firm Acer in April 1998. In future, Siemens PCs will be produced by Acer.[29] All but one of Siemens other semiconductor plants are joint ventures. It was Tyneside's misfortune that contractual difficulties would have arisen from closures to its joint-venture semiconductor production sites with IBM in France, Motorola in the USA and Mosel Vitelic in Taiwan.[30]

With the example of the last-named plant, we can see that the factor of location of decision was heavily against Wallsend. Wallsend was overly dependent on Mosel Vitelic orders. Without support from other companies or other communities, Wall-send was the most vulnerable to closure. Siemens' only further solely owned micro-chip plant is in Dresden. Here the company is set to invest DM 2.7 billion by the year 2004 alone in a new chip factory in Dresden. However circa DM 800 million of this investment (30%) in the plant, the largest of its kind in Europe, comes from the state.[31]

There were powerful subjective reasons for Siemens preferring the Dresden lo-cation to Wallsend. Pierer was seen to have close links to Chancellor Kohl following German unification. Kohl, frustrated by 1992 with the insufficiencies of the privatiza-tion process in transforming Eastern Germany (see Part II of the companion volume of this work), nonetheless praised Siemens for the part it had played: "If all company boards had acted this way, we would be a bit further down the road."[32] Closing the Dresden plant would have cost the company even more in political, social and finan-cial terms than Wallsend.

In this examination of Siemens, we have seen that the firm's operations occur in an interdependent framework of community, markets and other firms. Observing this, we may make the suggestion that the greater number of relationships that one of these elements has, the less likelihood that its overall position as part of the framework will loosen, or even cease to be a constituent part of the framework. The strands linking Siemens to community in Germany and vice versa are many. They are also extensive links, being fostered still further, between Siemens and other companies in the sector. This was not the case with Siemens and Wallsend. Indeed, Wallsend was the latest and most vulnerable part of Siemens' operations, and because it was not linked in any way with other companies or other geographical communities, Wallsend was more vulnerable still.

In the previous section, we saw how Siemens is dependent on community. In this section, we have seen how Siemens tried to retain its company independence by subsidizing its semiconductor production. However, Siemens' insistence on independence also jeopardized the functioning coherence inside the company and in the geographical communities of its operation as a whole. Wallsend proved that this measure of independence is untenable. The Siemens Wallsend plant was as dependent on Mosel Vitelic as the Tyneside community was on Siemens, a precarious and questionable piece of irresponsibility, both on the part of the company and also the British government department that had decided to supplement Siemens' subsidized investment in the first place. We have already seen that The Netherlands government refused to subsidize further DASA production of Fokker as a bad business proposition, given the likelihood that DASA had more subjective loyalties to production sites in Germany. The wisdom of the Dutch government decision would seem to be borne out by the Siemens Wallsend episode.[33]

In view of the lack of market trust, we may note that, increasingly, Siemens is emphasizing its preparedness to cast aside self-conceptions of being an independent player in the international marketplace. Instead, the firm is moving to strengthen its links with other companies world-wide. Indeed, we have seen that Siemens is arranging cooperation agreements with other companies, extending to its German production sites also.[34]

The abandonment of the Wallsend plant heralded the company's recognition of its interdependence with sectoral community – that is, interdependence with other companies in the sector. Wallsend's fate showed that despite massive subsidy from government and company, there was neither the necessary interdependence of further investors nor a community present to secure its future. As we have seen in this section, transnational firms would do well to rid themselves of corporate behavior that has much in common with the hegimonial perceptions of power so damaging to states' relationships (discussed in Chapter 5). There are many geographical communities, like Wallsend, with a highly skilled and motivated pool of labor, which can profit from and bring profit to an increasingly global network of interdependent private enterprises. However, in the next section, by way of a consideration of the BMW-Rover crisis, we will see how the independence impulse in both state and company can inhibit the development of post-national social coherence.

INTERDEPENDENCE, SUBSIDISED LOCATION AND BMW

In this section we will discuss how public subsidy, as a response to the economic need of community, is only one part of a triumvirate. Along with the needs of community, we must consider the needs of firm and needs of capital also. With provisos of a stable capital interest and sectoral and community interdependence, we will see here with the example of BMW how the German model of consensus capitalism could provide equilibrium to this mutual community of transnational interest by its facilitation of links between and across geographical communities and firms. In other words, where a critical mass of interdependence between both sectoral and geographical community is present, public subsidy may succeed. However, with the example of BMW, we will see also that increasingly inappropriate elements of would-be independence hinder the extension of post-national social coherence. In the case of BMW's troubled investment in Rover, these redoubts of sovereign exercise of will were twofold, and found in both company and state. The first was the German-based company's insistence on its independence from larger rival firms. The second was the continued independent existence of the UK pound sterling outside the eurozone, which proved to be a barrier of rendering effective public subsidy in the interdependent European market.

BMW bought Rover in 1994 as a means of fulfilling two interrelated goals. First, Rover's product range, at the lower end of the automarket, was seen as an ideal complement to BMW's luxury series cars. By buying Rover, the firm obviated any risk of tainting the luxury aura of the BMW brand had it developed lower-range models on its own instead. Second, crucial to the firm's standalone culture, the Rover purchase meant that BMW could forgo the option of agreeing a fusion or cooperation agreement with other firms. An extended product platform would make the company a more robust player in the transnational marketplace.[35]

BMW's independence culture can be traced as a behavioral reaction to the smaller company's efforts at competing with its much larger rival, Daimler. The mindset is best summed up by the statement of former BMW head Eberhard von Kuenheim, uttered as a standard reply to queries about possible cooperation agreements with competitor firms. "At high altitude, the eagle flies best of all alone."[36]

However, by the beginning of 1999, it seemed that the eagle had flown too high in its pursuit of Rover, and as a further result, its eyrie was suffering from neglect too. The investment required at Rover was much more than previously forecast, – in February 1999 estimated at DM 12 billion compared with only 5 billion in 1994. Also, Rover sales had collapsed, both in its domestic British market and outside the UK.[37] In February 1999, therefore, the supervisory board fired company managing director Bernd Pischetsrieder, who had bought Rover.

Had Germany's company codetermination laws not existed, BMW investment in Britain would have become considerably less immediately upon Pischetsrieder's demise. The company rescue plan to be carried out by his successor-designate Wolfgang Reitzle foresaw a cut in all production at Rover in the UK with the exception of Minis and Land Rovers. A new mid-range car would be built instead, based on design platforms supplied by BMW rivals Ford or VW. The plan would have entailed 10,000 job losses in Britain, and the complete closure of the Longbridge car plant near Birmingham. In knowledge of the plan, Reitzle's appointment was opposed by the (German) employee representatives on the supervisory board. Works council head Manfred Schoch rejected Reitzle's appointment.[38] As *The Economist* article reporting the incident stated, "To Americans this might seem like socialism, but it is the way in Germany, whose car firms incidentally muster better labor relations and higher productivity than does General Motors in Detroit."[39]

As a consequence of German employee representatives' solidarity with their English colleagues (despite the latter's significant, perhaps unsolvable problems with productivity at Longbridge), Reitzle departed from the managing board as Pischetsrieder had done. Supervisory board chairman Eberhard von Kuehnheim could have used his casting vote to have appointed Reitzle but, together with the largest shareholder representatives on the supervisory board, was reluctant to jeopardize company stability with such a contentious appointment.[40] Moreover, Reitzle's plan, dependent on the external supply of design platforms, would have compromised BMW independence from other firms. Therefore, with the fundamental reason for its acquisition of Rover remaining (in contrast to the example of Siemens' investment at Wallsend) – the desire to expand from its upper-range market segment in car production, and its dependence within this segment on its lowest price 3-series model – it was the new employee-approved chairman Joachim Milberg who went on to negotiate a subsidy deal with the British government. Milberg threatened that without the subsidy, a considerable portion of Rover production would be switched to Hungary.[41]

In the section "The Global Business Application of the German Consensus Model" in Chapter 9, we reviewed how there are rational foundations for investment into new as well as existing firms. Investment will tend to locate in areas where there is already enough infrastructure and technology. Where this is lacking, it may be compensated for in terms of government subsidy, as a reflection of community needs. Additionally, with the examples of aid programs, we may see also that the community receiving the direct subsidy may not necessarily be governed directly by the government making the subsidy. The FRG government, for example, subsidized building the Shanghai subway transit system with circa DM 375 million, provided that German companies won the contract to build it.[42]

Nonetheless, as we saw in the previous section, Siemens Wallsend shows us that public subsidy, as a reflection of the core needs of community, and intended to increase social coherence by attracting private organization and capital, can only heighten the chance of stable long-term production, and functioning community, if it is matched by an equivalent appraisal of need on the part of other firms and the market. Even when public subsidy is matched by large investment by the firm, subsidy alone cannot induce a company to *stay* in one location if market needs are not met.

Probably subsidies can be seen as a valuable investment on the part of the community in cases where the production site is seen by the company concerned as a strategic part of its business operation. This was not the case with the Wallsend factory. Nor was it the case with DASA involvement in Fokker. By way of comparison, we can see that this was the case in serving the prolongation of BMW's investment in Rover. Contingent on production targets being met, the UK government agreed to pay BMW £152 million. In return for the subsidy, BMW undertook to place one-third of all company investment, circa DM 10 billion, in the UK until the year 2005.

We might see these two steps –the subsidy agreement between BMW and the UK government and the preceding act of transnational employee codetermination that made the second step possible – as an outstanding prototype example of post-national social coherence. Built upon foundations of German-based consensus capitalism, we may note that such steps can serve wider community interests, extending beyond narrower perceptions of nation-state.

Nonetheless, as is the case with so many of the genre, this prototype contained a fundamental design flaw. Both steps making up its constitution were not taken to foster interdependence but were made as the consequence of policies on the part of both company and British state aimed at maximizing independence from others. With the subsidy agreement, both parties found themselves in an interdependent relation-ship with influential strands of opinion present in both parties that were unwilling to admit the greater need for cooperation publicly. We have already seen that this was the reason for BMW buying Rover in the first place. In respect to the UK, in the longer term, post-Second World War administrations have consistently pursued in-dustrial policies independent of those pursued in continental Europe. The suspicion is that this policy of independence has contributed to the significant decline of manu-facturing industry during the same period. It is hard at any rate to envisage how a policy that recognized rather than scorned interdependence could have resulted in a greater decimation of UK manufacturing industry during this time.

In the shorter term, the portion of UK public opinion against joining the euro-zone was still high enough for the Blair government to equivocate about giving up the pound sterling. This was causing long-term planning problems for manufacturing industry throughout the whole of the UK. Furthermore, by the first months of 2000, the euro was worth only just over £0.61. At the beginning of 1999, it had been worth over £0.70. The subsidy to be paid to BMW by the UK government, amounting to £152 million, was rendered ineffectual by the high value of the pound, which saw BMW's income cut by £230 million in the same period. Meanwhile, manufacturing industry throughout the United Kingdom was faced with the problem of the strong pound. Consequently, other auto producers – Honda and Nissan – were considering considerable cuts to UK production. In May 2000, Ford announced the end of volume car production at its Dagenham plant in East London.[43]

For its part, on 16 March, the BMW supervisory board abruptly announced that it was to break up the Rover group and sell off the bulk of its UK interests. Land Rover was to be sold to Ford's luxury car division, Premier Automotive Group, now headed by Wolfgang Reitzle.[44]

In announcing the sell off, BMW continued to pursue its policy of independ-ence. It emerged that, in trying to find a buyer for Rover, BMW had broken off nego-tiations with Ford, General Motors, VW and Toyota as all had demanded a stake in the BMW group as a whole in return.[45] The pursuit of this option would have been an acknowledgment of a greater firm and community interdependence that was set to survive the crisis: BMW, along with VW, is involved in the future of Rolls Royce and Bentley car brands. BMW is also a partner in engines with Rolls Royce. BMW an-nounced in April 1998 that it was to invest DM 1 billion building a new engine fac-tory near Birmingham, safeguarding hundreds of jobs.[46] However, BMW was not able to accede to the needs of other firms' involvement. Only this U-turn could have ensured the success of the subsidized investment, in respect both to UK government subsidy to Rover and BMW's own even more considerable subsidy to Rover since 1994. To do so however, would have been to admit the failure of the purpose of the Rover investment, which was meant to buttress BMW's independence. For BMW, this was seemingly too great a step to take. Instead, it was left to the buyer of Rover, a UK Midlands-based consortium headed by former Rover Chief Executive John Towers, to find partner firms to help secure the future of Rover instead. Without doing so, many deemed the "new," "independent" Rover's prospects, without Land Rover, the new Mini, or its modern Cowley plant (retained by BMW to produce the new Mini) to be bleak. [47]

Nonetheless, it seems likely that the Rover crisis marks the beginning of the end of BMW as an independent company if it is to survive as a significant player in the transnational marketplace. Unlike Siemens, BMW has been less vulnerable to market pressures, because its long-term shareholders have either family reasons (the Quandts with a 45.6% constituent shareholding) or institutional reasons (for example Dresdner Bank, Allianz, R+V) for a stability in share price. Thus in 1999, initially there was an internal management, capital and employee coalition agreed that the company interests and identity as an independent entity were served best by retaining a broad level of transnational interdependence internal to the group. Further investment in Rover was favored to make transnational interdependence, and hence company independence, more robust. However, as the company's financial difficulties mounted into 2000, this coalition disintegrated. At the time that Pischetsrieder was fired, the Quandts were reportedly the objects of advances from other vehicle manufacturers: VW, Toyota, Fiat and Ford. [48] Leaden fuel was added to these rumors following the volte-face over Rover in March 2000. The head of the BMW works council Manfred Schoch was cited as stating that the family had requested chairman Milberg to identify tenable solutions to enable the continuance of the firm's independence. According to Schoch, if the Quandts judged that the chairman were unable to do so, the family would consider selling their shares. [49]

In closing this section, we may draw the following lesson from the BMW-Rover crisis: in practical terms, supposed independence in an interdependent world was worth little. We have seen that neither company nor British government gained. We may also see that BMW's major shareholders, the Quandts lost heavily also. It may be that such a patriarchal shareholding structure, almost feudal in character, while undoubtedly shielding the firm from market instability, is inappropriate for the operation of a firm active globally.

THE ESTABLISHMENT OF INTERDEPENDENT NETWORKS

In this chapter, we have seen that the stable development of both company and community is best safeguarded if both are part of a greater supporting framework, transcending company and community. Finally, to try to help understand these points, and link them with the points we uncovered in the previous chapter referring to DaimlerChrysler, I will conclude this chapter by means of a series of graphical models.

Characteristics of stable social coherence can be understood as depicted in an equilateral triangle of interdependent relationships between the interests of wider geographical community, market capital, and firm (Figure 1).

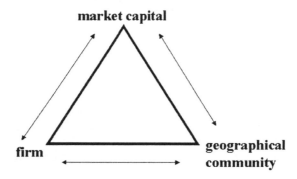

Figure 1. Interdependent Relationships

We can perhaps see that if there is any departure from the equilibrium depicted by this equilateral triangle, if two of the three elements depicted become closer to each other than the third, then the relationship of the former two to the third one becomes strained. The distance fosters the growth of mistrust. If this is the case, for example, with market capital becoming more distant from the other two, then as a consequence of its distance to the more relatively closely aligned firm and geographical community, it may find itself attracted to other firms and communities to constitute new triangles. We may see this to be the problem faced by Siemens and its employees. Thus, there is good reason for market capital to be depicted at the apex of Figure 1: from such a position it has the overview necessary to discern alternative location points for greater returns on its investment.

Movement is demanded to offset this possibility on the part of one or both of the points more closely arranged together to bring the third back, or else the triangle of mutual interest will cease to exist. However, where community and firm have become distant, or fear becoming distant, from the needs of capital, it is much easier for the firm to move than community. Democratic community must incorporate a variety of opinions to reach consensus on possible responses, which may take some time. The manager of a firm, however, must reach a decision far more quickly. In this respect, Siemens' managers were seen by capital to have waited too long for the arrival of consensus on movement in community, and so even although both moved, capital moved still further away. Relative distance between market capital and the other two points remained the same.

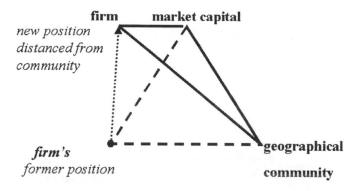

Figure 2. Daimler-Benz and Interdependence Imbalance

With the aid of the model in Figure 2 however, we can see the effect of Daimler-Benz management's overt demonstration in favor of a closer relationship to the market at the beginning of the Schrempp tenure. The ensuing distance to the communities of its operation caused resentments.[50] Indeed, as many Daimler-Benz shareholders were themselves members of the same geographical communities affected by the company's cuts, we may see that the distance between firm and community became greater in partial respect to the distance between capital and community. The resentments expressed by shareholders concerning high salary levels awarded to upper management could be seen as evidence for this point.[51]

Nonetheless, following the fusion with Chrysler, there were indications that the company desired a rapprochement (with community representative encouragement) towards the needs of community. It was in the interests of both firm and capital to accede to a placement of community at the apex of mutual relationships to establish a new equilibrium between two different company cultures. We can see their agreement on the paramount accentuation of community further illustrated by the dotted line arrow in Figure 3.

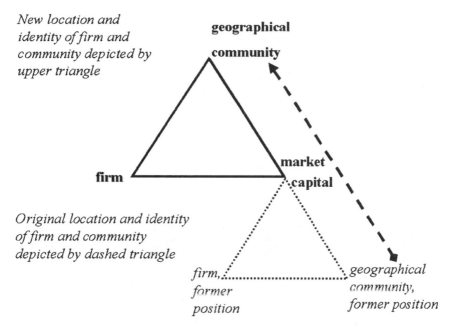

New location and identity of firm and community depicted by upper triangle

geographical community

firm

market capital

Original location and identity of firm and community depicted by dashed triangle

firm, former position

geographical community, former position

Figure 3. Mutual Interdependence and the Accentuation of Community

Figure 3 helps us see that not only is the framework of mutual interdependence following the fusion of the two firms greater. The new locations of both firm and geographical community in the model also help us see that the only constant in business is change. In respect to firm, we may recall the views of Nicholas Kaldor, as cited by Penrose. In a 1934 article on "The Equilibrium of the Firm," Kaldor defined the firm as a "productive combination possessing a given unit of coordinating ability ... all the theoretically relevant characteristics of a firm change with changes in coordinating ability. It might as well be treated therefore as a different firm."[52] Community too is subject to constant change.[53]

Nonetheless, it is more difficult for community to coordinate responses to change, without a diminishment of sense of community. We have seen that there was no prospect of Wallsend or Fokker moving to the triangular apex. To try to find an appropriate model that may help us account for methods of losing valuable elements of community, let us review further aspects offered by this series of models thus far. In doing so, we will be able to examine a final model, which will also help us conceive when subsidy of geographical community may be a viable method of compensation to offset the prospect of community exclusion.

Figure 1 was an attempt to reflect perceptions of market preeminence aided in part by supranational approaches, as discussed earlier in Chapter 8, in the section "Overcoming Obstacles to Closer Social Cooperation." Market capital is at the apex set above the other two. We have seen, however, with Figures 2 and 3, that market capital need not always be at the apex. Nonetheless, by virtue of our discussion, we have seen also how community and company are the "worker-bees," upholding equilibrium in these triangular relationship models. Market capital, it seems, is the omniscient beekeeper, moving from hive to hive at will. In contrast to the other two, it would appear to have a whole range of choices open to it. Furthermore, we have seen that community finds it far harder to move than the firm does. How can we best respond to this? We can do so by seeing that the model may be amended to incorporate further triangles in a non-hierarchical cell structure of interdependent relationships. A non-hierarchical cell structure opens up further possibilities for firm as well as community.

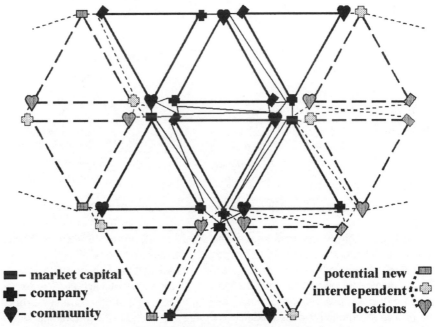

■– market capital
✚– company
♥– community

potential new ▦
interdependent ✤
locations ♥

Figure 4. Non-hierarchical Interdependent Relationships

The solid lines and black shapes in Figure 4 depict existing frameworks of interdependent relationships. The dotted lines and gray shapes depict potential new frameworks.

With the aid of this final model, Figure 4, we can see that there is a greater network of global relationships. As well as the two-dimensional depiction of the model, we may also perceive this framework in three dimensions. As well as the horizontal structures depicted here, we may remark that vertical and diagonal lines in the lattice connect local points to global points also. We can see that interdependence processes therefore cannot be seen as hierarchical. In truth, with such a wide framework, no point can become an apex for long. With such a non-hierarchical conception of relationships, we can see how the needs of geographically static community may also be met, community becoming a global point with enough variation of possible alternatives to counterbalance the geographically indeterminate global village of the markets.

This fourth model gives us an indication of the disequilibrium of Siemens and Wallsend. Both community and, to a lesser extent, company found themselves at the edge of this model. Siemens had the resources to back away from the edge, to seek other interdependent relationships elsewhere, and make new triangles, as represented by the dotted lines in the figure. The wider geographical community of Wallsend did not. The community of Tyneside will be left to attempt to reenter at a new point, probably once more by means of subsidy.

It is to be hoped, however, that this time the subsidy will be better thought out on the part of government, and occur with the participation of several companies, not just one. The model also helps us see how subsidy of community may work. It reminds us that we must consider which point and on which level community may best gain entry or reentry to the framework. To be a long-term part of the network requires a clear understanding between all concerned – firms, communities and market capital, – on what the goals and positioning of investments should be.

We can imagine the constituent parts of a post-BMW era Rover, for example, together with the innumerable supply-chain firms in the automotive and engineering sectors in the English Midlands region, somewhere at the center of this model. Most will be saved from detaching from the framework by a greater number of links with other points, either geographical, in terms of its links to many English communities, or functional, in terms of its links to customers, suppliers and partner firms worldwide. Indeed, the more triangles present in the non-hierarchical lattice, the more potential support each point on each triangle may gain. So much so, that some business relationships may survive, although perceived by outsiders as being without substance. In a theoretical analysis that has parallels to my analysis of the BMW-Rover crisis, Held, discussing the complexity of interdependence and the error of linking political community to nation-state structures, sees political communities as "multiple overlapping networks of interaction."[54]

We may therefore see that in addition to subsidized locations of industrial production, there is a subsidized location of decision also. We may surmise that if there is already a large quantity of existing points near at hand in the framework, then their existence supports the decision to continue economic activity in the area. However, as indicated by the criss-crossing link lines in Figure 4, it is some times difficult to discern how any one point acts upon another, in view of the complexity and manifold variety of the number of relationships in which each is involved. How may we best assess and therefore better calibrate the actions of one individual or group within the framework? How may we be better able to assess the social and economic transaction costs of these relationships? Without a capacity to do so, we may doubt the collective efficacy of the framework. In this respect, Held writes on frameworked links between communities, firms, employees and consumers:

> If such frameworks are to be effective, they need to constitute the basis for a routine and durable understanding among economic partners, for without this it is hard to see how enterprises could function successfully in the context of economic competition and the need to raise funds private or public, for their development.[55]

Held's solution is a UN-based global system of cosmopolitan law. We have already rejected Held's option however, because of its reliance also on nation-state conceptions, and the extent that its approach implies coercive intervention.[56] Let us therefore consider in the next chapter how we may avoid coercive approaches, and how we may encourage greater societal cooperation, by making some suggestions on possible amendments to perceptions and routines in the lobbying process.

NOTES

1. Buckley and Artisien, p. 152.

2. See 'Die 100 größten Unternehmen', 40. Folge (*FAZ* supplement), 7.7.1998. It should be further pointed out that market doubts about the company predated these figures.

3. See Wilfried Feldenkirchen, *Werner von Siemens Erfinder und internationaler Unternehmer* (Berlin: Siemens, 1992), pp. 142-147. Also see map depicting world telegraph lines in 1881, pp. 30-31. Feldenkirchen discusses both the then moral and practical reasoning for setting adequate rates of pay, as well as informal annual consultations at his home between the head of the firm Werner von Siemens with company masters and officials. A pensions scheme for all firm employees was introduced in 1872, the twenty-fifth anniversary of the company. After 30 years of company service, employees were entitled to a pension set at two-thirds of their working wage. Earlier, in 1868, Werner von Siemens had discussed the need to introduce a pension scheme specifically in relation to the company's copper mine near Tiblisi in Georgia.

4. David Marsh, *The New Germany*, p. 129. The cooperation with GEC did not prove to be wholly successful, and in 1998, Siemens and GEC announced the dissolution of dual shareholding arrangements in the two subsidiary companies they had founded jointly following their takeover of Plessey. See 'Siemens und die britische GEC gehen getrennte Wege', *FAZ*, 25.6.1998, p. 19.

5. See Angela Maier, 'Ausländer auf dem Weg an die Spitze', 'Die 100 größten Unternehmen', 40. Folge (*FAZ* supplement), 7.7.1998, p. B 9.

6. 'Funktion zählt mehr als Rang und Titel', Bundsanstalt für Arbeit (ed.), *Uni Magazin Perspektiven für Beruf und Arbeitsmarkt* Sept/Okt 6/96 (Mannheim: Verlag Transmedia 1996), pp. 25-27. Werner von Siemens' vision for his company was for it to establish itself as a "world business." See Feldenkirchen, p. 79.

7. Dietmar Lamparter, 'Auf Bewährung', *Die Zeit*, Nr. 31, 23.7.1998, p. 17. For details of the company's Time Optimized Process program, see company's 1996 annual report: *Siemens AG Jahresbericht 1996*.

8. Dietmar Lamparter, 'Sanierer mit Skrupel', *Die Zeit*, Nr. 47, 12.11.1998, p. 30.

9. Lamparter, *Die Zeit*, Nr. 47, 12.11.1998, p. 30.

10. Compare remarks of Herrhausen on what he himself saw as the political constituency of business. "Without the consent of our employees – the internal public – and our customers – the external public – we cannot achieve our goals." See Herrhausen, 'Wirtschaft und Presse', in *Denken – Ordnen – Gestalten*, pp. 73-79 (p. 73). We may further speculate that Siemens avoids the use of the term "shareholder value" because it was originally formulated by Jack Welch, the head of Siemens' US rival, General Electric. But bearing in mind also Herrhausen's remarks in the same speech cited in this note, that "open conversations end, public conversations begin," the likelihood is that such thoughts are likely to remain speculative only.

11. See ' "Sind wir schell genug?" ' *Spiegel* 7/97, 10.2.1997, pp. 80-84 (p. 81); "Kein Sozialunternehmen," also *Spiegel* 7/97, p. 84. The reports cite the views of member of the supervisory board, Peter von Siemens: "Even a milkman wouldn't bother

opening his corner shop for this sort of profit." The second article title is based on the response of a share analyst, asked whether radical change might lead to the loss of thousands of jobs. He stated that Siemens was no "social support undertaking."

12. 'Siemens verfehlt das Gewinnzeil wegen Halbleitergeschäftes', *FAZ*, 17.7.1998, p. 19.

13. See http://www.siemens.de/annualreport.

14. See *Reuters* news agency report, *FAZ*, 17.7.1998, p. 19. S & P reduced Siemens rating in July 1998, and Moody's downgraded the company in January 1999. See also interview with Alfons Graf: 'Siemens unter Druck: Die Betriebsräte verlangen von den Aktionären Geduld', *Die Zeit*, Nr. 4, 21.1.1999, p. 25. See Lamparter articles: *Die Zeit*, Nr. 31, 23.7.1998, p. 17; *Die Zeit*, Nr. 47, 12.11.1998, p. 30.

15. Lamparter, Fritz Vorholz interview with Maucher 'Big is beautiful', *Die Zeit*, Nr. 29, 9.7.1998, p. 21.

16. See interview with Graf, *Die Zeit*, Nr. 4, 21.1.1999, p. 25.

17. See Leinemann, *Spiegel*, 21/96, pp. 114-126. We can perhaps see reasons for the attractiveness of Schrempp's public profile for the markets summed up by Deutsche Bank and Daimler-Benz supervisory board head, Hilmar Kopper: "I have great respect for his ability to simplify things. Where else can you get that these days? I'm suffocated in complexity,"(p. 123). In contrast, Schrempp's predecessor enjoyed a reputation in the media as a philosopher-businessman who sought consensus. (Although his downfall may have been that he sought the limelight rather more.) See Hans Otto Eglau, *Edzard Reuter* (Düsseldorf: Econ Verlag, 1991). Further examples of difficulties at the onset of Schrempp's tenure: 'Schrempp hält noch weitere gravierende Entscheidungen für nötig', *FAZ*, 12.4.1996, p. 18; 'Die Dasa-Mitarbeiter halten "Dolores für Kolores" ', *FAZ*, 15.9.1995 p. 19.

18. See Mercedes Benz-Koordination/express-Redaktion (eds.), pp. 9-12 (p. 11).

19. This does not mean that these measures were without workforce tensions. Personal acquaintances of the author employed by Siemens' subsidiaries sold off in the printing and dental equipment sectors have been far from enamored by the firm's policy.

20. Sibylle Krause-Burger, 'Ein Beamter als Boß', in *Die neue Elite. Topmanager und Spitzenpolitiker aus der Nähe gesehen* (Düsseldorf: Econ Verlag, 1995), pp. 75-83 (pp. 80-81).

21. See *FAZ*, 17.7.1998, p. 19. Siemens' registration on Wall Street is planned for 2001. See http://www.siemens.de/annualreport.

22. See 'Toyota knüpft Investitionen an EWWU-Beitritt Großbritanniens', *Handelsblatt*, 31.1/1.2.1997, p. 1; Thomas Fischermann, 'Mit Sekt und warmen Worten', *Die Zeit*, Nr. 45, 29.10.1998, p. 37.

23. Fischermann, 'Mit Sekt und warmen Worten'.

24. See Hartmut Schumann, 'Wirtschaftliche Dimensionen der Außenpolitik', in Dieter Blumenwitz et al. (eds.), *Zeitschrift für Politik* Heft 2 Juni 1994 (Cologne: Carl Heymanns Verlag, 1994), pp. 146-156 (p. 147). Schumann cited the usage of the term "insurance premium" by then supervisory board head Hermann Franz, in *Wirtschaftswoche* 45/91, 1.11.1991, pp. 136-7.

25. See 'Siemens schließt Halbleiterwerk im englischen North Tyneside'; 'Briten verbittert über Produktionsschließung von Siemens', *FAZ*, 1.8.1998, p. 14.

26. *FAZ*, 1.8.1998, p. 14.

27. See John Zysman, 'Can Japanese Direct Investment Sustain European Devel-

opment in Electronics?' in Mark Mason and Dennis Encarnation (eds.), *Does Ownership Matter? Japanese Multinationals in Europe* (Oxford: Clarendon Press, 1994), pp. 331-362 (p. 342, p. 348).

28. See Ludwig Siegele, 'Das nächste Problem', *Die Zeit,* Nr. 26, 24.6.1999, p. 25. Like Siemens, Fujitsu had also announced the closure of a solely operated production facility in England, in Prime Minister Blair's Sedgefield constituency. See 'Mit Sekt und warmen Worten', *Die Zeit,* Nr. 45, 29.10.1998, p. 37.

29. Dietmar Lamparter, 'Lauter Gewinner' *Die Zeit,* Nr. 19, 29.4.1998, p. 24.

30. 'Siemens schließt Halbleiterwerk im englischen North Tyneside'; 'Briten verbittert über Produktionsschließung von Siemens', *FAZ,* 1.8.1998, p. 14.

31. 'Die Größten Spinner', *Spiegel,* 32/96, 5.8.1996, pp. 22-33.

32. Remarks cited in 'Kohl fordert weitere Hilfen für Ostdeutschland', *FAZ,* 18.11.1992, p. 15; see also Krause-Burger, 'Ein Beamter als Boß'.

33. See 'Siemens baut neue Chip-Fabrik in Newcastle statt in Dresden oder Villach', *Süddeutsche Zeitung* 5/6.8.1995, p. 23. Incentives supposedly given to Siemens to persuade it to invest at Wallsend as opposed to alternatives in Dresden or Villach in Austria included 100% deduction on building costs and on corporation and capital gains tax, and a ten-year waiver on the payment of business rates. Even the Saxons in Dresden could not compete with the temptations of such Anglo-Saxon "free-market" incentives of a tax- and rate-free site, along with lower wages, lower company national insurance contributions and lower training costs. The then President of the British Board of Trade Michael Heseltine rejoiced over the prospect of jobs success for Britain's once-thriving industrial north.

34. See Pierer's view on cooperation with other companies in his 'Letter to Shareholders', http://www.siemens.de/annualreport. There is nothing new in this strategy. Indeed, the overambitiousness of Siemens' wish to retain its independence in chip production can be seen even more starkly if compared to its cooperation activity in a high technology sector of a previous era. Together with AEG, Siemens formed the Gesellschaft für drahtlose Telegraphie m.b.H, better known as Telefunken, in 1903. The motivation for this then very high techology alliance was to be able to compete with the British firm Marconi. The founding of Telefunken, however, did not, by any means prevent the continued high levels of competition between Siemens and AEG in other sectors. See Gerhart Jacob-Wende, *Deutsche Elektroindustrie in Lateinamerika: Siemens und A.E.G. (1890-1914)* (Stuttgart: Klett-Cotta, 1982), pp. 33-34. See also Cawson, in Wallace and Young (eds.), pp. 185-205. Cawson implies that firms in the same sector may not be competitors (p. 185).

35. Dietmar Lamparter, 'Vollgas zurück', *Die Zeit,* Nr. 13, 23.3.2000, pp. 23-24.

36. See 'Joachim Milberg trägt an einer schweren Hypothek', *FAZ,* 17.3.2000, p. 16.

37. See Lamparter, 'Wer schleppt BMW ab?' *Die Zeit,* Nr. 7, 1.2.1999, pp. 19-20; Lamparter and Thomas Fischermann, 'Zu spät geschaltet', *Die Zeit,* Nr. 7, 1.2.1999, p. 20.

38. See 'Das ist der Gast', *Spiegel* 6/99, 8.2.1999, p. 92. Article quotes Schoch: "We cannot shut the Longbridge plant."

39. 'Barbarians at Bavaria's Gates', *The Economist,* 13.2.1999, pp. 23-25 (p. 23).

40. See Lamparter, *Die Zeit,* Nr. 7, 1.2.1999.

41. See Lamparter articles: *Die Zeit,* Nr. 7, 1.2.1999; 'Die Fitmacher, *Die Zeit,* Nr.

27, 1.7.1999, pp. 17-18.

42. See 'Auch bei zweiter U-Bahn-Linie in Schanghai deutsche Hilfe anbieten' in *Woche im Bundestag*, 24. Jahrgang Nr. 16, 28.9.1994, p. 17.

43. See Thomas Fischermann, 'Schmerzlicher Abschied: Das Dienstleistungsland Großbritannien verliert seine Industrie', *Die Zeit*, Nr. 13, 23.3.2000, p. 25; 'Vorwurf von Verrat und Sabotage', *Süddeutsche Zeitung*, 3.4.2000, p. 26; Will Hutton, 'There goes the family silver again', http://www.guardianunlimited.co.uk/ford/article/0,2763,219330,00.-html, 30.4.2000; Hugo Young, 'There's a conspiracy of silence about our over-valued pound', http://www.guardianunlimited.co.uk/ford/article/0,2763,219329,00.html, 4.5.2000; Nicholas Bannister, 'The end of the production line', http://www.guardian-unlimited.co.uk/ford/article/0,2763,219339,00.html, 10.5.2000.

44. See Lamparter, *Die Zeit*, Nr. 13, 23.3.2000.

45. Sophie Barker, 'MPs grill BMW over Rover deal', *http://www.telegraph.co.uk*, Issue 1770, 30.3.2000.

46. 'BMW gibt sich als stiller Sieger', *FAZ*, 30.4.1998, p. 20.

47. See Sophie Barker 'Rescuer's figures add up to rough ride', Barker, Maurice Weaver, George Jones, 'Rover saved by £10 sale to Phoenix', both *http://www.telegraph.co.uk*, Issue 1811, 10.5.2000. As the last title indicates, BMW sold Rover to the consortium for the symbolic sum of £10. BMW also agreed to loan the new company 1500 million.

48. See 'Wem gehört BMW?', *Die Zeit*, Nr. 7, 1.2.1999, p. 20; See Lamparter, '*Die Zeit*, Nr. 7, 1.2.1999, pp. 19-20.

49. See 'Ford will BMW übernehmen', *Spiegel Online*, 20.3.2000, http://194.163.254.145/wirtschaft/maerkte/0,1518,69644,00.html.

50. On assuming office as head of Daimler-Benz, Schrempp stated that he was striving for a "democracy of creativity ... everybody can participate in discussion. None-theless, ultimately there will be the dictatorship of decision." See 'Kommandowechsel auf einem Supertanker', *Handelsblatt*, 26/27.5.1995, p. 2.

51. See, for example, resentment of dissident shareholder representative Ekkehard Wenger following loss of court case he pursued to stop Daimler's share-options scheme evident in following quote: "Whoever takes Daimler to court in Stuttgart has to reckon that the case won't end there." See 'Wenger verliert auch Berufung gegen Daimler-Benz', *FAZ*, 13.8.1998, p. 16. See also criticism at last shareholders meeting of Daimler-Benz in 'Aktionäre fordern Änderung der Vergütung für Führungskräfte', *FAZ*, 28.5.1998, p. 27.

52. See Penrose citing Kaldor's 'The Equilibrium of the Firm', *Economic Journal*, Vol. XLIV, no. 173, March 1934, pp. 13-14.

53. See Linklater, p. 2.

54. Held, p. 225.

55. Held, p. 253.

56. See Held, p. 255, p. 258; see earlier discussion in Chapter 6 of this book.

12

The Multilateral Practices of Lobbying and the Privatization of Democracy

Let us examine now how private organizations' substantial role in growing transnational and transinstitutional interdependence might be linked more effectively with the needs and wills of communities. To do so, I would argue in favor of an adaptation of perceptions and practices of nation-state lobbying processes, incorporating a formal recognition of interest group rights, as a supplement to accepted rights of the individual in the democratic process. I will argue that these group rights in society will also entail duties.

I have titled this chapter "The Multilateral Practices of Lobbying and the Privatization of Democracy," because as we shall see, it is not just private business, employer and employee organizations, or interest groups that carry out lobbying, but public institutions too: in the EU for example, Commission, member state and sub-state level government. In this respect, lobbying can be understood as a part of the ongoing negotiation process. Furthermore, as we have seen in this book already, global interdependence is such that we cannot limit our discussion to the geographical borders of the EU. Hence, although I focus on European lobbying, we should bear in mind the permeability of geopolitical perceptions and practices (EU and member state institutions, along with firms from Europe lobby world-wide).[1]

In the first section, we will focus on how private organizations seek to influence society, and how society seeks to exert influence on private organizations. Having done so, in the second section I will emphasize the importance of a consideration of the scope of firms' activity to better understand and conduct the democratic process. An appreciation of TNE activity can help us find approaches towards wider frameworks that can better account for the role of business in the organization and governance of community. Nonetheless, in the third section, we will see that the legacies of prejudice about the role of transnational business still have to be addressed before we can do so. Having seen how these legacies might be overcome, I will sketch out a possible means providing for both the legitimization of the role of geographical community in business, as well as a business role in the community, as an example of the recognition, incorporation and active participation of sector group interests in democratic processes.

Seeing the need to legitimize lobbying channels for business and interest groups in general, what we might term as the privatization of democracy, will not only conclude our consideration of transnational issues of social coherence in transnational parameters. It can help us on two further points. First, the conscious incorporation of intergroup recognition and dialogue in democratic processes may better accommodate ethnic heterogeneity within states. Growing ethnic heterogeneity within states is an accompaniment to transnational economic developments. Second, it may aid the individual and collective processes both of European integration and of German unification, and help understand these in terms of multipolar and non-hierarchical parameters. The success of German unification, for example, depends ultimately not only upon greater private investment in Eastern Germany, but also upon the achievement of better understanding between Eastern and Western Germans.[2]

HOW PRIVATE ORGANIZATIONS AND PUBLIC INSTITUTIONS INFLUENCE EACH OTHER

In this section, we will see that the nature of the lobbying process makes it difficult to obtain a clear picture of whether interest group activity has a positive or negative effect upon the collective good.

Within this picture, we will see that both private business organizations and public institutions seek proximity to the other, in a mutual recognition of the influence that their actions have upon one another and society as a whole. However, processes of dialogue mostly occur without publicity, and so we may observe the tendency to display a general self-defense reflex in public statements by those involved in the political process. There is evidence on a daily basis in news media coverage of a reluctance to admit to doubt about one's self or one's group in public, shown in the tendency to blame the other side when agreement is not reached.

Thus, on the basis of the evidence offered in this chapter, I would suggest that both business organizations and public institutions have profound influence upon the behavior of the other, but the nature of their activity risks missing the general point: establishing the needs of society as a whole. We may liken the activity of business organizations and public institutions to that of two peacocks fanning their feathers in front of the bored hen, both failing to acknowledge the utility of the other, and both forgetting the hen. Were they to try to discover new forms of behavior, promoting cooperation between them, they might well discover that the hen would be able to make considerable use of the both of them, more often, to the mutual satisfaction of all parties.

We can see that there is a need throughout Europe to overcome perceptions and techniques of lobbying practice as discussed by Kurt Sontheimer in relation to West Germany:

Despite the solid foundation of pluralistic interests in post-war German society, its factual situation has not been dealt with properly theoretically. German political thinking, with its statist tradition, still finds discussion of "corporate powers" uncomfortable. It is still believed that ... the influence of societal interests upon political decisions is illegitimate.

Business associations also contribute to this situation, as they constantly portray their specific interests cloaked in the common good, and act in public as if heeding their interests would serve the good of all.[3]

In post-war Federal Germany, in the aftermath of the Weimar disaster, Article 21 (1) *Grundgesetz* outlined the status of parties as legitimate instruments for the articulation of public opinion. However, no such provision exists in the *Grundgesetz* for interest groups. In this respect, Ulrich von Alemann has claimed that there is a prudery in discussion and treatment of interest groups.[4] Yet these groups are looked to by the media and legislators alike for confirmation, or condemnation, of policy. As is the case within one member state of the EU, a similar trend can be discerned in the Community as a whole. At the EU level, any lobbying effort that is seen as European guarantees the best prospect of success.[5] At the national level, proposals lobbied for portrayed as serving the national interest have best prospect of success. There is an institutional forum for interest groups at the European level, the Economic and Social Committee (ESC), but it is the Commission or national governments as the hubpoints of the legislative process at their respective levels that are the focus of lobbying activity. As William Wallace has pointed out, "Interest groups and campaigning organizations naturally tend to play one level of government off against each other to their best advantage, without observing abstract principles too closely."[6]

In the case of large TNEs, for example, some 45 company heads have found membership in the ERT to be a useful discussion arena and lobbying platform. According to Cowles, ERT members meet with the new Council presidency at the beginning of every six-month term, and additional meetings occur where the occasion arises.[7] However, like other European business lobbying groups (see below), the ERT is a self-electing group, and bearing out Wallace's point, there is no point of principle to membership, and companies may see better prospects of return in lobbying elsewhere. In this respect, we may note that Europe's fourth largest company, VW, with production sites of significance to many communities inside and outside the EU, is not represented on the ERT. VW boss Ferdinand Piëch exploits his close relationship to German Chancellor Schröder instead.[8]

We may link Wallace's point with my earlier suggestion of a necessary modification of our understanding of corporatism. I suggested in "The Coalition of Interests between Business and the Community in Germany," in Chapter 9, that we conceive of corporations in Germany as forces that provide key support to *society* as a whole. In international society, we have seen that TNEs are acting increasingly without regard to state borders. TNEs, along with other transnational interest groups, are integral parts of a framework of intertwined negotiation processes, where they themselves may be the centers of decision in the first instance, deciding which negotiation table – local, regional, national or transnational – offers them the best prospect of return.[9]

We should bear in mind that in the light of the mass and complexity of decisions to be taken, legislators desperate for information but too pressed for time and/or resources to conduct their own research may become overly dependent on interest group lobbyists.[10] Indeed, in presenting itself to the public, the European Commission has stated that in preparing a proposal, it "listens to governments, industry, trade unions, special interest groups and technical experts before completing its final draft."[11] We can perhaps understand such an explicit admission of its malleability if we recall that the Commission's powers have been given by the member states' governments, only for the latter to criticize the former for daring to act like them as a result. Consequentially, the Commission is a body not held in high public esteem, and is thus perhaps more dependent on interest groups for legitimacy than any other public institution in the EU.[12]

In Brussels, with both Commission directorate staff and European parliamentarians the objects of the lobbyists' attention, a highly specialized and differentiated network of organizational and private company representative offices has evolved. Despite their affiliations to the pan-European business organization, UNICE, national business organizations such as the BDI also maintain their own offices in Brussels.[13] Through the advent of the SEA, the activity of national business organizations increasingly reflects overlapping agendas. They often find out about EU activity from individual firms. Indeed, Daimler's office in Brussels has more employees than that of UNICE. Additionally, reflecting the overall flexible approach, UNICE is becoming increasingly dominated by the TNE agenda, rather than reflecting concerns of businesses within states via affiliated national organizations. Since 1990, TNEs based inside and outside the EU have constituted the UNICE Advisory and Support Group.[14]

Within the EU, Kohler-Koch has judged that states' governments remain the "main interlocutors of interest groups, because their positions are decisive."[15] But we may recall her point, that we considered in Chapter 7, that the Community does not function hierarchically.[16] We can see furthermore that there can be no homogenous concept of state affairs, let alone Community affairs. Indeed, as state and Community institutions display differentiated, contradictory behavior among themselves, along horizontal as well as vertical levels of governance, we may doubt Kohler-Koch's judgement whether the positions of state governments are decisive on all issues.[17] This applies in the field of "foreign policy" too. Ministries once concerned with internal affairs are increasingly directing attention to external relations. In Germany, for example, two-thirds of total annual Federal government expenditure in this area (just under DM 12 billion) is not in the Foreign Ministry budget, but in the remit of other ministries. There are a total of 250 desks concerned with external affairs in other ministries compared to only 68 in the Foreign Office. Furthermore, the *Länder* have more representatives in Brussels than the Federal Foreign Office.[18] We can thus see the trend to a domestication of foreign policy.

The dynamic to greater global interdependence is having marked effects upon the nature of government. States form only a small minority in the greater cast of international actors, together with 300 intergovernmental organizations, 10,000 nongovernmental organizations and 40,000 transnational private companies.[19] ERT Chairman Maucher, also president of the International Chamber of Commerce, has explicitly highlighted the limitations of state-based perceptions in a 1998 interview. He declared "European thinking" to be "local thinking."[20]

Nonetheless, at the EU level, as Kohler-Koch has pointed out, the specialization in the Commission's Directorates General as well as in the Departmental Councils (i.e. ECOFIN, Environment, Agriculture, etc.) has served to facilitate the growth of narrowly based interest group organization rather than groups pursuing broader aims.[21] Accordingly, in the light of, first, the lobbyist's tendency to select which arena is most suited for the lobbying purpose; second, the specialization of lobbying effort; third, the sheer scale of lobbying effort, we may be skeptical whether the collective good is served by these compartmentalized efforts. The lobbyist deploys information shaped according to a preformed sectoral opinion, idea or need. Therefore, we may surmise that opinions, ideas or needs developed on the basis of general information are lacking, because where there is a surplus of information, we can never know definitively if the decision reached is correct.

Thus, we may conclude this section by noting that there is indeed substantial influence between private organization and public institution on each other. However, variance of participation points and participants in any single instance would seem to count against any guarantee in the wider global framework of the advancement of a collective good.[22]

Furthermore, in the light of growing specialization in the lobbying process, discussed above, we may agree strongly with Kohler-Koch's suggestion that "to associate with like-minded groups across borders is an act of integration, which ... necessarily provides disintegrating effects in the home environment."[23] Accordingly, it would seem to be unlikely that any further approaches to transnational integration can reach any more substantial improvement relevant to ordinary citizens' lives with additional public institutional organization at the supranational level, in the EU, or EU-affiliated bodies. On a wider scale, the 188 UN members can hardly aspire to be united with each other if the term "united nation" hardly applies to any one of them internally.[24] However, we should not forget that the association of like-minded interests at the transnational level, discussed by Kohler-Koch, has also had positive effects. The achievement of greater inner-state integration by curtailing the association of like-minded groups at the transnational level is undesirable as well as untenable. To partially offset the effects of inner-state differentiation therefore, we should try to find ways of legitimizing the lobbying process at the international level, to provide for mechanisms of mediation between groups of expertise.[25]

If there is greater dialogue across frameworks within which this process takes place, then we can suppose to know more definitively if the decision reached by a more limited number of participants at certain participation points is correct, or if it is not, how it can be corrected. However, before we do so, let us use a theoretical analysis of the lobbying process at nation-state level to correct insufficiencies of studies of the international policy process.

THE NEGLECTED RECOGNITION OF THE ROLE OF BUSINESS IN COMMUNITY GOVERNANCE

To try to find an approach towards solving the problem of legitimizing the transnational lobbyist, let us turn, as an initial guide, to a theoretical analysis of the domestic lobbying process. James Rosenau has discussed a model of an imaginary third legislature, in which besides the actual bicameral parliamentary system common in most liberal representative democracies, there is room for the leaderships of unions, firms, employers associations and citizens groups to make their views known. In discussing this model in a previous era, at the beginning of the seventies, Arnulf Baring saw the lobbying process regarding foreign policy matters as being much more limited in policy formulation, either providing support for the government or rejecting it.[26]

As we saw in the previous section, tracing the domestication of foreign policy, times have changed, and we may extend this model now to the transnational and transinstitutional arena. Nonetheless, other commentators have only partially seen links between the domestic and international policy process. Thus, practical applications of exploiting and adapting these links have so far been missed. The role of TNEs has been overlooked. In his much-praised recent work on international political theory, *The Transformation of Political Community*, Andrew Linklater, while arguing for the necessity of ending unjust exclusion practices and the desirability of overcoming "asymmetries of power and wealth," overlooks how practical economic actors may cooperate in this transformation.[27]

Robert Putnam, citing examples of Daimler-Benz, Japan's Mitsubishi and the USA-based IBM, at the "frontier of economic development" in his more practically based analysis, has identified resulting government policy dilemmas resulting from interdependence. However, while identifying the need for political policy makers to play "two-level games," reconciling the demands of domestic and international politics, Putnam ignores the fact that these companies, as we have seen in the previous chapters, are also players in such "games."[28] TNEs are at the frontier of political development also.

Sarah Collinson has tried to extend Putnam's two-level game model in respect to EU commercial policies, to incorporate a third level, her stated aim being to bring conceptual frameworks from international relations theory together with an empirical investigation of EU policy making and governance. But as she herself admits, her hierarchically couched analysis (level 1 = international level; level 2 = European Union level; level 3 = national level) fails to take account of the complexity of policy execution and negotiations between various competing and conflicting EU institutions. Furthermore, I find her discussion of EU commercial policy most frustrating because of its solely institutional, *non-commercial* focus. It would seem to me that a consideration of the core role of business actors must be an integral part of the "research agenda," as Collinson herself describes it.[29]

Moreover, we should remember that these "policy games" are in fact complicated political processes, becoming automatic at times, with implications for the lives of millions of people. In response to the complicated implications of these processes, many might be tempted to give up on democracy. It is sometimes difficult to discern how the wills of individuals affect these processes.[30] Consequently, we should take account of all the players in the game. *Not*, I would emphasize, to seek to bar TNEs from playing. By virtue of their creation of material wealth and jobs, they are too valuable, too skilled. Indeed, their ambition and organization have made the multilevel game possible. Accordingly, their skills should be accorded tangible recognition with a chair at the table (rather than have them stand behind one or several others, putting them off, or giving some players advantages over other players). In recognizing the contribution of TNEs to the game, this will serve to increase chances that the game will be continued successfully, and lessen the risk that other players will be forcibly removed by TNEs, impatient that the game is not being played as they envisaged it.

Furthermore, in making TNEs welcome full players, all the players will be better able to assess and give a candid consideration of everybody's weaknesses as well as strengths, to find techniques to prevent some players from having to miss a turn, or having to drop out altogether. Above and beyond this, we may hope also that this process of dialogue, incorporating the practical transnational organizational expertise of TNEs, could identify practical steps, as Linklater puts it, "to ameliorate the condition of the most vulnerable groups in world society."[31] In doing so, we may strengthen democratic processes in the global context. We may also hope to develop a greater understanding of how individuals may better follow how their actions influence political processes. Greater understanding reached in processes of dialogue will lead more people to see that these processes are not impervious to their wills, and therefore hopefully encourage greater societal participation.

However, to do so, we must first overcome the difficulties in legitimizing the lobbying role of interest groups in general. These are considerable. Who would take part? International pressure groups such as Greenpeace, for example, may very well be supported by traditional liberal left proponents of democracy, but their campaigning methods, whether reliant on spectacular direct action or on mail shots, have no legitimacy if seen in parameters of liberal parliamentary democracy. In the light of these, one commentator has claimed that Greenpeace's success in pressuring Shell not to sink the Brent Spar North Sea oil rig ended all "grassroots democratic ideals."[32]

I cannot pretend to be able to resolve such difficulties here. The resolution of eligibility criteria for transnational debate participation itself requires debate, constituted by as many of the greater cast of international actors cited in the previous section as possible. But in the light of the evidence considered in this chapter regarding the potential benefits of transnational economic activity, we can and should here address some of the difficulties of legitimizing the role of the business lobby.

OVERCOMING HINDRANCES TO COMMUNITY RECOGNITION OF TRANSNATIONAL BUSINESS

In Chapter 9, we saw how the incorporation of codetermination in German company law had strengthened the workings of business and contributed to the strength and stability of democracy within FRG society as a whole. As a corollary to this in this section, I would like to propose how societies world-wide may formally acknowledge, and thus be better able to make use of, private organizations' substantial role in frameworks of transnational and transinstitutional interdependence. In this section, I would argue that such an acknowledgement would redress past behavioral patterns, which have resulted in a partial confrontation between the interests of business and community. As we shall see, this will demand an exchange of mutual signals, symbolic and practical, on the part of both business and community, recognizing the worth of the other. We could see this acknowledgement serving the needs of a greater societal recognition of interdependence. We could perhaps envisage interlinked symbolic memorandums of understanding of codetermination by community in company, and company in community.

I would suggest that we may understand how to compensate for tendencies towards confrontation between business and community by tracing problems of noncooperational behavior present on both sides back to popular distrust of the role of TNEs in Europe during the seventies. I would suggest that this has resulted in behavioral tendencies in both community and TNEs not to acknowledge the validity of the other.

In "The global business application of the German consensus model," in Chapter 9, we have already considered arguments against the demonization of TNEs. Cowles discusses the origins of this demonization in Europe. She traces perceptions at Community level, echoing views in the Community at large during the seventies of TNEs as a potential threat to democratic society, particularly US-based firms, by virtue of their larger size in comparison to their European counterparts. These views culminated in 1980, with the EEC Commission's proposal to introduce measures of codetermination in companies, known as the Vredeling initiative, after Henk Vredeling, then commissioner for social affairs. The prospect of this directive being passed by the European Council led TNEs to organize to oppose the measure. UNICE was deemed too unwieldy and inefficient to serve their purpose. In response to what they perceived as a threat to their operations, a group including executives from BP, Fiat, Ford, Hoechst, IBM, ICI, Shell, Solvay and Unilever met in Brussels in 1980, a further objective of the meeting being to improve the efficacy of UNICE. The group became known as the European Enterprise Group. Other business interest groups also organized in reaction to the threat of European regulation: the EU Committee of the American Chamber of Commerce, and the ERT. The formation of these bodies marked a significant escalatory step in industrial lobbying organization in the EU. The membership transcends the EU in interrelated networks (many members of the European Enterprise Group are members of one of the other organizations).[33]

Thus, as a reaction to their methods being impugned by elements across the rest of European society, TNEs began to assume a group identity of their own.[34] Indeed, Cowles records the views of a figure she identifies only as a multinational enterprise representative, tracing the origins of this new transnational bonding, using the pronoun "we" not to mean his own company but TNEs as a group.[35]

Here, I would argue that we may draw useful pointers towards the extension of transinstitutional democracy by seeing that techniques advanced to overcome prejudices between ethnic groups may give us insights into overcoming potentially damaging perceptions of the role of TNEs in community and TNEs' perceptions of the role of community. In this respect, I would suggest that a mutual presumption of worth on both sides, in a process of dialogue, is a stage towards intergroup cooperation that can bring mutual benefits. Dialogue is the first stage in overcoming perceptions in one group of past injustices (perceived or actual) perpetrated by the other. In the absence of dialogue, the identity of one group cannot reflect the other's position, and it may evolve into a form that damages both sides. As Charles Taylor has remarked, the identity can turn into a "struggle against the things …significant others want to see in us."[36]

As a further example, we may see the views of Keith Richardson, an ERT spokesman, also as reflecting perceptions of TNEs of themselves as a single group. His remarks would seem to indicate that the identity of the group is strengthened by emphasizing the utility of the group at the expense of outsiders, – in this case, public institutions. Richardson has maintained:

Industry has a certain legitimacy at the European level. … Society needs the wealth that industry creates, and the individual companies that make up industry are directly accountable to customers, employees, shareholders, bankers and to political and social pressures of every shape and size. Such direct accountability is curiously absent from Europe's political institutions. When, for example, the European exchange rate mechanism fell apart on a summer's day some years ago it was a waste of time asking, "Who was in charge? Who was responsible? Who lost his job and is now in the streets begging for his bread?"[37]

We can adduce further evidence for damaging behavior patterns impeding dialogue, on the part of both public institutions and private business organizations, in that neither have promoted the functionality of the EU forum for intersectoral dialogue, the ESC.[38] The Maastricht Treaty weakened the ESC.[39] Nor do business interest groups appear to take the body seriously, a clear indication of the body's neglect given by the lack of first-rank business figures nominated to it.[40] I would suggest that both sides' shoddy treatment of the ESC shows the disinclination to communicate with the other, rather than the inappropriateness of the body itself. Were the latter in fact the case, the forum would have been disbanded or reformed years ago. The body's ill-use borders on the realm of outright non-cooperation, as elements on both sides indulge instead in megaphone diplomacy tactics with the public in between.

Indeed, a member of Jacques Santer's cabinet has argued in an interview with Cowles that "big companies are not going to create jobs in Europe."[41] This may be so, and we may indeed note with approval that to redress the balance of its closeness to large business lobbyists, the EU Commission has increasingly taken to finding out about the needs of small and medium-sized businesses.[42] But we may doubt whether the Commission's parallel practices of seeking to exploit differences between big business and smaller business interests, in Cowles' words, "to encourage industry positions closer to the Commission's liking,"[43] facilitate the collective good of the Community's economy. Such techniques are not "encouragement" however. They are coercion. I would argue that the Commission and the Council as representatives of community should at least demonstrate a preparedness to investigate methods of job creation with TNEs, and not dismiss any possibility out of hand. A process of dialogue may also redress cost-cutting pressures from big companies on smaller and medium sized supplier firms.

This is not to say that a process of dialogue does not occur. But as we have already seen, there is no audit on the effects of the dialogue. ERT members, for example, meet with the new Council presidency at the beginning of every six-month term, and additional meetings occur where the occasion arises.[44] However the content and aim of the meetings receive no wide media attention or transsocietal debate. What do they talk about?

As we have seen, the membership of ERT is not alone a representative sample of business interests, even within the narrower scope of TNE criteria. If we consider figures for Europe's 100 largest companies ranked in terms of turnover in 1997, only an arbitrary cross-section of 24 make up the total number of 45 ERT members. However, this cross-section of 24 men (all 45 ERT members are men) oversaw a total of just under DM 1,500 billion turnover in 1997.[45] Therefore, it is in the wider public interest to hear what they have to say. After all, it seems to me that the ERT plan for the internal market can be judged to have been an overwhelming success. On the other hand, a cross-section of a group making up roughly one-half of Europe's inhabitants, women, may wish to ask ERT members why all of them are men. The exclusion of women from elite business circles is even more comprehensive than in the political arena, an area also dominated by men. However, given a greater process of dialogue, both sides may be able to find out better how to serve the general interest better.

The reinforcement of public institutions by businesses taking on formal responsibility would be no dramatic departure. We have seen how private companies are important parts of our community. Where they are missing, there is less sense of community. Moreover, it would seem that awareness of interdependence of economic and social interests is becoming clearer. Maucher's interview comments cited in Chapter 11 give us an indication of the existence of a growing awareness within companies of their role. Communities could give further encouragement to companies to admit to their role as an integral and valued part of a free and wealthy societal order.

But in the light of the evidence so far, what could be the criteria for establishing interest groups' rights in the transnational policy process? There are all sorts of criteria for the influence that a company has upon society. We may eliminate quantitative criteria in determining whether private organizations should be accorded recognition as valued participants in the public policy process. Company size and profit change constantly, and size criteria would rule out small business organization from participation. Accordingly, we must seek qualitative criteria for participation. In the last section of this chapter, I will make some suggestions, which will be founded upon a mutual exchange: on one hand a recognition by private organization of the duties owed to the community, on the other hand, the community's extension of an official recognition of interest group rights.

In this section, I have argued that the facilitation of greater public recognition of the worth of business activity may not only strengthen democracy but strengthen democratic practices of business also. I would define this as a greater mutual recognition of the rights and duties brought by companies' activity in society. I would argue that were such a conception to become more widespread, it might help overcome the frequent mutual lack of understanding brought by often diverse needs of employers and employed, which have constantly hindered the establishment of greater social coherence in Europe.

On the basis of our understanding of transnational economic activity, and recalling Rosenau's conception of an imaginary third chamber, we can make some suggestions about how we might conceive of such a forum in transnational reality. In line with my emphasis that we do not require any further level of supranational public institutional organization, our conception should not be so that it exists as an institution housed in a building, but so that it exists firmly in the imagination. However, how may we extend this imagined construction from the narrower abstract conceptions of political science to make it more appealing to interest groups and individuals in society? In short what could the mutual incentive be for such a commitment to follow such a code of practices?

TOWARDS A FRAMEWORK ACCOUNTING FOR THE ROLE OF BUSINESS IN THE GOVERNANCE OF COMMUNITY

In this section, we can state baldly that the most effective incentive that will encourage the participation of private interest groups in public policy process will be money.

We could envisage the introduction of a democracy tax. Companies with a level of employee representation and/or a preparedness to participate in processes of democratic dialogue with the wider public could be rewarded with lower levels of corporate taxation. We could envisage that communities inviting a private organization's participation in policy processes would conduct an audit scheme based on qualitative criteria on the suitability of the organization as a potential democratic participant. The qualitative criteria could be established by wide-ranging dialogue within the community. As well as financial incentives, we could see that firms would have a further incentive to take part, knowing that obtaining the audit would make them more appealing to their customers. We could envisage the audit having a similar kind of benchmarking effect in democratic terms as audits conducted under the aegis of the International Organization for Standardization (ISO). Such audits are seen as beneficial to a company in regulating its relationship with its peers. The most commonly known are the generic titles ISO 9000, applying to quality management, and the more recent ISO 14000, applying to environmental management. As ISO itself points out, ISO's management systems do not define the content of the processes, merely an understanding of the mechanisms necessary to ensure its optimum attainment: "Both ISO 9000 and ISO 14000 concern the way an organization goes about its work, and not directly the result of this work. In other words, they both concern processes, and not products."[46]

I would argue that this auditing step, or something like it, is an urgent necessity. As Svein Andersen and Tom Burns have pointed out, although legislative and political responsibility remains formally with institutions, their practical authority is declining.[47] It is difficult for states to be signatories to agreements on pollution, for example, when they are not the direct beneficiaries of material wealth that accrues from practices that damage the environment. Nor are states often in the position to directly ensure compliance on these matters. But in an interdependent relationship, states and communities within these states, along with TNEs, may see compelling reasons why all parties in international society should participate in negotiating an ethical set of principles, which could cut the abuse of human and global resources, and set long-term goals of their elimination.

In terms of general public opinion, obligations to wider humanity are sensed in our knowledge of famine and other natural disaster world-wide. There is a long history, as Watson points out, of non-state bodies such as religious organizations being agents of obligation to wider humanity, and not just those inside a more narrowly defined parameter of geographical jurisdiction.[48] Perhaps we can apply this to companies too.

The principles, as opposed to interests that states declare themselves to follow, are expressed in contractual obligations in international law. Can we extend this form of regulation to apply just as much to companies too? Can there be a collectively agreed ethical form of conduct for companies? In view of the combination of a potential wide range of responses from individual persons and companies and interdependence, can there be an underlying ethical framework for business operations? In view of the arguments in this chapter on transnational and transinstitutional interdependence, I would argue that there could be. Such an ethical framework may not provide a solution to problems in itself, but it could help establish benchmarks as a foundation against individual insecurities that themselves are instrumental in causing divisive behavior.

In this respect, we could recall that interdependence in the community of states found its expression despite the Cold War in the Helsinki agreement, where Soviet bloc states were also signatories to commitments upholding individual human rights. The Helsinki agreement and the subsequent CSCE process can be seen to have provided a means for dissident groups to articulate opposition across Eastern Europe. Charter 77 in Czechoslovakia was perhaps the most prominent example. Thus, can we perhaps envisage a future sort of Helsinki agreement where transnational companies also commit themselves to undertakings embodying similar principles as made by governments at Helsinki? This is not to say that a transnational company should in any way be compared with a totalitarian regime. Nevertheless an external commitment would be of significant value in spreading responsibility.

In this chapter, we have focussed on transnational influence activity; but with our emphasis on non-hierarchical aspects of transnational processes, we can conceive of access points to Rosenau's imaginary third chamber not only at transparent transnational levels, but at local, regional and nation-state levels also. We would do well to move *our* interests groups out of the lobby, whether at local, national or supranational levels, and place them in the light of a spacious debating chamber founded upon agreed ethical principles so that we might foster better a process of coherent dialogue with greater public accountability. Let us now turn to linking this thought with the findings of this book as a whole.

NOTES

1. Cowles, in Wallace and Young (eds.), p. 132, for example, reports 14 ERT members meeting with French Prime Minister Edouard Balladur to emphasise the urgency of the Uruguay Round of GATT negotiations.

2. I discuss these issues in greater detail in *Post-National Patriotism*, the companion volume to this work.

3. Kurt Sontheimer, *Gründzüge des politischen Systems der Bundesrepublik Deutschland* (Munich: Piper, 1989), pp. 185-186; see also Ulrich von Alemann, *Organisierte Interessen in der Bundesrepublik* (Opladen: Leske + Budrich, 1987), pp. 16-17.

4. Von Alemann, p. 36.

5. See Wolfgang A. Dietz and Christiane Glatthaar, *Das Räderwerk der EG-Kommission* (Bonn: Economica Verlag, 1991), p. 169. As a specific example, Cawson, in Wallace and Young (eds.), p. 199, reports that in 1995, Philips arranged a visit of Commission staff to the company's Eastern European production centers to underline the

company's commitment to EU policy on bolstering former Communist states' economies.

6. W. Wallace, *Regional Integration*, p. 79.

7. Cowles, p. 131-132. Members listed p. 138.

8. See, for example, Wolfgang Hoffmann and Roland Kirbach, 'Kontakthof der Macht', *Die Zeit*, Nr. 28, 8.7.1999, pp. 21-22.

9. See also W. Wallace, *Regional Integration*, p. 49.

10. At the nation-state level see Hans-Peter Ullmann, *Interessenverbände in Deutschland* (Frankfurt/Main: Suhrkamp, 1988), p. 269; at the EU level, Cawson, p. 198.

11. http://europa.eu.int/inst/en/com.htm#work.

12. Kohler-Koch in Kreile (ed.), p. 111-112; Dietz et al., p. 166.

13. See Wolfgang Wessels, 'Growth of Multi-Level Networks', in Wallace and Young (eds.), pp. 17-41 (p. 31). On the relationship of Commission to interest groups, see Irène Bellier, 'The Commission as an Actor: An Anthropologists View' in the same volume, pp. 91-115. Logically, she finds that lobbyists' influence is greater "if they are active ... when the decision is being prepared" (p. 110).

14. Cowles, p. 132.

15. See Kohler-Koch, in Wallace and Young (eds.), p. 60. Kohler-Koch applies her judgement to issues covered by QMV on the Council.

16. Kohler-Koch, in Wallace and Young (eds.), p 53. See also section 'The European Union Treaty' in Chapter 7 of this book.

17. At the EU level, this was most ironically illustrated in 1998 by the circa DM 2 billion annual subsidy given to tobacco farmers in the Community on one hand, and the ban on tobacco advertising agreed in the EU on the other. See 'Das Europäische Parlament entscheidet über ein Werbeverbot für Tabakwaren', *FAZ*, 13.5.1998, p. 6; 'Grüne Stengel für den blauen Dunst', *FAZ*, 14.8.1998, p. 17.

18. Jochen Buchsteiner, 'Das Ende einer Erfolgsstory', *Die Zeit*, Nr. 29, 9.7.1998, p. 3.

19. Buchsteiner.

20. Lamparter, Vorholz interview with Maucher 'Big is beautiful', *Die Zeit*, Nr. 29, 9.7.1998, p. 21.

21.Kohler-Koch, in Wallace and Young (eds.), p. 48.

22. Kohler Koch, in Wallace and Young (eds.), pp. 49, 55-56, has identified MEPs as natural allies of broader interest groups, because parliamentarians favor attracting the broadest possible support to ensure their reelection. In a 1996 survey, 80% of MEPs stated that they valued interest group activity because they supplied them with expert information. But, as we may judge from our discussion in the section 'The European Parliament' in Chapter 7, the low MEP attendance figures at EP debates would seem to indicate that many MEPs have not used the information available to them to have developed an opinion.

23. Kohler-Koch, in Wallace and Young (eds.), p. 52.

24. UN   membership   as   of   1.5.2000.   See   http://www.un.org/Overview/-unmember.html.

25. See Kohler-Koch, in Wallace and Young (eds.), p. 48: "inter-expert bargaining is the essence of the game of successful interest intermediation."

26. See Baring, p. 317.

27. Linklater, p. 206.

28. Robert Putnam, 'Two-level games: The impact of domestic politics on Transatlantic bargaining', in Helga Haftendorn and Christian Tuschhoff (eds.), *America and Europe in an Era of Change* (Boulder: Westview Press, 1993), pp. 68-83 (pp. 76-77).

29. Sarah Collinson, ' "Issue-systems," "multi-level games" and the analysis of the EU's external commercial and associated policies: a research agenda', in Jeremy Richardson (ed.), *Journal of European Public Policy*, Vol. 6, no. 2, June 1999, pp. 206-224.

30. For a discussion of relationship of individual will to political processes, see discussion of the fall of the wall and the German unification process in Chapter 5 of my *Post-National Patriotism*.

31. Linklater, p. 206.

32. See Rudolf Maresch, 'Medientechnik. Das Apriori der Öffentlichkeit', *FH/NG* 9/1995, pp. 790-799 (p. 796).

33. See Cowles, pp. 118-130.

34. Needless to say, Communist Eastern Europe attacked big business as an ideological matter of course.

35. Cowles, p. 122, quotes the MNE representative's views thus: "We recognized that if it came to a crunch in the Council, and we [the MNEs *(Cowles' clarification)*] were persuading one of the government to hold their support, there would be a high danger of a trade-off."

36. See C. Taylor, *Multiculturalism and 'The Politics of Recognition'*, p. 33. I extend this discussion concerning issues of recognition between groups, linking it also with Giddens' concept of dialogic democracy in Chapters 15 and 16 of my *Post-National Patriotism*.

37. Keith Richardson 'Introductory Foreward', in Wallace and Young (eds.), pp. xvii-xxiv (p. xxiii). Richardson overlooks the firing of the UK Chancellor of the Exchequer a year after the British government was forced to withdraw from ERM.

38. For details of ESC, set up under the Treaty of Rome, 1957, see Bundeszentrale für politische Bildung (ed.), 'Europäische Union', *Informationen zur Politischen Bildung 213*, p. 36; 'Neue Zusammensetzung im WSA', *FAZ*, 25.9.1998, p. 30. ESC consists of 222 members, representing three functional sectors: employers' groups, trades unions, and "other interests," the latter being crafts, expertise and consumer group interests. Commission and Council are obliged to consult ESC, which meets ten times a year, on CAP, transport, internal market, social policy, education, consumer affairs, regional and structural policy, industrial policy and research.

39. See Westlake, pp. 50-51. We may agree with Westlake's judgement simply if we consider that 135 Community administrators, employed to support the work of ESC, have additionally served the work of the Committee of the Regions since its creation under Maastricht. See also *FAZ*, 25.9.1998, p. 30.

40. See 'Deutsche Interessenvertretung in der EU: Die 24 Mitglieder im Wirtschafts- und Sozialausschuß', *FAZ*, 25.9.1998, p. 30. For example, BdA, BDI, and German Association of Chambers of Industry and Commerce (DIHT) all send rank-and-file employees delegated to ESC, not presidium members, or the organization heads themselves. Unions and expertise interest groups tend to send higher-ranking personnel.

41. Cowles, p. 136.

42. See 'Die Wirtschaft soll in die EU-Gesetzgebung einbezogen werden', *FAZ*, 7.8.1998, p. 22. The report details small and medium sized businesses being lobbied by

the Commission to take part in its Business Test Panel scheme to find out the effects of Community market legislation.

43. Cowles, p. 136.

44. Cowles, p. 131-132.

45. List of ERT 1997 membership in Cowles, p. 138. One hundred largest companies in 'EUROPAS GRÖSSTE UNTERNEHMEN IN ZAHLEN' in *FAZ* supplement 'Die 100 größten Unternehmen', p. B. 7. My calculation of total turnover of 23 the largest companies in the ERT also appearing in the *FAZ* list includes the 1997 turnover of Telecom Italia, not a participant on the ERT, but taken over by Olivetti, a participant, in 1999. Until then however, Olivetti was not one of Europe's largest companies according to turnover. By comparison, Cowles figure that the combined of ERT's total 45 companies would seem to be an underestimate. She cites a sum of €500 billion, circa DM 1,000 billion (p. 131).

46. See http://www.iso.ch.

47. Andersen and Burns, in Andersen and Eliassen (eds.), p. 238.

48. Watson, p. 100.

13

Some Conclusions about Transnational Activity Transcending States

In Chapter 12, I suggested that the limitation of public institutional democracy may be corrected by incorporating private interests formally in the public policy-making process. We had already seen, by our consideration of DaimlerChrysler, Siemens and BMW, that there are elements of private policy making very much in the public realm, and which have also been served by the advent of employee codetermination.

We have seen in this book as a whole that there would seem to be a complex of democratic political and social values among European businesses and business leaders that would be amenable to such developments. Over the course of Part II especially, we have examined how the limitations of liberal representative democracy faced with the advent of transnational organization and growing importance of transnational business may be corrected.

In tracing the history and current dilemmas of European integration in Part I, we saw that European integration was a valid response to the divisions of nationalism and the threat to freedom posed by totalitarianism. Nevertheless, it has now created the potential for new and greater divisions in the world-wide state system. Here, we saw that, in view of the transnational reach of business, there are increasingly compelling reasons for the abandonment of undifferentiated institutional approaches to international unity. We discussed the territorial and conceptual limits of intergovernmentalism and supranational federalism. In Chapter 6, we saw that not only does nationalism handicap such approaches to integration, they have much in common with it also. Both intergovernmentalism and federalism rely on criteria of inclusion and exclusion too.

Conversely, in the light of increasing difficulties in drawing demarcations in international society, we saw that Mitrany's functional views, developed originally in the 1930s, are still apt. In view of the ongoing blight of unemployment, a greater accentuation on functionalism in pursuit of greater post-national social coherence would be attractive. The certitudes of functionalism may foster a sense of worth and cooperation between individuals and groups more than the creation of new abstract political structures. Nonetheless, I also argued that functionalist approaches would only succeed if we rejected hegemonic concepts of power. For example, EMU will only succeed if conceived of in these terms.

Moreover, in introducing the theme of EMU and discussing growing interdependence between states in Chapter 5, I suggested that we should question traditional conceptions of sovereignty. Human rights are not only threatened by the dictatorship of a single individual, but also by the effects of the actions of one group upon another, both in terms of interstate relationships and in respect to states' authority over individuals and groups within their borders. Thus, in an interdependent world, I would suggest that we could rein in conceptions of states sovereignty just as the populations of states once reined in monarchs, as indicated by the term "constitutional monarchy." We can envisage a similarly symbolic role for sovereignty, with the term "constitutional sovereignty."

In Part II, with an analysis of the possibilities of social benchmarking stemming from the mechanism for closer cooperation in the Amsterdam Treaty, we have seen that we could conceive of an extension of social coherence occurring world-wide, via a deployment of transinstitutional differentiated approaches to functional problems, based on dialogue. In Chapter 9, I argued that transnational enterprises, which have both local and global aspects to their operations, could become the agents of global mediation between functional and geographical communities of interest. Furthermore, here we saw that such firms based in Germany had special reasons for setting high social benchmarks, to escape from the specters of the past, which still haunt present conceptions. By considering the contrasting paths of DaimlerChrysler and Siemens, we saw that the global application of German consensus capitalism is by no means a straightforward process. Nonetheless, we saw that a recognition of TNEs as well as geographical communities as legitimate participants in worldwide processes is essential to the effective reconciliation of diverse global interests.

Although I have argued consistently in favor of functionalism, we may see also how this work has exposed limitations of representative democracy within EU states. One of these demands immediate correction. Following the Maastricht Treaty, states were obliged to give EU citizens resident for over three months the vote at the local community level, and these individuals may also choose to vote in European elections in their country of residence rather than country of origin. However, it makes little sense to have the vote at district and European levels, but to be denied the vote at national or regional levels in between. Furthermore, the fact that students, studying in a community for only a semester, before returning whence they came, may decide on the future of a community's transport or education policies, but a Turk, for example, long-term resident in Germany, and with every hope of seeing his or her grandchildren grow up there, cannot is absurd. Following the Maastricht Treaty, Berlin, the location with the largest Turkish population outside Turkey. 140,000., became the first *Land* government in Germany to introduce local voting rights for its 52,000 EU residents.[1] This fact is an ironic echo of A.J.P. Taylor's comment during the first days of the Cold War: "We are led to hope that one day the German people may rule in Berlin. That outcome is, in the long run, unavoidable; it will be tolerable only if there also rules in Berlin an awareness of a community of nations."[2]

But thus far there is only a partial awareness of nations, not only in Germany, but also throughout the whole of the EU. We may wonder why non-EU citizens, working in the Community and contributing to its economy in some respect, or in the case of US servicemen in Europe, its security, are not able to contribute to discussion about the society in which they live. TNEs and their employees may act towards changing state-based citizenship conceptions. With the American colonialists' slogan in mind, "No taxation without representation," many may wonder why they have no say in the affairs of their state of residence.[3]

We may connect the future of individual businesses with the future of individual democratic systems. If both survive in partnership based upon processes of dialogue, each may flourish individually. We may see that just as democracy encourages business, so can business encourage concepts of democracy.

Post-Cold War changes might not have seen the advent of a stable world political system that can be understood clearly. However, we can see the value of growing interdependence if we liken recent developments challenging traditional, more easily understandable practices and perceptions of nation-state to the development of avionics. Aircraft were formerly designed with stability during flight paramount. Technology controlling the aircraft was rudimentary: a motor directly linked to a propeller for propulsion and cables linked the pilot's hand-controlled column and foot pedals to flaps to adjust altitude and direction. However, recent developments in aeronautic technology have favored innate instability. Instability fosters both airframe maneuverability and speed. Drawing an analogy with the contemporary international political order, it may be, that increased interdependence of many global subsystems can serve more people more efficiently and speedily without crashing. The drawback is that more people would be affected by any crash should anything go wrong. Moreover, such are the complications of interdependence that we may also have difficulties in knowing if things *are* going wrong. But in processes of collective dialogue, which maximize the inclusion of individuals' questions on the agenda, we may at least hope to minimize the consequences of individual failings, and avoid societal crash.[4]

I would recall Popper's views discussed in Chapter 1 concerning the salience of uncertainty in our world. Doubt in one sense is linked to a lack of certainty. Thus, I hope to have shown that open processes of dialogue may combat existential uncertainty. Additionally, dialogue may facilitate the elimination of tensions from potential conflict between segmentary territorial focuses of identification on one hand and the functional primacy of interdependent albeit diverse economic needs on the other. Centers of political governance are still conceived in segmentary geographical terms, but it may be that the unfulfilled hopes of many people post-Cold War may better find fulfillment if we attempt to learn lessons from functional areas, science and technology, as well as business. This would involve extending our conceptions of democracy to these functional areas, making them more accountable also, as discussed in Chapter 12.[5] Nevertheless, doubt is also linked to a lack of belief. Therefore in another, positive sense, I would hope to have shown that there is every reason to doubt the validity of nation-state conceptions of societal organization.[6]

I have based my observations in this book on a study of the actions of German companies acting transnationally. But what is happening within Germany in the light of this increasing transnational activity? The scope of this book has excluded giving answers to these questions. Even so, in the light of our survey of growing economic, political and social interdependence at the global level thus far, from a cosmopolitan viewpoint, there should be no particular reason for exhibiting a measure of solidarity between communities merely because they have nationality and citizenship in common.[7] Nonetheless, this has been the case in substantial measure right from the onset of the German unification process. In the companion volume to this work, *Post-National Patriotism and the Feasibility of Post-National Community in United Germany*, I investigate further why this should have been so, along with the limitations and benefits arising from this exclusivity.

NOTES

1. DPA report, *Das Parlament*, 3.3.1995, Nr. 10, Jahrgang 45, p. 1.

2. A.J.P. Taylor, 'The Ruler in Berlin', in his *From the Boer War to the Cold War* (London: Penguin, 1996), pp 108-115 (pp. 114 – 115).

3. In the FRG, there are circa 1.9 million *non-German* EU residents. In respect to those living in the city *Länder*, they may vote only in local districts; they may not vote for the city mayor. There are over 5 million *non-EU* citizens in Germany without any prospect of voting rights at all. [Figure of EU citizens based on that given by Martin Schulz, 'Deutschland-Daten', in Werner Weidenfeld and Karl-Rudolf Korte (eds.), *Handbuch zur deutschen Einheit* (Frankfurt/Main: Campus Verlag, 1996), pp.769-803 (p. 773).]

4. See Mitrany, p. 267: "The life of our society is now ruled by ... marvels of technical and scientific skill, skills easily passed on in space and time ... in itself that is right; but not by itself. For human nature has not moved in step with and in relation to that mechanistic advance."

5. See Niklas Luhmann, 'Die Weltgesellschaft', in *Soziologische Aufklärung 2: Aufsätze zur Theorie der Gesellschaft* (Opladen: Westdeutscher Verlag, 1975), pp. 51-71 (p. 58).

6. Michael Williams, 'Doubt', in *Routledge Encyclopaedia of Philosophy Volume* 3, pp. 464-465.

7. See Linklater's critique of overlaps between cosmopolitan and communitarian stances on changing political community, pp. 50-55. A consideration of these terms does not form part of this book. But I would hope that adherents of both perspectives would find much in this work which is appealing. My suggestion in *Post-National Patriotism* of the development of a post-national patriotism could, I suppose, be defined as cosmopolitan communitarianism.

Bibliography

BOOKS

Alemann, Ulrich von. *Organisierte Interessen in der Bundesrepublik.* Opladen: Leske + Budrich, 1987.

Andersen, Svein and Eliassen, Kjell (eds.). *The European Union: How Democratic is it?* London: Sage, 1996.

Anderson, Benedict. *Die Erfindung der Nation: zur Karriere eines folgenreichen Konzepts [Imagined Communities: Reflections on the Origins and Spread of Nationalism].* Frankfurt/Main: Campus Verlag, 1988.

Archibugi, Daniele and Held, David (eds.). *Cosmopolitan Democracy: An Agenda for a New World Order.* Cambridge: Polity Press, 1995.

Baring, Arnulf. *Im Anfang war Adenauer: Die Entstehung der Kanzler-Demokratie.* Munich: Deutscher Taschenbuch Verlag, 1971.

Barr, Nicholas. *The Economics of the Welfare State* 3rd ed.. Oxford University Press, 1998.

Beck, Ulrich; Giddens, Anthony; Lash, Scott. *Reflexive Modernization.* Cambridge: Polity Press, 1994.

Beck, Ulrich (ed.). *Politik der Globalisierung.* Frankfurt/Main: Suhrkamp, 1998.

Beetham, David (ed.). *Defining and Measuring Democracy.* London: Sage, 1994.

Begg, David et al. (eds.). *EMU: Prospects and Challenges for the Euro.* Oxford: Blackwell, 1998.

Benz, Wolfgang. *Die Gründung der Bundesrepublik: Von der Bizone zum souveränen Staat.* Munich: Deutscher Taschenbuch Verlag, 1984.

Benz, Wolfgang.(ed.). *Die Geschichte der Bundesrepublik Deutschland Band 2: Wirtschaft.* Frankfurt/Main: Fischer Taschenbuch Verlag, 1989.

—— *Sieben Fragen an die Bundesrepublik.* Munich: Deutscher Taschenbuch Verlag, 1989.

Berghahn, Volker. *Unternehmer und Politik in der Bundesrepublik.* Frankfurt/Main: Suhrkamp, 1985.

Boyer, Robert and Drache, Daniel (eds.). *States against Markets: The limits of globalization.* London: Routledge, 1996.

Brunkhorst, Hauke. *Demokratie und Differenz.* Frankfurt/Main: Fischer Verlag, 1994.

Buckley, Peter and Artisien, Patrick. *North-South Direct Investment in the European Communities: The Employment Impact of Direct Investment by British, French and German Multinationals in Greece, Portugal and Spain.* London: Macmillan, 1987.

Bülow, Friedrich. *Friedrch List: Ein Volkswirt kämpft für Deutschlands Einheit.* Göttingen: Musterschmidt-Verlag, 1959.

Bull, Hedley. *The Anarchical Society: A Study of Order.* London: Macmillan, 1980.

Bullock, Alan. *Ernest Bevin, Foreign Secretary, 1945-51.* London: Heinemann, 1983.

Carter, April and Stokes, Geoffrey (eds.). *Liberal Democracy and its Critics: Perspectives in Contemporary Political Thought.* Cambridge: Polity Press, 1998.

Casson, Mark. *The Economics of Business Culture: Game Theory, Transaction Costs, and Economic Performance.* Oxford: Clarendon Press, 1991.

Chubin, Sharam (ed.). *Germany and the Middle East.* London: Pinter, 1992.

Cole, John and Francis. *The Geography of the European Community.* London: Routledge, 1993.

Collinson, Sarah. *Europe and International Migration.* London: Pinter Publishers, 1993.

The Commission on Global Governance, The Report of. *Our Global Neighbourhood.* Oxford University Press, 1995.

Crouch, Colin. *Industrial Relations and European State Traditions.* Oxford: Clarendon Press, 1993.

Däubler, Wolfgang. *Das Arbeitsrecht 1.* Reinbek: Rororo, 1993.

—— *Das Arbeitsrecht 2.* Reinbek: Rororo, 1992.

Deutsche Bundesbank. *Die Geldpolitik der Bundesbank.* Frankfurt/Main: Deutsche Bundesbank, 1995.

Dietz, Bertold et al. (eds.). *Die soziale Zukunft Europas.* Giessen: Focus, 1994.

Dietz, Wolfgang A. and Glatthaar, Christiane. *Das Räderwerk der EG-Kommission.* Bonn: Economica Verlag, 1991.

Dunning, John and Robson, Peter (eds.). *Multinationals and the European Community.* Oxford: Basil Blackwell, 1988.

Eglau, Hans Otto. *Edzard Reuter.* Düsseldorf: Econ Verlag, 1991.

Ehrmann, Michael. *Die Geschichte des Werkes Sindelfingen der Daimler-Motoren-Gesellschaft und der Daimler-Benz AG.* Stuttgart: Historisches Institut, Stuttgart University doctoral thesis, 1998.

Ellwein, Thomas and Bruder, Wolfgang (eds.) with Peter Hotelich. *Ploetz Die Bundesrepublik Deutschland Daten, Fakten, Analysen.* Darmstadt: Wissenschaftliche Buchgesellschaft, 1985.

Erhard, Ludwig. *Germany's Comeback in World Markets.* London: George Allen & Unwin, 1954.

Feldenkirchen, Wilfried. *Werner von Siemens Erfinder und internationaler Unternehmer.* Berlin: Siemens, 1992.

Feldenkirchen, Wilfried et al. (eds.). *Wirtschaft Gesellschaft Unternehmen: Festschrift für Hans Pohl zum 60. Geburtstag. 1 Teilband: Wirtschaft.* Stuttgart: Franz Steiner Verlag, 1998.

Feyerabend, Friedrich-Karl (ed.). *Europa 1992, Binnenmarkt, Europäische Union.* Giessen: Verlag der Feber'sche Universitätsbuchhandlung, 1993.

Ford, Glynn. *Report of Committee of Inquiry on Racism and Xenophobia. European Parliament 1991.* ECSC -EEC EAEC, Brussels-Luxembourg, 1991.

Franzke, Hermann (ed.). *Industriebau Bosch: Standorte Bauten Technik.* Basle: Birkhäuser, 1991.

Fukuyama, Francis. *The End of History and the Last Man.* London: Penguin Books, 1992.

—— *Trust: The Social Virtues and the Creation of Prosperity.* London: Hamish Hamilton, 1995.

Gall, Lothar and Pohl, Manfred (eds.). *Unternehmen im Nationalsozialismus.* Munich: Beck, 1998.

Genscher, Hans-Dietrich. *Deutsche Aussenpolitik ausgewählte Aufsätze 1974-1985.* Stuttgart: Verlag Bonn Aktuell, 1985.

George, Stephen. *Politics and Policy in the European Union.* Oxford University Press, 1996.

Giddens, Anthony. *The Nation-State and Violence.* Cambridge: Polity Press, 1992.

—— *Beyond Left and Right: The Future of Radical Politics.* Cambridge: Polity Press, 1994.

—— *Beyond Left and Right* [*Jenseits von Links und Rechts*]. Frankfurt/Main: Suhrkamp 1997.

Grauwe, Paul de. *The Economics of Monetary Integration.* Oxford University Press, 1992.

Greiffenhagen, Martin and Sylvia. *Deutschland: ein schwieriges Vaterland.* Munich: Paul List Verlag, 1993.

Grosser, Alfred. *Das Deutschland im Westen.* Munich: Carl Hanser Verlag, 1985.

Grupp, Claus D.. *Europa 2000.* Köln: Omnia Verlag, 1996.

Guéhenno Jean-Marie. *Le Fin de la Démocratie* [*Das Ende der Demokratie*]. Munich: Artemis & Winkler Verlag, 1994.

—— *The End of the Nation-State* [Revised (ed. of vol. above]. Minneapolis: University of Minnesota Press, 1995.

Gysi, Gregor (ed.). *Wir brauchen einen dritten Weg: Selbstverständnis und Programm der PDS.* Hamburg: Konkret Literatur Verlag, 1990.

Haas, Ernst. *Beyond the Nation State.* Stanford University Press, 1964.

Habermas, Jürgen. *Die Neue Unübersichtlichkeit.* Frankfurt/Main: Suhrkamp, 1985.

—— *Die moderne ein unvollendetes Projekt.* Leipzig: Reclam, 1992.

—— *Vergangenheit als Zukunft.* Munich: Piper, 1993.

—— *Die Normalität einer Berliner Republik.* Frankfurt/Main: Suhrkamp, 1995.

—— *Die Einbeziehung des Anderen.* Frankfurt/Main: Suhrkamp, 1996.

Haftendorn, Helga and Tuschhoff, Christian (eds.). *America and Europe in an Era of Change.* Boulder: Westview Press, 1993.

Handschuch, Konrad. *D-Mark ade! Das Maastrichter Experiment.* Frankfurt/Main: Fischer, 1994.

Heine, M; Kisker, K.P.; Schikara. A. (eds.). *Schwarzbuch Binnenmarkt: Die Vergessenen Kosten der Integration.* Berlin: Sigma Rainer Bolm Verlag, 1992.

Held, David. *Democracy and the Global Order: From the Modern State to Cosmopolitan Governance.* Cambridge: Polity Press, 1995.

Herrhausen, Alfred. *Denken – Ordnen – Gestalten.* Berlin: Wolf Jobst Siedler, 1990.

Hesse, Joachim Jens and Wright, Vincent (eds.). *Federalizing Europe? The Costs, Benefits, and Preconditions of Federal Political Systems.* Oxford University Press, 1996.

Heywood, Andrew. *Politics.* London: Macmillan, 1997.

Hof, Bernd. *Europa im Zeichen der Migration: Szenarien zur Bevölkerungs- und Arbeitsmarktentwicklung in der Europäischen Gemeinschaft bis 2020.* Köln: Deutscher Instituts-Verlag, 1993.

Hopmann, Barbara et al.. *Zwangsarbeit bei Daimler-Benz.* Stuttgart: Franz Steiner Verlag, 1994.

Hornstein, Walter and Mutz, Gerd. *Die europäische Einigung als gesellschaftlicher Prozeß: soziale Problemlagen, Partizipation und kulturelle Transformation.* Baden Baden: Nomos Verlagsgesellschaften, 1993.

Hyman, Richard and Ferner, Anthony (eds.). *New Frontiers in European Industrial Relations.* London: Blackwell, 1994.

Industrie- und Handelskammer zu Berlin (ed.). *Die Bedeutung der Rationalisierung für das Deutsche Wirtschaftsleben.* Berlin: Verlag Georg Stilke, 1928.

Isenee, Josef (ed.). *Europa als politsche Idee und als rechtliche Form.* Berlin: Duncker & Humblot, 1993.

Jacob-Wende, Gerhart. *Deutsche Elektroindustrie in Lateinamerika: Siemens und A.E.G. 1890-1914.* Stuttgart: Klett-Cotta, 1982.

Jaeger, Hans. *Geschichte der Wirtschaftsordnung in Deutschland.* Frankfurt/Main: Suhrkamp, 1988.

Jaeggi, Urs. *Macht und Herrschaft in der Bundesrepublik.* Frankfurt/Main: Fischer Taschenbuch, 1969.

Jaspers, Karl. *Vom Ursprung und Ziel der Geschichte.* Munich: R. Piper, 1949.

Jonas, Hans. *Das Prinzip Verantwortung.* Frankfurt/Main: Suhrkamp, 1984.

Kavanagh, Dennis and Seldon, Anthony. *The Major Effect.* London: Macmillan, 1994.

Kennedy, Paul. *Preparing for the 21st Century [In Vorbereitung auf das 21. Jahrhundert].* Frankfurt: Fischer, 1993.

Khan, Daniel-Erasmus (ed.). *Vertrag über die Europäische Union mit sämtlichen Protokollen und Erklärungen. Vertrag zur Gründung der Europäischen Gemeinschaft (EG-Vertrag) in den Fassungen von Maastricht und Amsterdam.* Munich: Deutscher Taschenbuch Verlag, 1998

Kohl, Helmut. *Ich wollte Deutschlands Einheit. Dargestellt von Kai Diekmann und Georg Reuth.* Berlin: Ullstein, 1998.

Kleist, Heinrich von. *Werke in einem Band.* Munich: Carl Hanser Verlag, 1966.

Keohane, Robert J. and Hoffmann, Stanley (eds.). *The New European Community.* Boulder: Westview Press, 1991.

Keohane, Robert J. and Ostrom, Elinor (eds.). *Local Commons and Global Interdependence: Heterogeneity and Cooperation in Two Domains.* London: Sage, 1995.

Korte, Karl-Rudolf. *Die Chance genutzt?: Die Politik zur Einheit Deutschlands.* Frankfurt/Main: Campus Verlag, 1994.

—— *Deutschlandpolitik in Helmut Kohls Kanzlerschaft. Regierungsstil und Entscheidungen 1982-1989.* Stuttgart: Deutsche Verlags-Anstalt, 1998.

Krause-Burger, Sibylle. *Die neue Elite: Topmanager und Spitzenpolitiker aus der Nähe gesehen.* Düsseldorf: Econ Verlag, 1995.

Kreile, Michael (ed.). *PVS Sonderheft 23 1992.* Opladen: Westdeutscher Verlag, 1992.

Kreuder, Thomas and Loewy Hanno (eds.). *Konservativismus in der Strukturkrise.* Frankfurt/Main: Suhrkamp, 1987.

Küstes, Hanns Jürgen (ed.). *Dokumente zur Deutschlandpolitik.* R. Oldenburg Verlag, 1998.

Laqueur, Walter. *Europe in our time [Europa auf dem Weg zur Weltmacht 1945-1992].* Munch: Kindler, 1992.

Lenk, Hans and Maring, Matthias (eds.). *Wirtschaft und Ethik.* Stuttgart: Philipp Reclam jun., 1992.

Linklater, Andrew. *The Transformation of Political Community.* Cambridge: Polity Press, 1998.

Luhmann, Niklas. *Soziologische Aufklärung 2: Aufsätze zur Theorie der Gesellschaft.* Opladen: Westdeutscher Verlag, 1975.

McKim, Robert and McMahan, Jeff (eds.). *The Morality of Nationalism.* Oxford University Press, 1997.

Mako, Joseph and Stolz, Armin (eds.). *Demokratie und Wirtschaft.* Böhlau Verlag Wien, 1987.

Marsh, David. *Rich, Bothered and Divided.* London: Hutchison, 1989.

—— *The New Germany.* London: Century, 1990.

—— *Germany and Europe: The Crisis of Unity [Der zaudernde Riese].* Munich: C.

Bertelsmann, 1994.

Martin, Hans-Peter and Schumann, Harald. *Die Globalisierungsfalle: Der Angriff auf Demokratie und Wohlstand.* Reinbek: Rororo, 1996.

Mason, Mark and Encarnation, Dennis (eds.). *Does Ownership Matter? Japanese Multinationals in Europe.* Oxford: Clarendon Press, 1994.

Mercedes Benz-Koordination/Express-Redaktion (eds.). *Werktage werden schlechter. Die Auswirkungen der Unternehmenspolitik von Daimler Benz auf die Beschäftigten.* Offenbach: express, 1997.

Mitrany, David. *The Functional Theory of Politics.* London: LSE Martin Robertson & Co Ltd, 1975.

Mohn, Reinhard. *Erfolg durch Partnerschaft: Eine Unternehmensstrategie für den Menschen.* Berlin: Siedler Verlag, 1986.

Montgomery, John and Foster, Edward. *Beyond the Wall: German Unification and European Security.* London: Royal United Services Institute, 1992.

Moravcsik, Andrew. *The Choice for Europe: Social Purpose and State Power from Messina to Maastricht.* Ithaca: Cornell University Press, 1998.

Morokvasic, Mirjana and Rudolph, Hedwig (eds.). *Wanderungsraum Europa: Menschen und Grenzen in Bewegung.* Berlin: edition sigma, 1994.

Musil, Robert. *Mann ohne Eigenschaften I.* Reinbek: Rororo, 1978.

—— *Mann ohne Eigenschaften II.* Reinbek: Rororo, 1978.

Nelsen, B.F. and Stubb, A. C.-G. (eds.). *The European Union.* Boulder: Lynne Reiner, 1994.

Nicol, William and Salmon, Trevor. *Understanding the new European Community.* Hemel Hempstead: Harvester Wheatsheaf, 1994.

Oakeshott, Michael. *On Human Conduct.* Oxford: Clarendon Press, 1991.

Platzer, Hans-Wolfgang. *Gewerkschaftspolitik ohne Grenzen: Die transnationale Zusammenarbeit der Gewerkschaften der neunziger Jahre.* Bonn: Dietz Verlag, 1991.

—— *Lernprozeß Europa.* Bonn: Dietz Verlag, 1993.

Penrose, Edith. *The Theory of the Growth of the Firm.* Oxford University Press, 1995.

Phillips, Donald. *Post-National Patriotism and the Feasibility of Post-National Community in United Germany.* Westport, CT: Praeger, 2000.

Popper, Karl R. *Auf der Suche nach einer besseren Welt.* Munich: Serie Piper, 1987.

Robertson, Roland. *Globalization: Social Theory and Global Culture.* London: Sage, 1992.

Rosenau, James. *The Study of Global Interdependence: Essays on the Transnationalisation of World Affairs.* London: Frances Pinter, 1980.

—— *Turbulence in World Politics: A Theory of Change and Continuity.* Hemel Hempstead: Harvester Wheatsheaf, 1990.

Ruzio, Wolfgang. *Das politische System der Bundesrepublik Deutschland.* Leverkusen: Laske Verlag + Budrich GmbH, 1987.

Sbragia, Albert M. (ed.). *Europolitics.* Washington, D.C.: Brookings Institution, 1992.

Schäfer, Lothar. *Das Bacon-Projekt.* Frankfurt/Main: Suhrkamp, 1993.

Schleyer, Hanns Martin. *Das Soziale Modell.* Stuttgart: Seewald Verlag, 1974.

Schmidt, Helmut. *Handeln für Deutschland.* Reinbek: Rororo, 1994.

Schneider, Theodor. *Nationalismus und Nationalstaat.* Göttingen: Vandenhoeck und Ruprecht, 1991.

Schwarz, Hans-Peter. *Geschichte der Bundesrepublik Deutschland: Die Ära Adenauer 1957-1963.* Stuttgart: Deutsche Verlags Anstalt, 1983.

Seifert, Karl-Heinz and Hömig, Dieter (eds.). *Grundgesetz für die Bundesrepublik Deutschland Taschenkommentar 5. Auflage.* Baden-Baden: Nomos, 1995.

Siemens, Georg. *History of the House of Siemens; Volume II: The Era of World Wars.*

Freiburg/Munich: Karl Alber, 1957.

Smith, Anthony. *National Identity*. London: Penguin, 1991.

—— *Nations and Nationalism in a Global Era*. Cambridge: Polity Press, 1995.

Smith, Julie. *Voice of the People: The European Parliament in the 1990s*. London: The Royal Institute of International Affairs, 1995.

Sontheimer, Kurt. *Gründzüge des politischen Systems der Bundesrepublik Deutschland*. Munich: Piper, 1989.

Steger, Ulrich (ed.). *Industriepolitik: eine Antwort auf die japanische Herausforderung?*. Frankfurt/Main:Campus Verlag, 1993.

Sternberger, Dolf. *Verfassungspatriotismus Schriften X*. Frankfurt/Main: Insel Verlag, 1990.

Story, Jonathan (ed.). *The New Europe*. Oxford: Blackwell, 1993.

Stubbs, Richard and Underhill, Geoffrey R.D. (eds.). *Political Economy and the Changing Global Order*. London: Macmillan, 1994.

Taylor, A.J.P.. *From the Boer War to the Cold War. Essays on Twentieth Century Europe*. London: Penguin, 1996.

Taylor, Charles. *Multiculturalism and "The Politics of Recognition,"* with commentary by Amy Gutmann (ed.). et al.. Princeton University Press, 1992.

Teltschik, Horst. *329 Tage: Innenansichten der Einigung*. Berlin: Wolf Jobst Siedler Verlag, 1991.

Thompson, John B.. *The Media and Modernity*. Cambridge: Polity Press, 1995.

Tsoukalis, Loukas. *The New European Economy: The Politics and Economics of Integration*. Oxford University Press, 1993.

Tugendhat, Ernst. *Philosophische Aufsätze*. Frankfurt/Main: Suhrkamp, 1992.

Ullman, Hans Peter. *Interessenverbände in Deutschland*. Frankfurt/Main: Suhrkamp, 1988.

United Nations Dept. of Public Information, *Basic Facts about the United Nations*. New York: United Nations, 1995.

Van der Wee, Herman. *Der gebremste Wohlstand: Wiederaufbau, Wachstum und Strukturwandel der Weltwirtschaft seit 1945*. Munich: Deutscher Taschenbuch Verlag, 1984.

Wallace, Helen and Young, Alasdair (eds.). *Participation and Policy–Making in the European Union*. Oxford: Clarendon Press, 1997.

Wallace, William. *Regional Integration: The West European Experience*. Washington, D.C.: The Brookings Institution 1994.

Wallace, William (ed.). *The Dynamics of European Integration*. London: RIIA 1990.

Wallerstein, Immanuel. *The Politics of the World Economy*. Cambridge University Press, 1984.

—— *Geopolitics and Geoculture*. Cambridge University Press, 1991.

Watson, Adam. *The Limits of Independence: Relations Between States in the Modern World*. London: Routledge, 1997.

Weidenfeld, Werner (ed.). `Strategien und Optionen für die Zukunft Europas Arbeitspapiere 1*. Gütersloh: Bertelsmann Stiftung, 1988.

—— *Maastricht in der Analyse*. Gütersloh: Verlag Bertelsmann Stiftung, 1994.

Weidenfeld, Werner and Janning, Josef (eds.). *Europe in Global Change: Strategies and Options for Europe*. Gütersloh, Bertelsmann Foundation Publishers, 1993.

Weizsäcker, Richard von. *Vier Zeiten: Erinnerungen*. Berlin: Siedler, 1997.

Westlake, Martin. *A Modern Guide to the European Parliament*. London: Pinter, 1994.

Zweig, Stefan. *Die Welt von Gestern*. Frankfurt/Main: Fischer Verlag, 1955.

JOURNAL ARTICLES

Abromeit, Heidrun. 'Ein Vorschlag zur Demoktratisierung des Europäischen Entscheidungssystems', in Vorstand der Deutschen Vereinigung für politische Wissenschaft (ed.), *PVS* 39, March 1998. Opladen: Westdeutscher Verlag, 1998.

Adam, Konrad. 'Nach seinem Bilde: Kohl, die Partei und die Europäische Gemeinschaft', in Bohrer, Karl Heinz and Scheel, Kurt (eds.), *Merkur* 5/98. Munich, 1998.

Begg, Iain and Peterson, John. 'Editorial Statement', in *Journal of Common Market Studies (JCMS)*, Vol. 37, no. 1, March 1999. Oxford: Blackwell, 1999.

Berthold, Norbert, Hilpert, Jörg. 'Global denken, lokal handeln', in Weidenfeld, Werner (ed.), *Internationale Politik* Nr. 5, May 1998. Bonn, 1998.

Blume, Georg and Mosdorf, Siegmar. 'Unternehmenskultur des 21. Jahrhunderts', in Glotz, P. (ed.), *Neue Gesellschaft/Frankfurter Hefte (NG/FH)*, 12/93. Bonn: Friedrich-Ebert-Stiftung, 1993.

Busch, Klaus. 'Die Wirtschafts- und Währungsunion in Europa', in Glotz, P. (ed.), *NG/FH*, 7/92, Bonn: Friedrich-Ebert-Stiftung, 1992.

Collinson, Sarah. ' "Issue-systems," "multi-level games" and the analysis of the EU's external commercial and associated policies: a research agenda', in Richardson, Jeremy (ed.), *Journal of European Public Policy*, Vol. 6, no. 2, June 1999. London: Routledge, 1999.

Dahrendorf, Ralf. 'Politik. Eine Kolumne: Geist und Macht', in Bohrer, Karl Heinz and Schell Kurt (eds.), *Merkur* 593, Heft 8, August 1998. Stuttgart: Klett-Cotta, 1998.

Frankenberger, Klaus-Dieter. 'Wo endet Europa? Zur politischen und geographischen Identität der Union', in Weidenfeld, Werner (ed.), *Internationale Politik*, Nr. 6, June 1998. Bonn, 1998.

Frost, Mervyn. 'Migrants, Civil Society and Sovereign States: Investigating an Ethical Hierarchy', in Moran, Michael (ed.), *Political Studies*, Vol. 46, no. 5, Dec 1998. Oxford: Blackwell, 1999.

Girndt, Cornelia. 'Im Dauerlauf zum Euro-Betriebsrat' in Hans-Böckler-Stiftung. pub.. *Mitbestimmung*, 5/99. Düsseldorf, 1999.

Glotz, Peter. 'Ausbruch aus der Wagenburg. Über die Zukunft der Gewerkschaften', in *NG/FH*, 11/88. Bonn: Friedrich-Ebert-Stiftung, 1988.

—— 'Editorial', in *NG/FH*, 7/92. Bonn: Friedrich-Ebert-Stiftung, 1992.

—— 'Europäische Visionen', in *NG/FH*, 7/96. Bonn: Friedrich-Ebert-Stiftung, 1996.

Guéhenno, Jean-Marie. 'Demokratie am Wendepunkt?' in Weidenfeld, Werner (ed.), *Internationale Politik*, Nr. 4, April 1998, Bonn, 1998.

Gutjahr, Lothar. 'Unternehmen Deutschland', in Bergmann, Theodor et al. (eds.). *Sozialismus*, 12/94. Hamburg, 1994.

Hänsch, Klaus. 'Wozu wir das vereinte Europa brauchen', in Friederich-Ebert-Stiftung, (ed.), *Internationale Politik und Gesellschaft* 1/97.

Hauser, Richard. 'Das empirische Bild der Armut in der Bundesrepubik – ein Überblick', in *Aus Politik und Zeitgeschichte*, B31-32/95 28.7.1995.

Henningsen, Manfred. 'Der deutsche Sonderweg am Ende?' in Bohrer, Karl Heinz and Scheel, Kurt (eds.), *Merkur* 5/95. Munich, 1995.

—— 'Die politische Verfassung Europas', in Bohrer, Karl Heinz and Scheel, Kurt (eds.). *Merkur* 5/98, Munich, 1998.

Hilz, Wolfram. 'Bedeutung und Instrumentalisierung des Subsidaritätsprinzips für den europäischen Integrationsprozeß', in *Aus Politik und Zeitgeschichte* B21-22/99, 21.5.1999.

Horster, Detlef. 'Porträt eines politischen Philosophen', in Glotz, P. (ed.), *NG/FH*, 6/96. Bonn: Friedrich-Ebert-Stiftung, 1996.

Johansson, Karl Magnus. 'Tracing the employment title in the Amsterdam treaty: uncov-

ering transnational coalitions and political parties and trade unions lobbying together' in Jeremy Richardson (ed.), *Journal of European Public Policy*, Vol. 5, no.
1, 1999. London: Routledge, 1999.

Jung, Matthias. 'Lob der Banalität: Sprache und Politik in europäischen Dimensionen', in
Glotz, P. (ed.), *NG/FH*, 12/97. Bonn: Friedrich-Ebert-Stiftung, 1997.

Kaufmann, Franz-Xaver. 'Globalisierung und Gesellschaft', in *Aus Politik und Zeitgeschichte*, B18/98, 24.4.1998.

Kostakopoulou, Theodora. 'Why a "Community of Europeans" Could be a Community
of Exclusion: A Reply to Howe', in Bulmer, Simon and Scott, Andrew (eds.),
JCMS, Vol. 35, no. 2, June 1997. Oxford: Blackwell, 1997.

Kostakopoklou, Dora. 'Is there an Alternative to Schengenland?' in Moran, Michael
(ed.). *Political Studies*, Vol. 46 no. 5, Dec 1998. Oxford: Blackwell, 1998.

Leaman, Jeremy. 'Diktatur der Bundesbank?' in Gaus, Günter et al. (eds.), *Blätter für
deutsche und internationale Politik* 7/93. Bonn: Blätter Verlag, 1993.

—— 'Maastricht-Karlsruhe und zurück' in Gaus, Günter et al. (eds.), *Blätter für
deutsche und internationale Politik* 11/93. Bonn: Blätter Verlag, 1993.

Lentner, Howard. 'Implications of the Economic Crisis for East Asian Foreign Policies'
in Park, Yon Kwang (ed.), *The Journal of East Asian Affairs* Vol. XIII, no. 1,
Seoul, 1999.

Maresch, Rudolf. 'Medientechnik. Das Apriori der Öffentlichkeit', in Glotz, P. (ed.),
NG/FH, 9/95. Bonn: Friedrich-Ebert-Stiftung, 1995.

Moravcsik, Andrew and Nicolaïdis, Kalypso. 'Explaining the Treaty of Amsterdam:
Interests, Influence, Institutions', in Begg, Iain and Peterson, John (eds.). *JCMS*,
Vol. 37 no. 1, March 1999. Oxford: Blackwell, 1999.

Neumann, Horst and Nolte, Dirk. 'Protektionismus in der Automobilindustrie' in *WSI
Mitteilungen*, 5/1993. Cologne: Bund Verlag, 1993.

Noël, Emil. 'Reflections on the Maastricht Treaty', in Ionescu, Ghito; da Madareiaga,
Isabel; Gellner, Ernest (eds.), *Government & Opposition*, Vol. 27, no 2. London:
L.S.E., spring 1992.

Nunnenkamp, Peter. 'Schreckgespenst Globalisierung: Chancen und Risikien für den
Standort Deutschland', in Weidenfeld, Werner (ed.), *Internationale Politik* Nr. 5,
May 1998. Bonn, 1998.

Nuscheler, Franz. 'Eine neue Weltpolitik: Multilateralismus statt Pax Americana', in
Weidenfeld, Werner (ed.), *Internationale Politik* Nr. 11, November 1998. Bonn,
1998.

Pearce, Robert and Papanastassio, Marina. 'European Markets and the Strategic Roles of
Multinational Enterprise Subsidiaries in the UK' in Bulmer, Simon and Scott, Andrew (eds.), *JCMS*, Vol. 35, no. 2, June 1997. Oxford: Blackwell, 1997.

Philippart, Eric and Edwards, Geoffrey. 'The Provisions on Closer Co-operation in the
Treaty of Amsterdam: The Politics of Flexibility in the European Union', in Begg,
Iain and Peterson, John (eds.), *JCMS*, Vol. 37, no. 1, March 1999. Oxford: Black-
well, 1999.

Pierer, Heinrich von. 'Die deutsche Debatte', in Weidenfeld, Werner (ed.), *Internationale
Politik* Nr. 5, May 1998. Bonn, 1998.

Rieger, Elmar and Leibfried, Stephan. 'Die sozialpolitischen Grenzen der Globalisierung,
in *PVS* 38, 1997 Heft 4. Opladen: Westdeutscher Verlag, 1997.

Schumann, Hartmut. 'Wirchaftliche Dimensionen der Außenpolitik', in Dieter Blumenwitz et al. (eds.). *Zeitschrift für Politik* Heft 2, Juni 1994. Cologne: Carl Heymanns
Verlag, 1994.

Spicker, Paul. 'Exclusion', in Bulmer, Simon and Scott, Andrew (eds.), *JCMS*, Vol. 35
no. 1, March 1997. Oxford: Blackwell, 1997.

Sitte, Ralf and Zegler, Astrid. 'Partnerschaft in Europa. Warum werden Gewerkschaften nicht an der EU-Strukturpolitik beteiligt?' in *WSI Mitteilungen* 12/1994. Cologne: Bund Verlag, 1994.

Wagner, Helmut. 'Asiens Finanzmisere: Profiteure und Bankrotteure der Globalisierung' in Welttrends e.v., Instytut Zachodri Poznań (eds.), *Welttrends* Nr. 19 Sommer 1998. Berlin, 1998.

—— ' The "Invisible Hands": Who paid the bill and who made a bargain in the Asian financial meltdown?' in Yon Kwang Park (ed.), *The Journal of East Asian Affairs* Vol. XII, no. 2. Seoul, 1998.

Walwei, Ulrich and Werner, Heinz. 'Europäische Integration: Konsequenzen für Arbeitsmarkt und Soziales' in *Mitteilungen an der Arbeitsmarkt – und Berufsforschung Heft 4 1992*. Stuttgart: Verlag W. Kohlhammer, 1992.

Weede, Erich. 'Arbeit und Wachstum in den westlichen Industriegesellschaften', in Blumenwitz, Dieter et al. (eds.), *Zeitschrift für Politik*, Heft 1 März 1999. Cologne: Carl Heymanns Verlag, 1999.

Wiener, Antje and Della Sala, Vincent. 'Constitution-making and Citizenship Practice – Bridging the Democracy Gap in the EU' in Bulmer, Simon and Scott, Andrew (eds.), *JCMS*, Vol. 35, no. 4, Dec 1997. Oxford: Blackwell, 1997.

Zwickel, Klaus. 'Für den Euro und eine europäische Beschäftigungspolitik', in Glotz, P. (ed.), *NG/FH* 6/97. Bonn: Friedrich-Ebert-Stiftung, 1997.

NEWSPAPERS

As can be discerned from the footnotes, a wide variety of daily and weekly newspaper publications were consulted while researching this book. Principally, these were: *Das Parlament, Der Spiegel, Die Frankfurter Rundschau, Die Süddeutsche Zeitung, Die Tageszeitung, Die Welt, Die Wirtschaftswoche, Die Woche, Die Zeit, Financial Times, Frankfurter Allgemeine Zeitung, Handelsblatt, The Economist.*
Other daily and weekly publications provided a further ambient input, the scale of these sources is reflected in various footnoted references.

LEAFLETS/BROCHURES, REFERENCE WORKS

Brockhaus Enzyklopädie. Mannheim, 1990.; various volumes

Bund Freier Bürger LV Hessen, *Freiheit statt Sozialismus*. Linden: Jan. 1995.

—— , *Wenn die D-Mark stirbt ...* Linden. Oct 1995.

Bundeszentrale für politische Bildung (ed.). *Informationen zur Politischen Bildung*. Various issues.

Commission of the European Communities, *Legal instruments to Combat Racism & Xenophobia. Comparative assessment of the legal instruments implemented in the various member states to combat all forms of discrimination, racism and xenophobia and incitement to hatred and racial violence* (Directorate General Employment, Industrial Relations and Social Affairs. 200, rue de la Loi, B-1049 Brussels, Dec. 1992.

Craig, Edward (ed.). *Routledge Encyclopaedia of Philosophy*. London, 1998; various volumes.

Federal German Finance Ministry. *Europäische Wirtschafts- und Währungsunion: Der Euro stark wie die Mark*. April 1996.

—— *per Saldo*. 1998.

Historische Kommission bei der Bayerischen Akademie der Wissenshaften (ed.). *Neue Deutsche Biographie*. Berlin: Duncker & Humblot, 1982; various volumes.

Kommission der Europäischen Gemeinschaften, *Wachstum, Wettbewerbsfähigkeit, Beschäftigung. Herausforderungen der Gegenwart und Wege ins 21. Jahrhundert.*

Weißbuch. Brussels: Bulletin der Europäischen Gemeinschaften Beilage 6/93, 1993.

—— *Eine Währung für Europa – Grünbuch über die praktischen Verfahren zur Einführung der Einheitswährung.* Luxemburg: Amt für amtliche Veröffentlichungen der Europäischen Gemeinschaften, 1995.

—— Regierungskonferenz 1996: Stellungnahme der Kommission – Stärkung der Politischen Union und Vorbereitung der Erweiterung. Luxemburg: Amt für amtliche Veröffentlichungen der Europäischen Gemeinschaften, 1996.

Committee for the Study of Economic and Monetary Union, European Council, *Report on Economic and Monetary Union in the European Community.* HC241.2 E854. 1989.

Löffler, Klaus. *Euro unsere stabile Zukunft.* Bonn: Europäisches Parament, Informationsbüro für Deutschland, 1996.

Löffler, Klaus (ed.). *Der EU-Reform Kompaß.* Bonn: Europäisches Parlament Informationsbüro für Deutschland, 1995.

Lutz, Bernd (ed.). *Metzler Philosophen Lexikon: von den Vorsokratikern bis zu den Neuen Philosophen.* Stuttgart: Verlag J.B. Metzler, 1995.

The New Encyclopædia Britannica. Chicago: Encyclopædia, inc, 1993; various volumes.

Siemens AG Jahresbericht 1996.

Sills, David (ed.). *International Encyclopaedia of The Social Sciences.* London: the Macmillan Company and The Free Press, 1968; various volumes.

Wer ist wer? Lübeck: Verlag Schmidt-Römhild; various years' editions.

INTERNET PAGES

The Daily Telegraph, available, http://www.telegraph.co.uk
The Economist, available: http://www.europe.economist.com
European Union, available http://europa.eu.int
The Financial Times, available, http://www.ft.com
The Guardian, available, http://www.guardianunlimited.co.uk
Süddeutsche Zeitung, available, http://www-dw.gmd.de.sz

Additionally, as can be discerned from the footnotes, a wide variety of TNE, state and institutional internet pages were consulted.

Index

Page numbers in italic script denote names and terms cited in chapter notes.

About the Author

DONALD G. PHILLIPS has variously worked as a lecturer at the Humboldt University of Berlin, as a research analyst with a political consultancy firm in London, and in the public relations department of the European Space Agency. Currently he is with the European Space Operations Centre in Darmstadt, Germany.